Kilimanjaro Porters and Guides

African History and Culture

SERIES EDITOR
Peter Alegi, *Michigan State University*

African History and Culture is a book series that builds upon and expands Michigan State University's commitment to the study of Africa. The series features books on African history, anthropology, sociology, and political science, as well as interdisciplinary studies, works on the African diaspora, and digital scholarship.

Kilimanjaro Porters and Guides

HISTORY AND TOURISM ON AFRICA'S HIGHEST MOUNTAIN

Leslie Anne Hadfield, Kokel Melubo, and Festo Mkenda

Michigan State University Press | East Lansing

Michigan State University Press
East Lansing, Michigan 48823-5245

LIBRARY OF CONGRESS CATALOGING-IN-PUBLICATION DATA
Names: Hadfield, Leslie Anne author | Melubo, Kokel author | Mkenda, Festo, 1968– author
Title: Kilimanjaro porters and guides : history and tourism on Africa's highest mountain /
Leslie Anne Hadfield, Kokel Melubo, and Festo Mkenda.
Other titles: African history and culture
Description: East Lansing : Michigan State University Press, 2026. |
Series: African history and culture |
Includes bibliographical references and index.
Identifiers: LCCN 2026008766 | ISBN 9781611865820 cloth |
ISBN 9781611865837 paperback | ISBN 9781609178352 | ISBN 9781628955903
Subjects: LCSH: Mountaineers—Tanzania—Kilimanjaro, Mount—History |
Chaga (African people)—Tanzania—History |
Tourism—Tanzania—Kilimanjaro, Mount—History
Classification: LCC GV199.44.T342 K5543 2026 |
DDC 796.52209678/26—dc23/eng/20260210
LC record available at https://lccn.loc.gov/2026008766
Porters making their way to Barafu camp, 2023.

Cover photo: Porters making their way to Barafu camp by Leslie Anne Hadfield.

Visit Michigan State University Press at *www.msupress.org*

Contents

Acknowledgments

THIS BOOK PROJECT STARTED WHEN JEFF DURRANT SENT LESLIE HADFIELD TO FIND Kokel Melubo at the College of African Wildlife Management (CAWM) at Mweka in 2017. Durrant had started a study abroad program taking Brigham Young University (BYU) students to Kilimanjaro and Mweka and recruited Hadfield to participate and help with some research about Chagga porters. Melubo was one of very few who had published about Kilimanjaro porters. He graciously spoke with Hadfield when she showed up unannounced at his door. Durrant's project morphed into a volume edited by BYU and CAWM professors Jeffrey O. Durrant, Emanuel Martin, Kokel Melubo, Ryan Jensen, Leslie A. Hadfield, Perry J. Hardin, and Laurie Weisler—*Protected Areas in Northern Tanzania: Local Communities, Land Use Change, and Management Challenges* (2020). When working on a chapter for *Protected Areas in Northern Tanzania,* Hadfield found rich sources available to uncover the history of mountain crews that was generally unknown. Hadfield and Melubo then recruited Festo Mkenda to draw from his previous doctoral research and contribute needed expertise in Chagga history to this project.

It has been quite a journey constructing this history and putting the manuscript together. We would like to particularly thank those who played key roles at important junctures. First, we thank the mountain crews that facilitated Hadfield's various treks up the mountain and first participated in interviews that led to the bigger project. Andrew Marandu, tour operator for Kilimanjaro Tanzanite Safaris DMC, organized the humble and experienced Joshua Mwakalinga to lead BYU groups. He and his son, Hudson Mwakalinga, and nephew, Enock Mwakalinga, as well as Batchi Donat and many other capable and caring crew members, gave Hadfield her first exposures, first interviews, and carried on conversations years after. This continued with Enock Mwakalinga's company, Impatiens Tours. Melubo also hiked Kilimanjaro four times with CAWM students, supported by porters and guides hired by the college.

The Brice-Bennett family at the Marangu Hotel also provided crucial support, insight, and access to the Kilimanjaro Mountain Club archive, seasoned guides, and other contacts without which this book would not have been possible. Anthony, Fionnuala, Seamus, and Desmond welcomed Hadfield in 2019 and 2021. Desmond continued to keep Hadfield updated on the Marangu Hotel and put her in touch with the Lany family through Peter von Lany. Peter opened up another world into this history with insights into his family history as well as access to published sources in Czech and German. He also provided illustrative images. The current Kilimanjaro Mountain Club has also facilitated access to sources, provided connections, and engaged us in fruitful discussions. Munira Hassuji, the club's efficacious secretary, has faithfully kept us in the loop. We would also like to thank other club officers over the years: Wilfred Moshi, Irene Verhuis, Niek Hoorweek, and Simon Mtuy. Bodil Ashton shared the digitized sources from her home in the United Kingdom to Hadfield in the United States when everyone was grounded because of the COVID-19 pandemic.

From these connections and Melubo's research, we found many willing interview and survey participants. We thank all those porters, cooks, guides and others who gave of their time and of themselves to provide critical perspectives to this project. In that endeavor, we owe a big *asante* to our four research assistants who conducted most of the oral history interviews and completed the transcription of these interviews: Edward Simango, Rehema Assenga, Ester Mramba, and Faisal Omary. They worked expertly and quickly to produce an important part of the research that shaped the narrative that follows (although the three authors are responsible for the analysis and writing). Edward Simango played a particularly important leadership role in this and in conducting follow-up interviews. Brian Githehu came through in a pinch to provide English translations of several transcripts to speed up the analysis and writing process, for which we are also grateful.

At the Evangelical Lutheran Church in Tanzanian-Northern Diocese Archive in Moshi Town, archivist Reverend Enock Petro Makundi provided attentive help and advice, and Huguette Umurerwa contributed an analysis of Kilimanjaro visitor's books as she was working on her undergraduate degree at Mweka.

Finally, other institutions and individuals provided funding and other important support. We obtained permission to conduct research from the Tanzania Wildlife Research Institute (TAWIRI) and the Tanzania Commission for Science and Technology (COSTECH). Much of the funding for the project came from various BYU sources, channeled through Hadfield. Samuel Badal, a participant of the BYU Kilimanjaro program, designed the maps as part of his work with the BYU Geospatial Services lab. The Ricci Jesuit Community in Moshi hosted meetings with Mkenda and Hadfield and Mkenda and the research assistants (for almost a whole day), even providing food. Finally, the Michigan State University African Studies Center, the Rocky Mountain Workshop on African History, and the African Studies Association of the UK (ASAUK) and participants provided opportunities for us to present our work and gain productive feedback—and Tendai Mangena from ASAUK directed us to the second Southern African Mountain Conference held in the Drakensberg South African mountains. It was a fitting last setting to present our research before finalizing the book for publication.

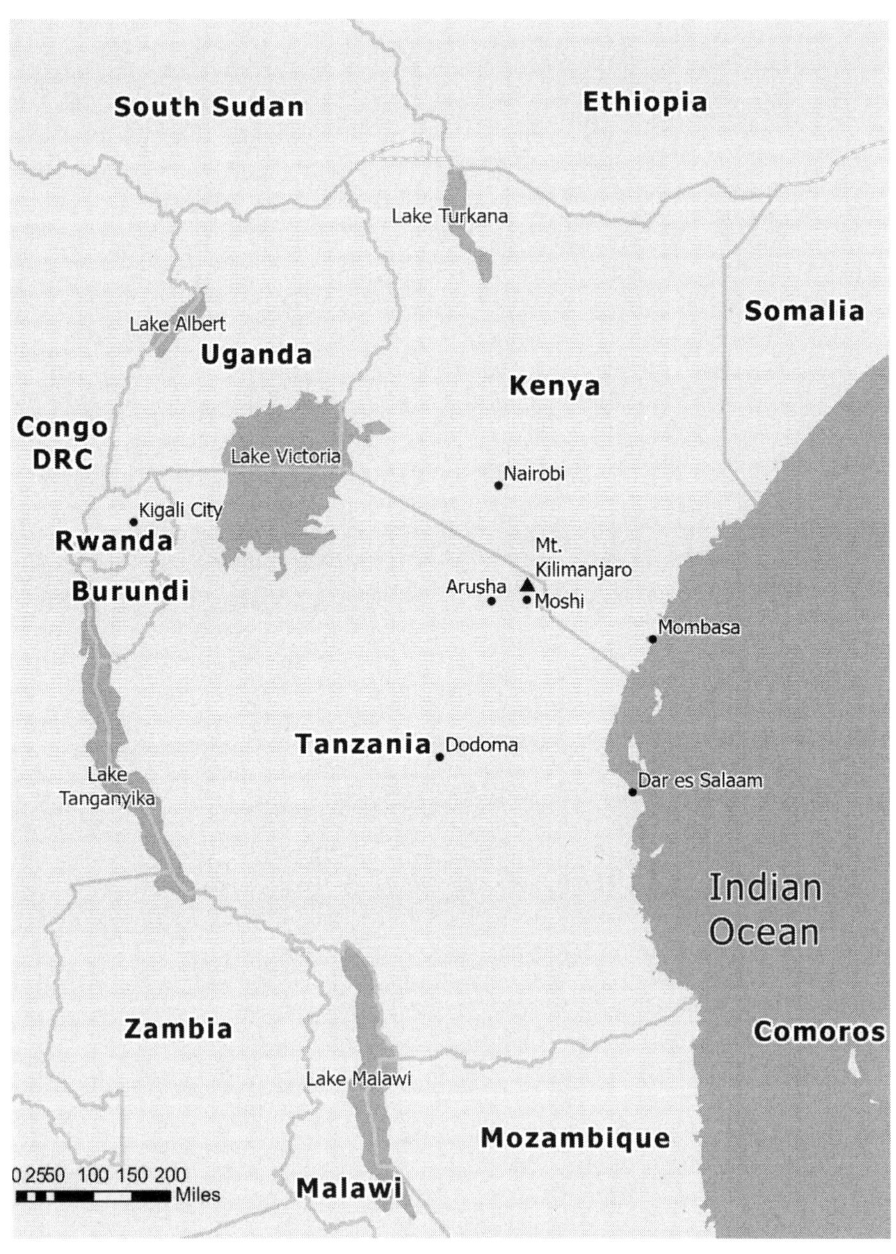

MAP 1. Kilimanjaro in East Africa. SAMUEL BADAL, BYU HBLL GEOSPATIAL SERVICES.

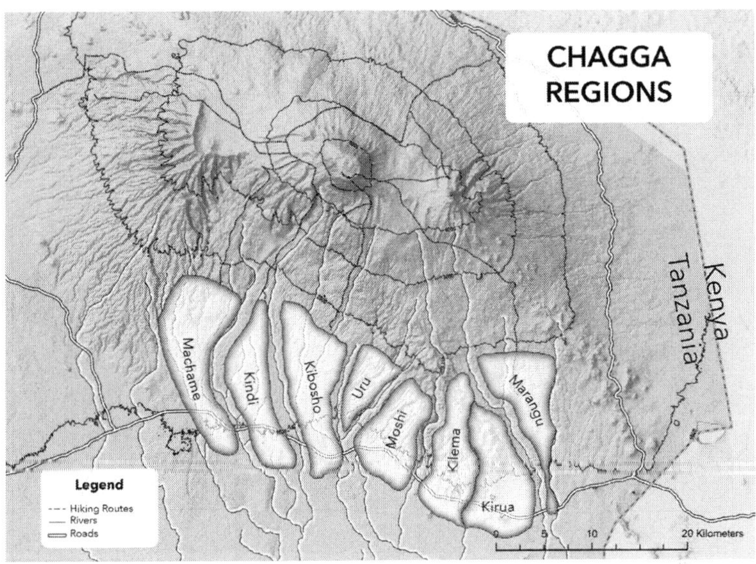

MAP 2. Chagga regions. SAMUEL BADAL, BYU HBLL GEOSPATIAL SERVICES.

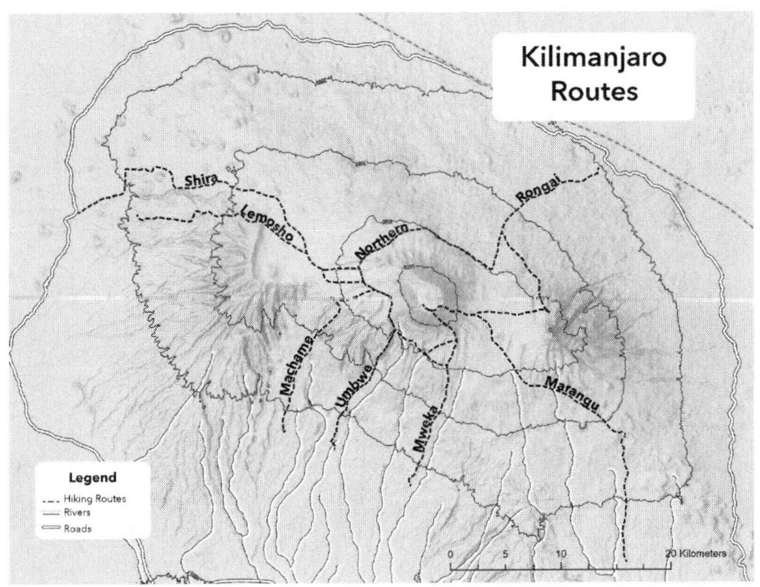

MAP 3. Kilimanjaro routes. SAMUEL BADAL, BYU HBLL GEOSPATIAL SERVICES.

CHAPTER 1

Mountain Crews, the World, and Mt. Kilimanjaro

"Pole pole" is a key Swahili phrase many tourists who hike Mt. Kilimanjaro learn. Those who heed this instruction from their guides to go "slowly" are more likely to have a better experience on the mountain. Walking slowly is key to acclimatization, one of the main challenges of reaching the highest peak on the African continent and the tallest free-standing mountain in the world. Visitors ascend anywhere from around 6,000 ft/1,830 m to 19,341 ft/5895 m in an average of five to seven days, tackling the last 4,000 ft/1,200 m in a grueling nighttime summit attempt that takes hours of the slowest hiking. Kibo, the mountain's largest volcanic cone with the highest peak, is both majestic and intimidating. Although Kibo looms over the trail and climbers' minds, climbers who proceed "pole pole" are also more likely to enjoy conversations and the scenery along the way. One of the attractions of Kilimanjaro is moving through different climatic zones as one ascends, passing the cultivated zone, through the tropical rainforest in the lush foothills, to the heath-moorlands, alpine desert, and arctic zones. Some porters and guides proudly assert that one can see the whole world on Kilimanjaro through these different zones. Some routes make the ascent even more interesting, taking climbers up different peaks and walls as they hike high and sleep low for acclimatization.

FIGURE 1. Crew packing up at Karanga camp in front of Kibo, 2021. PHOTO BY L. A. HADFIELD.

Those who work as porters, cooks, and guides on Kilimanjaro support crews see the whole world on Kilimanjaro in a different way. Rather than meandering "pole pole" to the next camp, porters and cooks power through with their heavy loads, passing the hikers on the trail to prepare the camp for the arrival of the guides and their clients. Rather than coming to the mountain for a once-in-a-lifetime adventure, they come for employment. They see the whole world through the tourists who come to them. Trekkers come from the United States, Europe, the Russian Federation, Africa (i.e., Tanzania, Kenya, South Africa, and Uganda), and more recently, Asia, especially China. Alex Lemunge became one of the first Kilimanjaro guides to come from the Arusha area in 1993 at the age of twenty-six. He started the work because he needed a job to support his mother while his father suffered from diabetes. His fruitful career guiding and then training guides also allowed him to educate his children. He explained that his main motivation was the pay, but that he enjoyed being on Kilimanjaro. Being a guide, he said, "It's the only job that gives you an opportunity to meet people from all over the world . . . from all walks of life."[1] Batchi Vitalis Donat turned to working on the mountain in 1999, when his teaching career was not paying enough. He decided to stick with mountain crew work and reflected twenty years later about how much he had learned to manage his money, build his life, acquire language skills, and "how to live with the different people" who come from different countries and parts of Tanzania to the mountain.[2] Born in a Chagga village on the foothills of Kilimanjaro, Simon Mtuy began working as a porter in his teenage years in the early 1990s and continued working on the mountain as a guide from the age of twenty-one. On February 22, 2006, Mtuy completed the fastest unsupported solo ascent and descent of Kilimanjaro, finishing in just over nine hours and twenty-one minutes. He formed his own guiding company and advocates for environmentally sustainable tourism and agriculture. He talked about how "people with different stories come to climb the mountain" and how he had seen all kinds of climates on the mountain. "I feel so connected to the mountain personally because I have seen the world in my eyes through Kilimanjaro," he concluded.[3]

Alex Lemunge, Batchi Vitalis Donat, and Simon Mtuy recounted what working as the crew means for them personally. The other side of their stories is what they do to support others who climb Kilimanjaro. For a successful climb, trekkers from around the world need the support of porters, cooks, and guides. Guides are responsible for overseeing the expedition and guiding the trekkers up the correct route to the mountain summit. This includes ensuring the trekkers' safety, advising on health and weather conditions, and providing information about the mountain itself. Cooks, often taken from the ranks of porters, are involved in meal planning, budgeting, food purchasing, preparation, and rationing. Porters transport tourists' luggage, food supplies, trash, and camping and specialized climbing equipment up treacherous terrain and in dangerous conditions both up and down the mountain. They set up and break down each campsite and may act as rescuers in case of a health emergency. For a five-day climb, ten individual trekkers would need forty porters as well as at least two guides and two cooks. In 2020, it was estimated that over nineteen thousand local Tanzanians were serving sixty-five thousand trekkers as porters, cooks, and guides. With this number of local labor forces, Mt. Kilimanjaro is said to be the most locally supportive and productive protected area in Tanzania's national park systems.[4]

The views of the myriad of individuals who perform the hardest and most valuable tasks on Kilimanjaro are critical to understanding the history and the current dynamics of mountain tourism on Kilimanjaro. To whom do endless numbers of foreign tourists from the late nineteenth century on owe their successful ascents? What do their histories tell us about climbing Africa's highest mountain? What do they tell us about the relationship of residents of Kilimanjaro to the mountain and the impact of the climbing industry on mountain workers and their communities?

What does their history tell us about the impact of the climbing industry on Tanzania as a modern nation state and how foreign climbers can contribute to a more responsible climbing industry in the future?

Authors who focus on tourism studies in Africa have highlighted the complex relationships local people have with national parks, nature tourism, and conservation. Tourism practitioners have talked about community conservation, searched out the views of local communities, and advocated for community engagement in tourism.[5] The nascent subfield of the history of tourism in Africa has also highlighted the different roles Africans play in tourism. Social histories of national parks and conservation along with works on tourism have addressed evolving ideas of wilderness and nature tourism, differing priorities between the state and local communities, and issues of livelihood.[6] Historians have also revealed the role of Africans in scientific knowledge production, including those who worked in conservation efforts and their complex relationships with the Europeans they worked with.[7] However, as geographer-historian Gordon Pirie and historian Todd Cleveland advocate, more histories of tourism in Africa need to delve into the important perspective of not just the visitors, but the visited, and need to bring in the complexities of history to understanding present day tourism.[8] This is particularly needed when understanding mountain tourism on Kilimanjaro. Despite its significance in the region, its historical and contemporary attraction to visitors, and the insights it could offer about mountain crews generally, little has been written about local people who work in Kilimanjaro mountain tourism. Although many company websites instruct future clients on how to prepare to climb the mountain, it was only in 2021 that a local guide born and raised in the foothills of Kilimanjaro published a guidebook.[9] Literature on Kilimanjaro has traditionally focused on conservation biology and climatology more than mountain-climbing crews. Moreover, as sustainable tourism development researcher Brent Lovelock has argued, "there has been more detailed coverage of the conditions for pack animals" than the conditions for porters in the literature about mountain guiding operations generally.[10]

By centering the perspective of Tanzanians, this book provides a fuller understanding of the Kilimanjaro mountain tourism industry as it spans the eras of European colonialism and African independence in a globalized world. By narrating the history from the mountain looking out, it does more than "make visible" the world of the mountain crews that is not generally known by those coming from outside. It also demonstrates how local communities and crews have shaped the industry in profound ways.[11] It argues that while the Kilimanjaro climbing industry developed in a colonial context, characteristics of which have persisted to the present day, local Tanzanian actors have played an integral role in determining access to and understanding of the mountain, climbers' successes, the nature of crew culture, and key industry features. Like historian Jacob Dlamini's history of tourism in the Kruger National Park in South Africa, this narrative "does not go in a straight line, with [Africans] starting out as powerless subjects and then growing into political citizens," but shows how Kilimanjaro mountain crew influence fluctuated, even as they asserted power at times during European colonialism and as they have struggled in the post-colonial period.[12]

Mt. Kilimanjaro's height, mass, climate, and ecosystem have fascinated humans for hundreds of years, drawing people from all walks of life to the mountain since time immemorial. Located in the northern part of Tanzania, immediately south of the country's border with Kenya, this ancient stratovolcano structure stands free of a mountain range. The two most prominent volcanic peaks pierce the sky, with the highest point, Uhuru Peak, on the top of Kibo (19,341 ft/5,895 m), facing opposite of the second highest, Mawenzi (16,893 ft/5,149 m). European interest in exploring and scaling Kilimanjaro closely followed the golden age of mountaineering and was deeply intertwined with the European colonial conquest of Africa, as was modern tourism and conservation.[13] The mountain-climbing tourism industry's roots lie in the history of mountaineering, which led to the development of the tourism industry and paralleled conservation efforts. The history of mountaineering—seeking to climb the highest mountains for the sport of it—was first written by those driving the sport and focused on the achievements of mountaineering pioneers. As more professional historians contributed to this history, they illuminated the origins of mountaineering among European naturalists, writers, and scientists in the latter part of the eighteenth century.[14] Many describe the flurry of efforts (especially by British climbers) to scale the Alps in the 1850s and 1860s as the "golden age" of mountaineering. Alpine clubs facilitating climbs and managing routes emerged out of that time, and mountaineering tourism spread to the Americas. Excellent work by historians has taken this history further by analyzing the links between nineteenth- and early twentieth-century mountaineering and European imperialism, nationalism, and notions of race and gender. This includes histories of early mountain clubs in South Africa that also arose at the same time as East African clubs while European mountaineers ventured into the continent.[15]

Because of its height and significance in the region, Kilimanjaro has attracted more attention. The first publications on Kilimanjaro mountaineering followed

European mountaineering, missionary, and explorer writing traditions, focusing on a European trajectory. In the journals of Johannes Rebmann (1820–76), the first European credited with sighting Kilimanjaro, there is a mention of climbers from the chiefdom of Machame who had possibly gone as far up as the mountain's snow level. However, the lack of other records makes it hard to understand with clarity possible earlier climbing by the local people and relegates the beginnings of the history of scaling Kilimanjaro to Rebmann himself. This historical narrative has persisted and often climaxes with the first recorded successful ascent of the mountain by German Geographer Hans Meyer (1858–1929) in 1889 (who even overshadows his companion, Ludwig Purstcheller).[16] Despite the broadening of mountaineering history, the history of the many crucial porters, cooks, and guides on Kilimanjaro has remained obscured. Although there has been some attention to Yohane Kinyala Lauwo as one of the first local guides on Kilimanjaro, most accounts of Kilimanjaro climbers published in academic journals and climbing and tourism literature remain largely stories about foreigners, mainly Europeans and Americans.

The highest mountain in the world, Mt. Everest, similarly has attracted more attention because of its prominence. The mountain range's extreme conditions pose greater challenges, adventure, and achievement. Unlike the histories of Kilimanjaro, much more has been written about the Sherpas in Himalayan mountaineering. There was an initial wave of interest in the Sherpa perspective in the 1950s because a Sherpa, Tenzing Norgay, was one of the first to reach the top of Everest along with New Zealander Edmund Hillary. As opposed to Meyer's 1889 summit of Kilimanjaro during the colonial scramble for Africa, Norgay and Hillary reached the summit of Everest in 1953, during the beginnings of decolonization in Asia and Africa. Norgay's achievement was immediately recognized—even held up as a point of Indian and Nepalese national pride (to Norgay's chagrin). Norgay's autobiography was published soon after the celebrated expedition.[17] Although proper recognition of many still lagged, other Sherpas gained greater recognition from foreign mountaineers than those who worked in the early years of the climbing industry on Kilimanjaro. Sherpas who performed their work with valor in the highest elevations earned the badge of "Tiger of the Snow" during their careers. On the other hand, it was only in 1989, the centenary of the first known summit of Kibo, that Lauwo was celebrated as possibly accompanying Meyer to the top in 1889. Other Sherpa autobiographies followed Tenzing's, though more so in the late 1990s and early 2000s after the disaster of the 1996 Everest climbing season drew more attention to the welfare of Sherpas.[18]

Mountain crews in the Himalaya and Kilimanjaro share some similarities in the economic and social aspects of the mountain tourism industries that have developed in the two places. Mountain crews in both places engage in the work for similar reasons with comparable impact, and they would recognize characteristics of a service industry that grew out of European mountaineering culture in either place. However, the climbing industry on Kilimanjaro has a longer history, rooted in its own colonial context and influenced by different economic, political, social, and environmental dynamics—not least the fact that conditions allow many more people to be involved in less technical mountain tourism on Kilimanjaro. Thus, fleshing out the history and present-day dynamics of this industry provides crucial understanding of the local context, a significant case study for the history of tourism in Africa and instructive comparisons for mountain tourism generally.

Mountain tourism became a global mass phenomenon with a continually growing number of trekkers for adventure or spiritual purposes in the early to mid-twentieth century. Kilimanjaro became a prime attraction during this period. Kilimanjaro can be ascended following seven different routes without technical skills, ice picks, or crampons, or really anything more than some warm clothes and good boots.[19] Because mountaineering gear and experience are not needed to reach Uhuru peak, coupled with commercialization of mountain-climbing tourism, tens of thousands of climbers ascend the mountain each year, bringing in an estimated 56 billion Tanzanian shillings (TZS) (about 50 million USD). The mountain is one of Tanzania's premier tourist attractions along with the Serengeti great migration of herbivores and the spectacular landscape of the Ngorongoro Crater. For most tourists, the trip to Tanzania would be incomplete without visiting these three attractions. Defined by its height, snow-capped peak, physical form, and surrounding environmental conditions, Kilimanjaro has also become one of Tanzania's natural United Nations Educational, Scientific, and Cultural Organization (UNESCO) world heritage sites, alongside Serengeti National Park, Ngorongoro Conservation Area, and Selous Game Reserve. Kilimanjaro is also Tanzania National Parks' (TANAPA) second highest-earning destination. Tanzania received over a million tourists in the 2019/2020 fiscal year, and 49,200 of those tourists specifically went for trekking and mountaineering to Mt. Kilimanjaro and Mt. Meru, the latter being another lone-standing stratovolcano in the north of the country. In the June 2023–June 2024 fiscal year, the number of tourists to Kilimanjaro was 63,650. Trekkers tend to stay on Kilimanjaro longer than visitors to any of the other six national parks

FIGURE 2. Machame camp, 2019.
Photo by Randall M. Hadfield.

and conservation areas in Tanzania's Northern Circuit. As a result, Mt. Kilimanjaro generates up to 45 percent of TANAPA's income which is necessary to fund the twenty-two other national parks throughout the country.[20]

While Mt. Kilimanjaro has come to represent endurance and determination, its significance extends beyond the value derived from global tourism and mountaineering.[21] It stands as a "giver of abundance and peace," the embodiment of blessings of plenty, as well as power, brilliance, superiority, and age.[22] Historian Matthew V. Bender argued, "Though impressive in its stature, the mountain has been of greatest value to human societies because of its water features."[23] The Kilimanjaro "waterscape," as Bender terms it, was a defining feature of the history and culture that developed on the mountain. Rains, rivers, and irrigation canals watered numerous mountainside gardens, sustained livestock, and provided for "cooking, bathing, and brewing."[24] Kilimanjaro also provides refuge for a variety of rare and endemic flora such as *Lobelia deckenii* and *Impatiens kilimanjari*. Animal varieties include the threatened charismatic species such as elephants, lions, and leopards. Moreover, this "African pole" is a critical source of food, fuel, building materials, and jobs for the Chagga community that currently inhabits the fertile middle zone around the mountain and several others far beyond. The Wadarimba (also referred to as Wakonyingo and Wataremba), first dwellers of the mountain, as well as later arrivals like the Chagga and the Maasai of Mt. Kilimanjaro, came for spiritual solace, farming, grazing, military conquest, medication, and education. They also came for other natural resources essential for livelihood, including timber, firewood, tannin, and charcoal.[25] The mountain, particularly the Kifinika parasitic cone, is a sacred but frightful peak that is believed by the Chagga people to possess spiritual powers and to be guarded by protective spirits. For the Maasai, the majestic Oldoinyo Oibor (White Mountain) is a cultural receptacle and ritual and cultural center for which people engage with utmost respect. Beyond the mountain, the well-watered slopes of Mt. Kilimanjaro are a primary catchment area for the Pangani River Basin, which drains the Pare and Usambara Mountain Ranges before reaching the estuary of the Indian Ocean. The mountain drains the Kikuletwa catchment that pours water into Lake Jipe and supplies the underground streams that keep Lake Chala filled up.

It is with this broader significance of the mountain that this history starts, privileging the local perspective, up through the present dynamics of the tourism industry. Although Chagga perspectives and the histories of other local Tanzanians have largely been left out of published works, previously untapped archives and oral history provide valuable windows into both the past and the present. Kilimanjaro Mountain Club records proved to be a gold mine with revealing scrapbooks, meeting minutes, and correspondence with hotels and government officials. Surviving reference books the guides were asked to carry and visitors' books left in huts on the mountain and at Gillman's Point and Uhuru Peak from the 1930s into the 1960s provided clues about the work, characteristics, and the relationships with visitors of early mountain workers. Oral history interviews with sixty-five guides and porters who worked anywhere from the late 1950s into current times most significantly fleshed out both the history of the earlier guides as well as the events of the past fifty years. Oral history interviews added to participatory observation and tourism research into contemporary conditions and efforts to ameliorate persistent challenges. Tourism research tapped into porters' unions, including interviews with five union leaders and twenty-seven porters, corroborated with information from mountain industry representatives and related archival materials, including recent visitors' books.

The book begins its narrative from the initial inhabitants of the mountain. Chapter 2 lays the foundation by providing a condensed history of the Chagga peoples' relationship with Mt. Kilimanjaro. It explains how the people occupied, understood, and interacted with the mountain. With this background, the Chagga people naturally acted as stewards of the mountain which thus led to them serving as the first guides for those who would come from afar seeking to explore the mountain. The Chagga component of the Kilimanjaro story remains significant throughout the development of the mountain tourism industry even as others from near and far add a different perspective to the more recent accounts. Chapter 3 investigates the beginnings of porter and guide work on Kilimanjaro as it was linked to the long-distance caravan porter work already established in Eastern Africa and as it was then linked to European exploration in the mid- to late nineteenth century. These explorers tapped into Chagga knowledge to access Kibo. Accounts of European expeditions reveal the colonial and scientific aspects of their caravans that shaped the character of these early European-led journeys. Early European expeditions to Kilimanjaro were colonial in purpose, seeking to know, claim, and conquer African land. It is in this context that the acclaimed first European conqueror of the mountain came from Germany, the first European country to colonize the area. These early expedition leaders also had a sense of racial and cultural superiority that they brought to their relationship with their crews.

Yet relationships with local political leaders determined access to the mountain. For example, Marangu became the main gateway to the great peaks of Uhuru and Mawenzi primarily because of good relations that existed between Chief Marealle I of that area and the German colonial authorities in the late nineteenth century. This relationship was crucial not least because the local chief recruited the African labor required for the ascent. Besides the advantage of having started early, Marangu was and remains one of the most direct ascents and friendliest routes down from the mountain. As such, it has also attracted significant investments related to the industry, including roads, hotels, and other tourist facilities.

Chapter 4 traces the emergence of the climbing tourism industry on Kilimanjaro from the early part of the twentieth century and analyzes the industry's relationship with the mountain crews. It begins with an account of the way the Kilimanjaro Mountain Club, in conjunction with Kibo and Marangu Hotels, managed the scheduling of climbing groups, worked with Chagga chiefs to hire porters and guides, and regularized the employment of porters and guides into the 1950s and 1960s. The chapter also explores the characteristics, motivations, skills, contributions, and conditions of the early porters and guides and their relationships with the hotels, climbing clubs, and clients. As the industry developed, many colonial customs continued. The support crew was expected to attend to every need of the visiting climbers, even at the expense of their own welfare. Porters, cooks, and guides developed unmatched expertise, established crew culture, negotiated pay and work expectations, and ensured the success and even survival of climbers. They seemingly did this without seeking the recognition foreign climbers received.

Beginning in the late 1960s, the industry outgrew the Kilimanjaro Mountain Club. At this point, the club sought to turn management over to the public parks system of the new Tanzanian nation-state, independent from 1961. Chapter 5 considers the impact of the development of Kilimanjaro climbing tourism on porter and guide work in the late twentieth century, particularly as it changed after Tanzania's independence and as the number of tourists and private companies offering climbing packages steadily grew. The new government eventually stepped in to become an important player, establishing the Kilimanjaro National Park (KINAPA) in 1973 and increasingly overseeing the industry. Near the turn of the century, the stage was set for the mushrooming of private companies and an expansion in the kind of people who engaged in Kilimanjaro mountain work, including more Tanzanians from various regions and more women. These changes made the mountain belong to the whole of Tanzania rather than only to the Chagga people. At this point, the book's focus shifts from distant history to recent developments in regulations, economic forces, and current porter and guide experiences. Greater numbers of people on the mountain put pressure on resources and working conditions. A subsequent rise in awareness of the plight of porters led to efforts to change their working conditions, necessitating the drawing of new regulations and the establishment of international and local porter organizations. The role of crucial laborers gained more attention, returning some influence to those constituting the backbone of the industry on Kilimanjaro. The quest for the improvement of working conditions continues to this day, even as new industry dynamics mix with old colonial characteristics. After the book has offered this deeper understanding of the dynamics that shape labor relations in the Kilimanjaro mountaineering industry, Chapter 6 draws on Melubo's tourism research and personal experience to analyze recent changes and current conditions. Based on that same research and experience is a list of practical recommendations appended to this book. Proposed for the improvement of the condition of porters and guides and for a more satisfying and ethical adventure in climbing Kilimanjaro, these recommendations make the book transition from a source of knowledge about Africa's highest mountain to a practical manual for its aspiring climbers.

Various parts of the world meet on Kilimanjaro. Some come for the adventure, some the quick money, others to prove themselves, and others because—as one

Kilimanjaro guide's shirt quoted the mountaineer and naturalist John Muir—"the mountains are calling." Everyone who participates is bound up in an industry with features tied to various strands of history and present-day developments. This does not mean it is a tangled mass inevitably leading to continued exploitation and degradation. It also does not mean that the relationships forged between mountain crews and tourists cannot be genuine. As it dives into the complexities of these relationships and developments, this history helps us go beyond simplified stories of the triumph of tourists and the trials of porters. As the story of a developing industry in its local context and some of the most important, but overlooked, people who made it, this book invites us all to take responsibility in paying respect to the mountain and the people who work on it with an eye to making a better future.

CHAPTER 2

Inhabitants of the Mountain

KILIMANJARO MOUNTAIN CLIMBING IS NOT THE FIRST ENGAGEMENT HUMANS HAVE had with Africa's tallest geological monument. The mountain is a constitutive element of the identity of the Chagga people who have inhabited its slopes for centuries. Their historical culture and economic activities are so completely entwined with the mountain that it might even be possible to say the mountain helped them carve a shared identity. Oral tradition and cultural linkages with neighboring groups suggest that migrants from different parts of the greater eastern Africa region came to the mountain, settled on its well-watered slopes, and, with time, became Chagga. In turn, through their cultures and traditions, the Chagga provide the earliest sources for understanding Kilimanjaro before the colonial period. Since the Chagga people also supplied the earliest porters when the Kilimanjaro climbing industry emerged and are still the main suppliers today, their story remains entwined with the mountain, allowing for a continuous history with elements from the distant past and from the present.

The history of the Chagga people before the nineteenth century is difficult to know in detail. However, thanks to oral traditions of the Chagga themselves and those of their neighbors, a level of speculation is possible. These traditions found their way into early accounts of missionaries and travelers who were attracted to

Kilimanjaro by factors ranging from evangelization and good climate to opportunities for trade and geographical curiosity. Beginning from such clues, later studies of the people—such as those by British colonial officer Charles Dundas in 1924 and academic historians Cathleen Stahl in 1964, Susan Geiger in 1972, and Sally Falk Moore in 1986—widely employed oral history to retrieve what existed in tradition and record what was remembered from experience. This wealth of research allows for a reconstruction of the process through which men and women from varied backgrounds colonized Africa's most prominent land mass, invented common cultural elements, and became the community of people referred to as Chagga. This Chagga identity developed around a certain geography, evolved around the mountain, and finally resulted in a dynamic political culture.

The Geography of Identity

The Chagga have sometimes been called "mountain people." This is not entirely without justification, for their mountainous environment is a key factor in their sense of identity. The Chagga "make surrounding nature a reflection and echo of all their moods," argued the German missionary Bruno Gutmann, their twentieth-century ethnographer and evangelizer.[1] In Stahl's view, "one striking feature which characterizes the Chagga themselves is an old precise deep-rooted sense of place."[2] Speaking fondly about the mountain, Thomas Marealle, once paramount chief of the Chagga, said: "I treasure a feeling of attachment to it that cannot be eradicated by sheer geographical distance," adding that even "a stray Mchagga who has had to spend his life away from it" found reason to appreciate it more.[3]

A stratovolcano with rocks as old as three million years, the mountain's history is obviously deeper than that of the Chagga. Mentions of a white-caped mountain somewhere in the tropics off the coast of East Africa go back at least nineteen centuries. Ptolemy (c. 100–170 CE) mentioned the existence of such a mountain at Rhapta, a location believed to have been somewhere on the East African coast. A Chinese chronicler of the twelfth and thirteenth century China–East Africa trade noted the existence of a great mountain west of Zanzibar. After he had visited the East African coast, the thirteenth-century Syrian geographer Abū al-Fidā (1273–1331) also spoke of a mountain white in color. Finally, Martín Fernández de Enciso (c. 1470–1528), Spanish author of the 1519 *Suma de Geographia*, wrote of an "exceedingly high" Mt. Olympus west of Mombasa—likely to be Kilimanjaro, although Mt. Kenya could also be a close competitor for that description. None of these early authors was recording first-hand experience and none used the name Kilimanjaro, let alone Chagga. Nevertheless, the grandeur of the mountain they described in the East African interior warrants the conclusion that it is most likely today's Kilimanjaro. Later travelers would view this conclusion as somewhat obvious.[4]

Since the early knowledge of a mountain in the interior was gathered from the East African coast, these accounts point to contacts between the interior and the coast from quite early on in history. Moreover, the weakness of silence as evidence notwithstanding, the accounts also suggest that the names Kilimanjaro and Chagga were probably not in currency before the sixteenth century.

The Chagga people used this common name for themselves, but in variations that ranged from Mchaka/Mshaka (singular) to Vachaka/Vashaka (plural). Other neighboring communities also referred to the mountain dwellers with some similar variations. Such, for example, was the case with the Wapare neighbors with a strong traditional joking relationship with the Chagga, who referred to them as Mwaagha (singular) and Vaagha (plural). The earliest written version of this group name is to be found in the journals of the German missionary John Rebmann (1820–75), who spoke about the mountains of "Jagga." Subsequent authors tended to use Chaga or Chagga, and the latter spelling is now the most used version in the English language.[5]

With their ancestries pointing to multiple directions, the Chagga lacked the myths of a common origin that are so common among other peoples. It would appear that those who shared sufficiently in a large pool of social and cultural attributes that were thought to be Chagga came to be referred to as *Wachagga* in plural, the singular being *Mchagga*. Their closely related dialects, all sharing a Bantu structure, became *Kichagga*, and the mountainous land they occupied became *Uchagga* or, more appropriately, *Uchaggani*. Nearly every migrant who remained on the mountain long enough and shared in the culture around it became Chagga.

The gradients that characterize the habitable middle belt around the 19,341 ft/5,895 m mountain, coupled with the numerous streams running parallel from its top, limited movement on Kilimanjaro to almost only two directions: up and down. This was a limitation with significant social and political implications. Up to the nineteenth century, for example, the patterning of political aggregation followed the up-down direction.[6] Moreover, in absence of pumps, water furrows—an ancient Chagga specialization of considerable scholarly interest—were made to obey gravity through the up-down direction, using what Dundas called the native's eye for grade.[7] The furrows were shared by those living next to them, from up the mountain downwards. They were managed by a *mmeku wa mfongo*, an elder in charge of a furrow, whose social and political significance cannot be exaggerated. He ensured fair distribution of water, resolved water disputes, and called for joint labor to maintain channels. In addition, the rich, well-watered volcanic soils made the region agreeable to the hunter, the gatherer, the animal keeper, and the gardener, as well as determined what could be hunted, gathered, kept, or gardened. By determining how people obtained their livelihood, the geography of Kilimanjaro controlled the starting point of their cultural fermentation.

The mid-nineteenth century offers a more explicit reference to both "Kilimanjaro" and "Chagga." From this date on, visitors at the coast heard of the silver mountain called Kilimanjaro in a place called Chagga, the two words appearing in various spellings. By this time, they had become familiar geographical names at the coast. The earliest written record by an eyewitness to both the mountain and the people who lived on it is that of the missionary John Rebmann. Rebmann visited the region three times between 1848 and 1852, when he talked of the "mountains of Jagga" in plural, apparently referring to the two major peaks of the same mountain. More specifically, he used the name "Kilimanjaro" up to eleven times in the diaries containing the accounts of his journeys "to Jagga." He saw "the lofty summits of the mountains of Jagga and the outline of their connection and separation." It was the "Suahili" (the Swahili-speaking peoples at the coast) who called it Kilimanjaro, said Rebmann, for "the inhabitants of Jagga called it Kibo, snow."[8] Writing after visiting the mountain nearly forty years after Rebmann, British explorer Henry Hamilton Johnston (1859–1927) upheld the coastal use of "Kilimanjaro" and noted its absence in the interior.[9]

To date, the search for the meaning of Kilimanjaro continues, and everyone's guess reads as good as that of everyone else.[10] It is very likely that, living on the mountainside, these "inhabitants of Jagga" had names for each peak separately and no single name for the whole massif. This was also the judgment of early Catholic missionaries who arrived in the region toward the end of the nineteenth century.[11] Besides the permanently snow-covered Kibo, the second major peak is Mawenzi and the third, less prominent, Shira. Unlike the singular name Kilimanjaro for the whole mountain, the individual peak names Kibo and Mawenzi existed in Chagga mythologies. One of them was the popular attempt to explain the rugged face of old Mawenzi as resulting from a thrashing by young Kibo.[12] Because in the past, the name was not used by the Chagga themselves, recent suggestions that it was derived from *Kidhema Kyaaro*, the Chagga phrase for "a journey impossible to attempt," would also seem to lack historical merit.

Rebmann used the term "Jagga" mainly as a place-name. His journeys were "to Jagga"; there was an "ordinary route to Jagga"; Kaptei, a country proper to the Wakuafi, lay "to the north of Jagga"; and the "wilderness between Teita and Jagga" was full of elephants.[13] John Ludwig Krapf, Rebmann's contemporary and missionary colleague, used the name in the same way, speaking frequently of "mount Kilimanjaro in Chagga" and "the snowy mountain of Chagga." He also pointed out that Wakuafi and Wamasai lived in the vicinity of Chagga.[14]

This spatial usage of the name Chagga agrees with later records. R. Thornton's 1865 account contains a reference to "Jagga range of mountains."[15] On his part, Johnston wrote in a footnote that "*Čaga* (which is pronounced Chaga) is the native name for the inhabited belt, between 3,000 and 7,000 feet, stretching around the mountain," and, "at the risk of reiteration," repeated the same note elsewhere in his book.[16] A later document mentions Moshi as a place "in Chagga."[17] In 1890, Catholic missionaries decidedly took the route to "Tchaga" and said such was the name by which the southern part of Kilimanjaro was designated.[18] In the following year, the German geographer Hans Heinrich Josef Meyer (1858–1929), who is credited with being the first known European to have enjoyed the support of African porters and guides all the way to the top of Kilimanjaro, talked of Marangu as "one of the small states forming part of the district of Jagga, the cultivated zone which runs round the southern half of the mountain."[19] Ten years later, the British colonial administrator Alfred Claud Hollis (1874–1961) visited Taveta on the Kenyan side of the border and learnt about families "from Chaga," about places like Usseri and Mwika "in Chaga," and, in a footnote, explained that "Chaga is a local name for Mount Kilima Njaro,"[20] further indicating that the name Kilimanjaro itself was foreign to those who inhabited the mountain. Even as late as 1916, British journalist and author Frank Richardson Cana (1865–1935) still talked of the well-watered country known as Chagga.[21]

Besides its reference to place, the name Chagga appears obscurely in two other peculiar uses. The first is Thornton's mention of "the River Jagga" which flowed from Lake Jipe and joined River Pangani.[22] The many, mostly seasonal, rivulets which fit this description make it impossible to determine which one was Jagga. The second is a rather confusing reference by British military officer Christopher Palmer Rigby (1820–85) to "an ancient city" marked as "Jaca" in an inscription in the fort of Mombasa, which some travelers pointed out to him as "Chagga of Kilimanjaro," and the ruins of which he saw near the mouth of the River Ozi, north of Mombasa.[23] All these uses make us ask whether originally "Chagga" meant a place, a mountain, a river, or an ancient city.

And yet there is another use of the name to consider. Rebmann also used the name Chagga when referring to people. Hence, "among the Jagga people who were with [him] there was a rain-maker" who failed to stop the rain, and so "the Jagga erected a hut of banana-leaves" which proved to be too small a shelter for his entourage.[24] Once he used the full name "Wajagga," saying it was a Swahili designation of the local "Wakirima."[25] While there is a locality in Kilimanjaro known as Kirima (hence its residents are Wakirima), the term "Wakirima" could be understood more generally as mountain dwellers. On his last visit to "Majame," Rebmann and his team of Wanika were so mishandled by the king of the place that, when they finally obtained leave to depart, the Wanika "would not even wait for the Jagga soldiers who, at my desire, were to have accompanied us to Kilema."[26]

Later writers used the term "Wachagga" more directly. The most explicit is "Wa-tchaga or Tchagas" by Catholic missionaries, with an additional detail that they "inhabit the massif."[27] Meyer used the name "Wa-Jagga" even more frequently.[28] Later, Hollis talked more explicitly about "the Wachaga of Kilema."[29] The use of "Chagga" or "Wachagga" for people becomes more frequent with time.

It is the use of Chagga as a place-name that stands prominent in these early writings, often referring to a region larger than specific localities on the mountainside. Machame, Moshi, Kilema, Mwika, and Usseri are all named as places in Chagga. Its use with reference to people is also significant, though slightly less prominent probably because of a noticeable interest in physical geography more than in people. It is very likely that these two senses of Chagga existed together from the moment the term emerged. This would agree with a regional linguistic practice, still common today, in which people are named after places and vice versa. The Wachagga would have lived in Uchaggani (Chaggaland), just as the Maasai would have lived in Umasaini and the Wapare, Upareni.

Contrary to so much historical evidence, there have been suggestions that "Chagga" was a place-name with no reference to people and that the farming population on Kilimanjaro started to bear the "tribal name" only from the 1890s.[30] It is interesting to note that British colonial administrator Charles William Hobley (1867–1947), who paid as much attention to people as to places and prospects in British East Africa, registered that "Wa" was simply the Bantu prefix for "people" and used terms like Kikuyu and Wakikuyu more liberally, as he also mentioned Wachagga.[31] Krapf, too, had noted that the "Wanika" who lived south of Mombasa were called "Wadigo" and their country "Udigo."[32] According to this Bantu linguistic practice, whenever Chagga was a place with inhabitants in it, those inhabitants were Wachagga. When, in a prayer for Rebmann, King Maina of Taita referred to the Kilimanjaro region as "Kirima," he also called its inhabitants "Wa-Kirima."[33] Rebmann translated "Kirima" as "Jagga" and "Wa-Kirima" as "People of Jagga," which he could have rendered "Wa-Jagga." As already suggested, by "Kirima" and "Wa-Kirima," King Maina likely meant "Mountain" and "Mountain-dwellers," respectively. Of equal linguistic importance is Johnston's use of the term "Ki-čaga" with reference to "the language of the country," which would ordinarily mean the language spoken by Wa-čaga, the latter term which he also used.[34]

Peopling Kilimanjaro

Archaeologists Henry Anthony Fosbrooke and Hamo Sasoon pointed out that, though the historical significance of archaeological findings on Kilimanjaro could not match those at Olduvai Gorge, they presented "some very tangible evidence of man's more recent occupation in the days before written history."[35] Such early humans on Kilimanjaro tell us about the Chagga no more than early humans in Olduvai Gorge tell us about present-day Tanzanians. Further evidence from archaeology and tradition also suggests that, as mentioned in the introduction, hunter-gatherers that are generally referred to as Wakonyingo (also referred to as Wadarimba, Wataremba, and Umbwang'ao), roamed the mountainside freely before they were pushed out or absorbed into a larger population of new immigrants.[36] If absorption is what happened, then the Wakonyingo contributed something indigenous to an obviously mixed Chagga population that is made of multiple immigrants.

The more recent inhabitants of Kilimanjaro who became main players in the mountain tourism industry are a mixture of migrants and indigenous people whose coming together initiated a process of social, cultural, and political fermentation, resulting in what has been called Chagga. Several studies have placed the initial encounter somewhere between sixteenth and seventeenth centuries in the common era. In one case, it has been suggested that "the Tanganyika hill tribes, which include the Chagga, came up from the planes about 1600–1760," with climate change proposed as explanation for this movement.[37] In another study, non-decorated pottery at Matunda and Marangu on Kilimanjaro, which could be interpreted as undeveloped, has been dated back to the middle of the last millennium.[38] This may also suggest initial settlements in the area around that period.

More interestingly, findings based on oral tradition have placed major migrations to Kilimanjaro roughly around the sixteenth century. In 1902, German Pastor

Heinrich Leonhard Adolphi (1852–1918), who worked as a missionary in the area, wrote down an account of the Lutheran mission there and speculated that 1660 was the year present Chagga people moved to Kilimanjaro. He arrived at this date from the simple fact that, at the time of his inquiry some elderly people could name between eight and ten generations back. He took this to mean back to the first elder of the *ukoo* (or *kishari*, loosely meaning "clan") to enter the country.[39] His method has been largely upheld by subsequent scholars.

For her part, in 1961, Stahl was of the opinion that migrations to Kilimanjaro took place three centuries earlier, which confirmed Adolphi's dating.[40] In 1971, Norwegian archaeologist and anthropologist Knut Odner (1924–2008) determined that six to thirteen generations of rulers were remembered in each of the major chieftaincies on Kilimanjaro. Taking thirty years to be the average for a generation and allowing some time for initial organization, Odner concluded that "we may conjecture that the Chagga have lived for more than four hundred years in their country."[41] This suggests a century or more earlier than Adolphi's calculation, but strengthens argument for a date between sixteenth and seventeenth centuries. Six years after Odner's writing, and working with Odner's date in mind, Moore preferred to talk about successive waves of migration to Kilimanjaro, starting at least five or six centuries back and possibly much earlier.[42]

Although the convergence of archaeology and tradition favors the sixteenth- and seventeenth-century timeframe, this period was probably a moment of intensification in Moore's successive waves of migration, not an initial stage. Nor should it be seen as the final date of migrations onto Kilimanjaro. Even today, one meets men and women who are only second or third generations on the mountain and whose identity as Chagga is not a subject of local dispute. The timeframe simply helps to deter imaginations of exaggerated antiquity. To the extent that the Chagga people were an identifiable group in the nineteenth century when written records about them were first created, they were still a culturally young and rapidly changing community. Theirs was a "habit of absorbing new comers" who brought with them new blood, new crops, and new skills, all of which contributed to an ever-growing identity.[43]

They came, wrote Stahl, Wakamba from the north, Wataita and Wamasai from the plains, and Wasambaa from the Usambaras, to settle on the mountain slopes and, "brought together by custom, to evolve by slow stages into a united Chagga people."[44] The list continues, including Wakahe and Waarusha, Wakikuyu and Wapare, and Wagweno and Wazigua, among other minority groups. These communities lived in the vicinity of Kilimanjaro, which stood at their center in the region between 350 and 410 east and 00 and 60 south.

Favorable climatic and soil conditions on the mountain were obvious pull factors that attracted migrants, especially those giving up nomadic pastoralism for a more sedentary farming lifestyle. The pastoral Maasai on the plains north and west of Kilimanjaro may have pushed such populations up the mountain. Moreover, pressure on populations elsewhere, such as that caused by the Oromo in the north around the sixteenth century, may also have sparked a wave of readjustments in the greater East African region and pushed surrounding communities to move up the mountain. Some authors have posited the theory that the impact of the Oromo migrations was felt as far south as the coastal regions of today's Kenya, which has strong historical connections with Kilimanjaro.[45] Linguistics and tradition further suggest that Bantu-speaking communities east of the Rift Valley and on both sides of today's Kenya-Tanzania border originated from the coastal region, even if they were not directly linked to the Oromo migrations. The Taita area in today's Kenya is also posited as an important dispersal point, probably connected to stirrings at the coast, whether caused by the migrations of the Oromo or by the Portuguese who were active in the region within the sixteenth century.[46]

While the geographical location of Kilimanjaro in reference to surrounding communities and historical accounts of migrations within the broader region provide reasons as to why people would have migrated onto the mountain, stronger arguments for their actually having moved there is to be retrieved from tradition. Rather than having myths of common origin, the Chagga themselves have myths of migrations onto Kilimanjaro. As if to confirm the westward movement from the coast, Dundas was told of some mythical Umbo people, who were driven out of their country and, moving via Usambara, came to settle on Kilimanjaro. They allegedly left stone markings on their way, which he could still be shown for proof. In an exaggeration typical of mythology, Dundas, writing at the beginning of the twentieth century, was told that "the horde was so vast that it took seven days for the whole mass to pass."[47]

More concretely, family genealogies point to a myriad of ancestral directions. Of the 732 patrilineal clans counted by Dundas at the beginning of the last century, 170 claimed Taita descent, 160 Kamba, 146 Masai, 51 Pare, 30 Sambaa, and 27 Kahe and Arusha, with the remaining made up of those who claimed to have always existed on the mountain and the most recent being Kikuyu and Meru arrivals.[48] Additionally, it is not entirely far-fetched to imagine a hint of Nyamwezi and Swahili blood among the Chagga as Stahl and Anon did, especially in the nineteenth century when the mountain became an increasingly important destination for the East African trade networks.[49] Stories also exist about light-skinned people, probably from the coast, who, "long ago in the time of the first ancestors," roamed in search of ivory for a certain "Serima."[50] That this ancestral diversity was an acceptable element of Chagga identity is revealed again in their myths and beliefs. For example, a key attribute of their *Ruwa* (God) is *moparla wandu*, meaning one who broke something open and, behold, humanity was released![51] The Chagga story thus suggests that, for the communities in this region of eastern Africa and possibly well beyond, common descent (in today's terms, biological or genetic relatedness) was not an important factor in determining a shared cultural identity. The Chagga identity evolved over time, becoming the strongest when many Chagga themselves described their identity in an attempt to define it.

Becoming Chagga

The Swahili poet and scholar Ali Jahadhmy proposed that the way people obtain their means of livelihood is the starting point of their cultural fermentation.[52] Indeed, on Kilimanjaro, the mountain environment had a determining impact on Chagga community identity. Yet, lest we render the mountain people passive, we must state that at issue is a combination of nature and humanity, a question of what human beings have done in their environment and with the natural resources at their disposal.

New immigrants may have arrived on Kilimanjaro singly or in family groups. Reaching there, they did not remain closed to themselves. There is substantial evidence for localized population mixture. Most obviously, some clan names spread across the whole mountain, albeit with minor variations. The opinion is that these names, or at least most of them, refer to the earliest ancestors who settled in a particular place. As families grew and economic and political pressure intervened, clans split and their offshoots moved to settle in other localities on the mountain, even as others went yonder to become Taita, Kamba, Meru, Masai, etc.

Besides names of people, there is also a notable repetition of place-names, suggesting that groups resettling in a new locality retained memories of old homes. There is Maua in the central division of Vunjo and another Maua in Kibosho, further west. The area immediately after the eastern division of Rombo is called Mwika, and there is another Mwika at Mbokomu, further west. There is Kirua in Rombo, and another Kirua in Vunjo. There is Mkuu in Rombo and Nkuu in the western division of Hai. There is Machame in Rombo and another Machame in Hai. There is Mrao in Rombo and Mrau in Hai. There is a Kitimbiriu at Rombo's Mkuu and another Kitimbiriu in Moshi, the latter famous as the first Lutheran station on Kilimanjaro. There are two places named Keni in Rombo. Although we cannot confirm which of these places were named first, the likelihood is that major movement was from the eastern and southeastern parts of Kilimanjaro to its western and northwestern parts. The fact that nearly all repeated names are found in Rombo argues more for migrations from there to the diverse localities than for the reverse.

Moreover, the northeastern areas are thought to have been settled first while the southwestern areas of Moshi, Kibosho, and Machame are probably the most recently settled.[53] Tradition holds that Kamba ancestors of the Lyimo clan of Marangu first settled at Usseri in the easternmost part and from there moved westward through the forest above the inhabited belt around Kilimanjaro.[54] Ancestors of the Mmari clan, thought to be of Kikuyu origin and the first to settle at Kibosho, also had their first settlement at Usseri.[55] It is also near Usseri that we find the Wangassa whose dialect is so different from other Chagga dialects that sometimes it is considered a separate language altogether. The Wangassa claim to have been there "since time immemorial."[56] Moreover, if local migrations also implied gradually giving up pastoralism for more crop farming, then the westward trend is further strengthened by the fact that Rombo was the last to make a complete switch to farming. It was ultimately forced to do so by the colonial border between Tanzania and Kenya, which denied people access to pastureland across the imaginary line. Together, these details make a strong case for a major westward trend of localized migrations without necessarily excluding minor movements in all other directions.

Even when clans settled in a particular area, they could not avoid mixing with others. In fact, it was necessary that they interact outside of their clan, for these patrilineal Chagga clans were—and still are—strictly exogamous. Incest was an improper sexual combination that was understood to bring about death instead of life.[57] The circle of unmarriageable relatives extended to practically the whole clan. Notions of aunt, uncle, nephew, and niece in the patrilineal line were completely absent. Instead, all siblings of parents were mothers and fathers, and all children of those parents were considered sisters and brothers. Thus, marriage outside of one's own family necessarily forced clans to interact. Although a child was closely related to the father's family, the mother's relations were still important. In life as in death, "uncles"—generally meaning one's maternal relatives—retained an irreplaceable ritual role in everyday life of Mchagga. One could not name a child without the knowledge of the uncles. Nor could one circumcise without their permission, marry without their approval, or bury in their absence. In fact, just as one's father had a right to the *kidari* (the breast) of every slaughtered animal, one's uncles were entitled to the *moongo* (the back) of all slaughtered beasts. At death, the recent dead habitually sought refuge among those of *umoosoni* (of the left, meaning "the uncles") in the spirit world, from where their living relatives had to ritually redeem them and reconcile them to their patrilineal ancestors.[58] In this way, ritual networks extended vertically along the patrilineal line and horizontally along the matrilineal line. The horizontal connections could be indefinitely extended, for the wider Chagga community was never strictly endogamous, and one's "uncles" could be Wakamba, Wataita, or Wamasai.

Ritual activity remained largely within family and clan networks. If this limited interactions, markets allowed less restricted social and economic exchange. It is said that Chagga youth spotted their lovers in the market.[59] Rebmann noted that these open *sangaras* defied clan and chiefdom boundaries. "Just as traffic brings many of the powerful tribes into frequent contact," he observed, "so do the Jagga meet together at their Sangaras, or market-places, with their nearest neighbours, the Dafeta, the Ugono, and the Kahe."[60] Frequented mainly by women and the youth, the *sangaras* had become important supply stations and had allowed exchange among the Chagga themselves and between them and their neighbors well before the colonial era. In the late nineteenth century, Johnston could see Maasai women and elders at Taveta and Moshi exchanging honey and vegetables.[61] Moreover, ancient routes across forests, extending from the easternmost to the westernmost parts of Kilimanjaro, point to a possibility of exchange across very long distances around the mountain.[62]

Through the markets, the Chagga consumed foreign products like clay pots, iron tools and *mbala*; that is, natron or *magadi* in Kiswahili.[63] Obtained from Kahe on the plains below Kilimanjaro, the latter product became an important nutritional substance and attained ritual significance among the Chagga. One also saw items from the coast, including cloth and beads.[64] The markets further helped traders to identify specifically Chagga tastes to know what goods to carry for barter when heading to Kilimanjaro. As Meyer learnt, there one took small pink or light blue Venetian beads, not the medium-sized crimson, dark blue, or white ones liked by other neighboring communities.[65]

What this population mixture reveals is an intense exchange of people, products, social ideas, and cultural practices, brought to Kilimanjaro from disparate directions and harmonized to form a community. Here, community does not mean a homogeneous group of people. Rather, the Chagga became a community in social and political scientist Karl Wolfgang Deutsch's (1912–92) sense of "a group of persons who are able to communicate information to each other effectively over a wide range of topics."[66] Such communication, it should be stressed, is made possible not so much by words as by an open set of shared symbols that are imbued with cultural significance. The Chagga evolved "a cluster of related dialects," Bantu in structure and closely associated with other languages in the region.[67] Like the Maasai, they practiced circumcision as a physical mark of initiation. Again like the Maasai, they ate *mlaso*, which was blood carefully drawn from necks of living cattle. There has been considerable opinion that these two practices originated from Cushitic-speaking societies further north, pointing to another layer of cultural interaction between the Chagga and other peoples within the broader region.[68] Furthermore, some keen observers have noted that the Chagga manifested an appetite for meat uncommon among farming societies, probably an element that was carried over from a more cattle-based existence elsewhere.[69]

Ultimately, whatever we may call "Chagga culture" today necessarily consists of layers of diverse origins, carefully laid down as if by a great master planner. Yet diversity of origin need not imply lack of originality. Elements appropriated were not necessarily used in the same way. For example, like the Taita, the Chagga wore the *kishong'o* ring made out of skin but did this for different purposes. In 1849, Chagga chiefs gave Rebmann the *kishong'o* as a token of friendship, but later Hollis noted that, unlike the Chagga, the Taita used it as a symbol of matrimonial bond.[70] In fact, the Chagga may have used the *kishong'o for* a myriad of other family rituals, as Dundas and the culturally keen Chagga chief Petro Itosi Marealle (d. 1982) observed.[71] Again, the Chagga and Maasai practice of circumcision may have a common origin, but still missionaries noticed a physical difference in the way the Chagga and the Maasai circumcised their sons, finding offence in the style of the latter.

Moreover, cultural creativity is better appreciated by observing the use of local items in ritual and in everyday life. Bananas—varieties of which, as Judith A. Carney and Richard Nicholas Rosomoff have argued, became indigenized in the region before the recorded transoceanic travels of the fifteenth and sixteenth centuries—were indispensable to the life of the Chagga.[72] A myriad of dishes were made out of green bananas. Ripe ones were served as fruit. Banana juice was mixed with an important local grain, *mbeke* (*Eleusine coracana*), and the mixture was fermented to make a brew that was essential for ritual and entertainment. These days the brew is called *mbege*, a name that has replaced the older *wari* that now refers to any alcoholic drink. Attributing the earlier-mentioned native skill in artificial irrigation to the need to grow *mbeke*, Dundas said, "the Chagga tribe presents the unprecedented instance of economic and social welfare vigorously furthered by the vice of alcoholism."[73]

Dundas's view aside, an even more important item in Chagga ritual was the *isale* (plural: *masale*; that is, the *Dracaena steudneri* plant). This evergreen plant was used to mark boundaries of a *kihamba*, the land on which a banana grove was established and identified as a family property under its male head. The *isale* was also used to seal contracts and to reconcile the estranged. In no way could an *isale*-bearing envoy be harmed anywhere on Kilimanjaro, except by the most heinous breach of custom.[74] When Rebmann was summoned to meet Masaki, chief of Kilema, in 1846, Rebmann's guide put "grass" into his hand, and he found the chief holding some as well.[75] This "grass" was most likely the *isale* leaves. Stahl would later call it "the old Chagga plant of peace and pardon," "the sacred Chagga plant," and "the Chagga holy plant"—all very accurate descriptions without any exaggeration.[76]

A man's *kihamba* was, in a way, the summary of all that it meant to be Chagga. Surrounded by a *masale* fence, each had an entrance called *mengele* or *kichumi*. This led to the center of the *mnda* (banana grove) where a homestead for each nuclear family was established. Reflecting this setting, a 1955 letter to the editor claimed, "We all know that a Mchagga is one with *Kihamba*, *Isale* and *Nyinda*," the latter word meaning banana plant.[77]

Traditionally, the Chagga homestead included one or two conical-shaped huts thatched by dry banana leaves or grass.[78] In this house, the father's seat at some respectable place and the mother's fireplace at the center were ritually installed.[79] Animals too found space in the house. Stall-fed, these animals were valued less for their meat than for their dung, which fertilized the intensely cultivated *kihamba*. The animals were also the Chagga symbol of wealth, which, in that one house, meant "fecundity, prosperity and comfort, all under one roof."[80] Near the house was a barn, artistically made and well covered, in which the family's *mbeke* and other valuables were preserved.[81] In later times, an *itongo*—a square, often single-room, Swahili-style house—was added on the compounds of the well-off. In the *itongo*, the homeowner slept or the *mbege* was kept.

A more-or-less typical nineteenth-century Chagga homestead was thus complete. Children could play outside, women could go to the market, and men could be out in the fields, but, come evening, all returned to this private home. It was also in this home that the dead were buried, sometimes indoors and always facing Kilimanjaro, signifying complete ownership of the land and unity of family members, living and dead.[82] The Chagga exhumed ancestral skulls and gathered them in a *mbuo*, the *masale*-made clan or family shrine that constituted the most sacred family space within the banana grove.[83] For the Chagga, it was those that did not stay in this kind of home environment that were not Chagga.

The Chagga referred to these others as *Kyasaka* or *Mmwai* (plural: *Wamwai*), simply meaning someone "from the wilderness" or "from the bush."[84] Interestingly, this derogatory way of regarding others as "from the wilderness" was not peculiar to the Chagga. "Shambaa" is said to mean "the place where bananas thrive," and the drier areas neighboring the old Shambaa Kingdom were called *nyika*, meaning wilderness.[85] Until the 1940s, most communities in the hinterland of Mombasa bore the name *Wanyika*, but this was changed to "Miji Kenda" in the mid-twentieth century because the former was considered too derogatory.[86] The root *saka* from which *Kyasaka* derives is the Chagga equivalent of *nyika* from which Wanyika comes, as Dundas also observed.[87] In Kikamba and Kikuyu, the root would be *thaka* (or *theka*), rendering into *Wathaka* what the Chagga called *Kyasaka*. From this point of view, there is a likelihood, once proposed by the notorious German colonizing agent Carl Peters (1856–1918) and unconvincingly rejected by Charles Hobley that the words "Dsagga" or "Dshagga" had some connection with both the Kamba and Kilimanjaro.[88] If this were indeed the case, the Chagga may have retained for their name a Kamba version of what they themselves called others derogatorily. Given the Kamba preponderance in Chagga history, this is not an inconceivable possibility.

So far, this narrative may appear to create an impression of social and cultural homogeneity among the Chagga. Without presuming to be exhaustive, it has focused on the elements that afforded them a community identity. Yet this need not mean lack of diversity in localized detail. For example, ancestral diversity, which has been dealt with in some detail, has sometimes been used to explain differences, from amounts of dowry paid to language specifics.[89] Be that as it may, the aspect of the Chagga story that stands out is that, out of so much diversity, so much commonality was possible.

The social and cultural identity expressed through ritual networks across families and clans were not coterminous with any Chagga polity. Individuals prayed when they needed to, and publicly organized religion was a rare practice in Chagga life. Families performed rituals according to need, and clans, joined by friends and neighbors, organized marriages and funerals. Rather than a solemnized ordination, seniority of age was the necessary quality of those who presided over ritual.[90]

The *mangi* (chief; plural: *wamangi*) had little or no role at all in the ritual life of his people. For example, although he could determine the date for circumcision that marked the beginning of a new age group, his action was not needed to validate the rituals involved but simply to exercise control over and add prestige to the group through the presence of his own sons in it.[91] Even the sons had no ritual responsibilities, for the ceremonies could be (and often were) performed without them. Moreover, families and clans sacrificed to their own ancestors according to their own customs and procedures.[92] Occasional public rituals and sacrifices could be necessitated by an evil that befell an entire chiefdom. Rather than preside over such rituals, the most a *mangi* could do was to provide animals and other items required for the purpose and order the rituals to be carried out by the elders in his own family or in different families and clans under his jurisdiction.[93] Unless he merited it by age, the *mangi* was not a ritual elder even within his own family, let alone in his chiefdom.

The limited ritual significance of the Chagga chief makes it difficult to view him as a "universal kinsman" as Moore once suggested, even in a restricted sense.[94] His role was mainly political, and not every one of his actions can be explained in terms of tradition and culture. This observation becomes clearer as we now focus on nineteenth-century politics on Kilimanjaro.

Chagga Political Organization

There are various schools of thought about the origin of chieftaincy among the Chagga. Some think it evolved naturally from the clan system, with one clan conquering and subduing others.[95] This theory fails to explain some details. Chagga chieftaincy rested wobbly upon the clan networks that predated it and survived its demise in post-independence Tanzania. Clan relationships continued to have greater cultural and ritual bearing on individuals than did their political chiefdom affiliations. In a war between opposing chiefdoms, for example, two engaging warriors broke away with remorse if they realized they were clansmen.[96] On the contrary, chiefs exercising their political mandate did not hesitate to seek help from neighboring communities like the Maasai, the Waarusha, or the Wataita in order to settle scores with fellow Chagga chiefs. This political behavior defies conventional expectation. For example, prominent English social anthropologist E. E. Evans-Pritchard (1902–73) viewed the "tribe" as the largest territorial unit whose members combine in war against an outside enemy and settle internal scores by arbitration, a principle the Chagga clearly defied.[97]

Wimmelbücker attributes an eastern Nilotic origin to the Chagga term *mangi* and considers it to have been introduced to Kilimanjaro in the 1600s when it replaced an older designation *ntemi* or *mtemi*. Alongside this proposition is a great likelihood that, unlike the east-west migration trend, the "*mangi* tradition" followed a west-east trend, reaching Rombo last.[98] Of interest is Wimmelbücker's association of the term with an age-set system where the *mangi* was leader of the warrior *rika* (age group; plural: *marika*). This was the theory implicitly favored by Bruno Gutmann, who saw state consciousness as developing at the point where "the tension between associations based on kinship and those based on age brings about a change of balance, and leadership begins to pass to the latter, age-class becoming a warrior class which outgrows the clan and subjects kinship-groupings to its own leaders."[99]

This age-set system, which had disappeared from Kilimanjaro in the later part of the nineteenth century, had connections with a region-wide socio-political tradition probably championed by the Maasai.[100] According to Dundas, early Chagga *marika* bore the same names as those of the Maasai, and the two could even be cross-dated.[101] However, the warrior group being politically the most important *rika* in the society, its installation was more likely a matter of local control than mere response to a regional rhythm. For example, Chagga chiefs handed over power to their senior sons, a transfer often made to coincide with the stepping down of a warrior *rika* in favor of its successor age group.[102]

A *rika* was formed along generational lines, not clan lines. Made of newly initiated *wasoro* (men; singular: *msoro*), the warrior *rika* constituted the *watengo* who were the chiefdom's crucial defense force.[103] It supplied labor for digging *mreshe*, the defensive dugouts which could hold up to whole villages together with their cattle.[104] It maintained old furrows and made new ones. For all these reasons, the birth of a *msoro* brought great delight to the chief. "As soon as they can do without a mother's care," said Rebmann, "all male children are compelled to live together, to be trained early to serve the king as guards and their country as engineers."[105] The chief needed their labor to dispense the services expected of him by his people.

In turn, he reserved the right to collect tribute from his people, often in the form of beasts and brew. He used a large part of the tribute to look after the *wasoro* that served him. He preferentially looked after those from poor families at initiation and provided them with bride wealth at marriage.[106] He had to strike good balance between services offered and tribute demanded, otherwise people deserted his chiefdom and shopped around for a better chief.

As an institution, Chagga chieftaincy changed rapidly and constantly. The chief changed from being the leader of a *rika* to the man (very rarely the woman) who had the ability to keep himself in power and also remained chief for as long as he could continue to do so. Support mechanisms shifted from members of a *rika* to members of a clan, giving rise to the notion of a chiefly clan in particular localities around Kilimanjaro. However, Chagga chieftaincy never became fully hereditary. There were as many clans seeking to seize the chieftaincy as there were individuals within ruling clans seeking to climb on the throne. The tradition of chiefs stepping down for their elder sons was a strategy to avoid contest by retaining and consolidating power in the chief's house. Moreover, stronger chiefs handpicked vassals and sometimes sent their own relatives to rule beyond home territory. Thus, a "ruling clan" among the Chagga meant a clan capable of sustaining one of its own members in power rather than one with undisputed royal blood.

It is also possible that, as regional and local migrations became more restricted because of land scarcity or simply attachment to space, chiefs could exercise more authority over their subjects. More certainly, as Kilimanjaro became increasingly incorporated into the nineteenth-century coastal caravan trade, the chiefs were equally increasingly interested in controlling their end of the trade, with less attention paid to dispensing traditional services to their people. Tribute continued to be collected, now not so much for the care of *wasoro* as for provisioning caravans that called on the mountain. Thus, tribute became increasingly extortionist, an attribute of Chagga chieftaincy most recalled today.

Organization of Nineteenth-Century Chiefdoms

Early Europeans who visited Kilimanjaro before the terms "chiefdom" and "chief" were conventionally reserved for African traditional polities and political leaders spoke of native states, kingdoms, and kings. For example, Rebmann reported reaching "the little kingdom of Kilema" where he was met by "a number of soldiers of Masaki, the King of Kilema."[107] From Rebmann we also learn that the earliest remembered (though disastrous) expedition to climb Kilimanjaro was commissioned by "Rengua, king of Majame."[108] Rebmann knew the local term *mangi* and used it thrice in his accounts, but he more persistently called them kings.[109] The Catholic missionary Le Roy also referred to Pfumba of Kilema as "Sa Majesté" and "le souveraign," albeit with a touch of cynicism.[110]

Similarly, Johnston talked of "the populous states of Chaga around the southern and eastern flanks of this mighty snow-crowned volcano."[111] He was envious of Rebmann, who passed through "the little *Čaga states*" unperturbed, since, in Johnston's view, Arab traders and the slave trade had not yet brought the curse of internecine war to the region.[112] Comparing these Chagga states with the political organizations of the Wanyika, Krapf found both to be extremes: "each Kinika tribe strikes off again into several under- or sub-divisions," he wrote, "as though they intended to carry their republicanism to the extreme, in opposition to the despotic monarchies of Chagga and Usambara and of other countries in Africa."[113]

The use of terms like kings and states provides insight into the spontaneous and unconventional judgment of those who pioneered the European mission in tropical Africa. They had every reason to think of states, whether monarchical or republican. The chiefs they encountered on Kilimanjaro were sovereign heads of independent polities. They were often men, and sometimes women, who reserved authority to raise armies and responsibility to provide security.[114] Early missionaries and explorers depended on the security provided to them by these African political rulers. The Europeans also needed their permission to enter, work in, or leave the Chagga chiefdoms.

These nineteenth-century Chagga chiefdoms were numerous; they may have numbered over a hundred in the unrecorded past.[115] However, as stronger chiefdoms absorbed weaker ones, their number went down steadily, with only forty recorded in May 1894.[116] Some of these chiefdoms were big, some small, and some militarily stronger than others over which they exercised hegemonic control. Their heads were assisted by "privy councillors" that were locally known as *njama*.[117] At Kilema, Rebmann identified "the king's vizier" whose name was Rehani, and "other chief men of the land." When he was summoned to meet Masaki, he shook hands with not only the chief but also the chief's "ministers."[118] A similar decorum was observed at Machame. There, the missionary was followed by "the king and his chiefs" who came to receive presents and to hear what he had to say. At Moshi, Rindi sent "his counsellors" to negotiate with Johnston the price for a building site.[119]

Moreover, Chief Mamkinga of Machame included a Swahili *muanga* (medicine man) on his council.[120] This was most likely a common feature that persisted through most of the nineteenth century. For his part, Chief Sina of Kibosho had at his service

Taita fortune tellers and medicine men.[121] A ceremony through which Chief Pfumba of Kilema and Catholic missionaries became blood brothers was presided over by a man variously described by the missionaries as "the king's old sponsor" and "the old sorcerer."[122] A more vivid example is that of Makimembe, a famous—or "notorious" in missionary eyes—medicine man who served Marealle of Marangu and probably extended his services to Shira, Machame, Kibosho, Moshi, Mamba, and Ugweno.[123]

Besides these councilors, the chief's mother was politically important in an unofficial capacity. In situations where the chief had more than one wife, mothers became particularly instrumental in preserving their own issue from harm and seeing that they inherited the chieftaincy, a practice that further suggests a lack of clear hereditary procedures.[124] Apart from Mashina of Mamba, herself a chief's widow, all women chiefs were mothers acting as regents, a practice which Le Roy considered to have been a general norm among the Chagga.[125] Another unofficial but influential group in the traditional Chagga political structure was that of *masumba*. These were big men in a chiefdom, often rich with cattle and land, upon whom the chief relied for emergencies that could not be covered by tribute.[126]

The Chagga chief was not distinguished by any external mark or dress, although later in the twentieth century, some chiefs sought this distinction by wearing animal skins on top of western suits. However, the chief's soldiers wore a distinct dress. As Rebmann observed at Kilema, some of the chief's men (most likely his soldiers) wore caps made from skins and long garments.[127] A similar observation was recorded by Meyer and later missionaries, who noted the marked difference in the dress of those ready for war.[128]

From these details, the organization of the nineteenth-century Chagga chiefdom can be well reconstructed. As head of a chiefdom, the chief commanded a group of *wasoro* organized mainly for defense. According to Rebmann, the *wasoro* under the command of Masaki of Kilema, a relatively small chiefdom in mid-nineteenth century, numbered about four to five hundred.[129] Those under Rindi of Moshi, a relatively strong chiefdom in the latter part of the same century, numbered about one thousand and, according to Johnston, constituted "the pick of Moši's manhood."[130] Those under Sina of Kibosho, another strong chiefdom, also numbered about one thousand in the early 1890s and included some instructors from Arusha.[131] Some chiefs placed their fighters under the command of a trusted individual. For this purpose, earlier in the nineteenth century, Rengua of Machame had his brother, Mwara, and later Marealle of Marangu had Sianga.[132] Moreover, besides the *njama* that directly advised the chief, there were *wachili* (singular:

mchili) who oversaw smaller administrative divisions and reported to the chief.[133] The *wachili* distributed land, collected tribute, settled disputes, and sat on the chief's lawn of justice.[134]

At the beginning of the twentieth century, the Chagga population was estimated at 125,000. A chiefdom could have a population of anything between one thousand and twenty thousand people.[135] This again confirms that none of the polities described was coterminous with the social and cultural networks that gave the mountain population a common identity. While clan networks extended beyond the often-changing chiefdom boundaries, each chiefdom contained a mere section of such networks.

Political Allegiance and Community Identity

Their diverse ancestry and decentralized politics have made the Chagga difficult to fit into conventional categories. Their sense of shared identity has sometimes been dismissed. Dundas, for example, had "A History of the Wachagga, Their Laws, Customs and Legends" as part of his title and noted that they had a "more or less common language" and their customs were "in the main identical, but varying in detail," then went on to write "there is no common name for the inhabitants of this mountain." His reasoning was that "they originate from various tribes, and even from different races," thus lacking in something he considered essential to group identities: a common ancestry.[136] Before Dundas, Johnston had been more optimistic: "Although these little states are perpetually quarrelling among themselves," he wrote, "they are nevertheless closely united by ties of blood and possess a common language, Ki-čaga, unless, indeed, the Warombo, as I have sometimes thought, speak a dialect of their own."[137] Johnston's latter part of his observation probably referred to the distinct Kingassa dialect in Rombo mentioned earlier.

For believers in social evolution, the nineteenth-century Chagga community offers an example of a society in the early stages of political centralization. At the end of her volume on Chagga ethnography, Stahl asked: "Had the Europeans not taken over the sovereignty of Kilimanjaro in 1886, would the Chagga themselves have united?"[138] Her response was in the affirmative. Unlike Dundas who thought centralization would have happened through either Rindi of Moshi or Sina of Kibosho, Stahl clearly judged that it was imminent through the latter chief who attained fame and notoriety through stratagem and force.[139] But what Stahl never asked was whether the Chagga should have united at all. Plurality of polities does not strike many as possibly a different way of political organization, which could have been perfected with time, but simply as a stage in some social-evolutionary wheel.

Before European colonization of Kilimanjaro, the Chagga resisted political centralism. There was not a mono-directional progression toward centralization, as chiefdoms united and split for various reasons throughout the nineteenth century. The rise of a strong, forceful leader occasioned unification, just as his demise was followed by split into smaller polities.[140] Besides, political unity did not necessarily translate into political strength. Often greater centralization implied political vulnerability on the part of the ruler, entailing suspicion of unyielding subjects and its attendant reliance on force.

Yet hegemonic control by a strong chief over some weaker ones was commonplace, making political competition on the mountain rife throughout the nineteenth century. Such was the dominance of Rengua and Horombo, the two most famous chiefs in the early part of the 1800s. Legend has it that they met at the Nanga River and agreed to divide Kilimanjaro into two, Rengua ruling from there westward and Horombo eastward.[141] However, theirs was a mere hegemonic overrule, not centralized bureaucracy. They intervened in the appointment of other chiefs—which further complicates notions of hereditary chieftaincy in Kilimanjaro—and demanded tribute from their vassals. Although Rengua had ceased to rule Machame about six years before Rebmann visited the chiefdom, his chiefdom's dominance over Kilema could still be sensed.[142]

It is Horombo who provides the most accomplished example of imperial attempt followed by total collapse. He is believed to have attempted to centralize and control the supply of ivory to Kamba caravans and to monopolize the distribution of commodities obtained in exchange. He made maximum use of a geographical advantage, as the northeastern part was better located for caravans between Mombasa and Kilimanjaro. The area was also rich with elephants. Horombo united all chiefdoms in the northeastern region of Kilimanjaro into one political unit under his leadership and bequeathed to it his own name, Rombo.[143] As if that were not enough, he extended his tentacles to the central-south region of Vunjo, reducing the chiefdoms there to tributary status and naming their chiefs. Horombo's success is partly explained by his ability to incorporate in his force warriors from each sub-chiefdom and to appoint loyal sub-chiefs. He died while fighting against the Masai, probably in the early 1830s. At his death, he had nearly two-thirds of the then Chagga population under his overrule.[144]

Horombo's empire did not survive his demise. Dissensions among his successors led to secessions of the different sub-chiefdoms, which were never to unite again.

But internal causes do not fully account for this imperial collapse. A growing Omani interest in Zanzibar slowly shifted the center of coastal trade from Mombasa to Zanzibar, leading to the ultimate subjugation of the Mazrui dynasty in 1837.[145] The caravans to Kilimanjaro now started from Pangani and Tanga, and the coastal Waswahili replaced the Kamba as the dominant middlemen. Moshi was the best mountain destination for these caravans. With trade, political drama on Kilimanjaro shifted from the northeast to the southwest. At the center stage were the chiefdoms of Moshi and Kibosho, especially in the last third of the nineteenth century.

The show of force between Rindi of Moshi and Sina of Kibosho is probably the most detailed story of Chagga political competition. More than any others at their time, the two competed for control of the Kilimanjaro segment of two interconnected regional systems: caravan trade and cattle raiding. From Kilimanjaro, coastal caravans obtained refreshments and provisions for their journey and exchanged cloth and guns for ivory and some war-captive slaves. Guns had a significant impact on the geopolitics of the region, not least on the practice of war and cattle raiding. Both Rindi and Sina used guns in their regular campaigns. At this point, raiding was fueled more by the need to provision caravans than by Chagga appetite for meat. It is said that the Chagga despised fowl meat, yet they even bred large numbers of fowls for selling to passing caravans, which implies a community that was open to new economic opportunities.[146]

Political success or even mere survival in these complex systems depended on a combination of factors, military strength being one of them. Sina's army was stronger than Rindi's, but the latter chief knew better how to negotiate for external support, especially from the Waarusha.

A second factor was the ability to make local and regional alliances.[147] One way Chagga chiefs did this was through the establishment of blood brotherhoods with fellow chiefs, as did Nkunde of Wanri in the west with Kinabo of Mkuu in the east.[148] So also did the youthful Shangali of Machame with Sina of Kobosho, when the latter had resisted every other effort to stop him from plundering his western neighbors.[149] Another way was through intermarriage among ruling families. Ndetia, Rindi's father, is said to have "strengthened his position by marriage, and espoused several princesses of the reigning families in the vicinity of his kingdom."[150]

A third factor was the skill to befriend foreigners, including Europeans, and to keep them away from competitors. This was an old trick. Rebmann was persuaded by the chiefs he met not to move on to other chiefdoms, and every time he showed intent to move on, he was plundered of his valuables.[151] This trick was eventually perfected by Rindi, whose general knowledge of the world highly impressed

Johnston. Rindi established contacts with the British consular in Zanzibar and requested for the Union Jack as a sign of British protection. He convinced coastal authorities that he was the paramount ruler of Kilimanjaro, a clear exaggeration of his powers.[152] He jealously guarded the Anglican missionaries he welcomed in 1885 because to him, they were a political asset. With the missionaries in his chiefdom, subsequent Europeans, whether travelers, traders, or colonizers, would have Moshi as their first stop on Kilimanjaro.[153] Rindi sent a letter to the consular in Zanzibar and received a golden ring as gift from Queen Victoria.[154] He sent Chagga envoys to Berlin, sent the German emperor "a fine tusk of ivory," and expected a gift in return. He also pestered his visitors for gifts, especially ammunitions, which he often got.[155] Noticing two small cannons in the chief's possession, the missionary Le Roy prayed that the imprudent gifts of the Europeans would not be turned against them.[156]

Finally, success depended on the skill to make political stratagems. When one felt too weak to confront one's opponent, one schemed to make that opponent collide with another stronger power. Often this involved supply of false intelligence, locally called *fitina*. It was a skill available to chief and commoner alike. In one case, a certain Merinyo, a high-ranking official and an intelligence officer in Rindi's army, did not like the clout gathering around Chief Marealle of Marangu. When he returned from a battle against Sina of Machame, Merinyo informed Rindi that among Sina's fighters were men speaking Kimarangu, the Marangu dialect of the Kichagga language. As this was interpreted to mean that Marealle supported Sina against Rindi, the latter chief granted Merinyo permission to lead a campaign against Marealle, even though Marealle was Rindi's son-in-law.[157] This incidence shows not only the power of stratagem but also the tendency of chiefly politics to override ties of blood. It warns against lumping of culture, tradition, and politics together in pre-colonial Chagga community.

With these details, a political map of Kilimanjaro just before it was taken over by Germans in 1886 can be fairly sketched. The whole mountain was virtually divided into two diplomatic blocks, one allied to Sina and another to Rindi. Most of the chiefdoms were vassalages of either one of these two powers. Attack on any vassalage easily translated into attack on the hegemonic lordship above it. Initially, German presence was seen as just another opportunity to be taken advantage of. Through German help, some chiefs strengthened hegemonic control, and others broke away from overrule as they had done in the past. It all started symbiotically, with some chiefs using the Germans against fellow chiefs while contributing men and provisions to the Germans' own expeditions in the region.

It was also with this kind of arrangement that the first European-led expeditions to scale the Kilimanjaro were provisioned and supported by Chagga men, who were commissioned by their chiefs. For the Chagga, this was just another new experience and opportunity, not entirely different from that of raring fowls to sell to foreigners or, in later years, growing coffee for the European market. As it had already happened over centuries, the mountain was attracting newcomers and, with them, new challenges and opportunities that the Chagga were willing to face and take by becoming expert climbers and helping others to climb Kilimanjaro.

CHAPTER 3

Facts and Fiction About Early Kilimanjaro Guides

SINCE THE EARLY NINETEENTH CENTURY, THE CHAGGA HAD BEEN CONNECTED TO long-distance trade routes that had developed in the East African region between the coastal hubs such as Bagamoyo, Saadani, and Mombasa and inland areas leading to Lake Tanganyika or passing through the Kilimanjaro region to Lake Victoria. Foreigners who became interested in exploring the higher reaches of the mountain first came via these routes. Missionaries and explorers often opened the way for colonial conquest in Africa, whether purposefully or inadvertently. German and British missionaries and explorers were the first Europeans to make inroads into Kilimanjaro and seek to conquer Kibo and Mawenzi. Once there, long-distance caravan work shifted to high-altitude mountain conditions where missionaries and explorers hired local Chagga guides and porters. The *mangi* supplied these visitors with guides and then porters. It is unclear who exactly were the first Kilimanjaro guides in the decades that Europeans started hiring them to hack their way through the forests and make their way to the saddle between Kibo and Mawenzi. The first guides employed in the nineteenth century were rarely named, and oral history has become muddled. Nonetheless, it is clear that they played a crucial role in the success of those early climbs. Mainly from Marangu, these men helped set the tone for the mountain-climbing industry that was to come. They acquired experience and knowledge from the mountain that became indispensable once the industry boomed. They passed on this experience and knowledge to relatives and neighbors as well as modeled ways to attend to clients with endurance, encouragement, and care, thus creating a cadre of potential porters and guides ready for hire when the industry needed them.

Long-Distance Caravans and European Colonial Expeditions

Since pack animals were too susceptible to trypanosomiasis spread by the tsetse fly in the East African region, caravans relied almost solely on human labor to carry their goods and supplies. A free wage labor market for porters had developed in the region by the early nineteenth century, although enslaved people were also used in long-distance caravans.[1] In this partly monetized economy, porter labor became commercialized with specialization and the rise of recruitment agents. The Swahili on the coast and the Nyamwezi in the region between the coast and Lake Tanganyika came to dominate this porter work. The Chagga were linked to these long-distance trading routes, yet engaged with trading caravans more so by welcoming them as visitors who came to trade and refresh in the more abundant mountain lands than by working as porters.[2] When Europeans came to travel to Mt. Kilimanjaro, enslaved individuals and ivory were the major trading items sent to the coast in exchange for cloth, beads, guns, and other imported goods.

The size and nature of caravans varied from small groups of a dozen people to huge caravans of hundreds of porters; from cooperative groups banding together to caravans run by commercial bosses; and from occasional to full-time porters. Porters were hired at various points along the trading routes but largely at either end of the long-distance routes as the larger caravans were organized at those points. Recruitment agencies and agents arose in coastal towns as more Europeans arrived there and created a bigger demand for porters in the late 1800s. Porters could register with agents or market their labor individually. They were paid a large percentage up front (in goods or money), then compensated for the rest of their work at the end of the trip. Some may have returned home at that point or hoped to obtain more work for the return trip. Nyamwezi men often engaged in this porter work to invest back into their homes and families. The structure of their society and agricultural and economic activities meant that they had access to labor in their homes, which allowed more men to leave to work as porters.[3] The seasons and agricultural conditions also determined when some were willing to work in trading caravans. Others may have engaged in porter work because of agricultural hardship or because the more urban coastal regions they originated from also facilitated this form of long-distance trade work.

In larger caravans, a culture of hierarchy, internal organization, and standard practices developed, influenced heavily, historian Stephen J. Rockel argues, by Nyamwezi, along with coastal groups. The caravan labor was organized through announcements in villages and towns, individuals searching for work, or recruitment agents. Once the laborers assembled, the loads were distributed and a division of labor established. Europeans described dividing provisions and goods into parcels weighing 50 to 70 lbs each, although certainly the loads varied in weight depending on the objects carried. Porters had to carry their assigned load along with some of their own equipment—even protection, such as a firearm or spear, if traveling through dangerous regions. Other porters carried food that was easy to transport and prepare, such as staples like beans, rice, or millet. Caravan officers and leaders managed large numbers of porters, with officers handling the recruitment, organization, and provisions for porters and guides or march leaders setting the pace and marking the path. Rockel also highlights the role of *mganga* or diviners in providing spiritual protection for Nyamwezi-led caravans.[4] As the caravan reached its destination each day, managers and officers directed the setting-up of camp and designated cooks to prepare food. After a morning or day's march, porters would have time to make any necessary repairs, attend to injuries, eat, and rest or entertain themselves before sleeping. As free agents, porters at times negotiated better working conditions, but at other times fell victim to hunger, thirst, and fatigue that came with this physically taxing work.

Beginning in the mid-nineteenth century, Europeans started to engage caravan teams to head into the interior with Kilimanjaro as their destination. Missionary Johannes Rebmann recruited a team of men for his 1848 journey.[5] Rebmann was followed by other German missionaries and British geographers and explorers, such as Richard Burton and John Hanning Speke in 1858, Karl Klaus von der Decken and Richard Thornton who reached snow on the mountain in 1861, Charles New in 1871, Joseph Thompson in 1883, Harry Hamilton Johnston in 1884, Samuel Teleki in 1887, and Meyer's trips of the same time (1887 and 1889). Accounts of their expeditions, written often by the lead Europeans, reveal the colonial and scientific aspects of their caravans that shaped the character of these European-led journeys. They were colonial in purpose—seeking to know, claim, and conquer African land—and also

FIGURE 3. Hans Meyer's 1889 caravan on its way to Kilimanjaro. HANS MEYER, ACROSS EAST AFRICAN GLACIERS: *An Account of the First Ascent of Kilimanjaro* (London, 1891), 44–45.

in holding a sense of European racial and cultural superiority. The exploratory and scientific purposes of expeditions up Kilimanjaro also changed the nature of porter work, increasing the time of the journey, changing the destination, and adding an element of specialization to certain porter roles.

Harry Hamilton Johnston and Hans Meyer's accounts portray the organization of porter work in their expeditions similar to the trade caravans of the time. They wrote about the effort that went into preparing for the expedition, including securing a team of porters through local contacts on the coast or individual porters they already knew. Johnston wrote that his 1884 caravan consisted of 120 men (thirty of whom were hired for one month to take them to the base of the mountain) who carried 50 lbs each.[6] In 1889, Meyer gathered men from various places for a total of around one hundred who carried about 60 lbs each (hiring sixty Swahili porters at Zanzibar).[7] They employed a hierarchy of managers and headmen among the crew and paid them according to the customs of the time. However, unlike trade caravans, they also sought people with particular skills and local knowledge and, rather than release all their porters at their final destination, encamped on the foothills of Kilimanjaro with some of their crew for further study or exploration.

Johnston complained of his troubles securing "collectors"—two men to help him gather his plant specimens.[8] Johnston, Meyer, and other European expeditions set up camps on Kilimanjaro among the Chagga for months, Johnston spending six months in 1884 and Meyer just over one month in 1889. Groups of porters were left for periods of time at lower camps as the Europeans ascended, with Johnston taking nine of his own men on his first ascent and three on his second, and Meyer and Purtscheller leaving two headmen, nine porters, and three Somali managers at a central camp, while taking Mwini Amani with them to their upper camp. The smaller number of porters who stayed with the explorers shifted from carrying loads to building and managing camps. Those who accompanied these explorers to higher elevations met different weather conditions with extreme cold temperatures and the physical risks of high altitudes.

Both expeditions also hired guides with valuable local knowledge of the mountain from different Chagga chiefs—Johnston taking six from Moshi and two from Marangu and Meyer writing about taking two from Marangu. These first expeditions relied on the good graces of the Chagga *mangi* to obtain local help. The practice of the *mangi* arranging for knowledgeable people to act as guides and later other laborers continued into the early twentieth century until certain men established careers of working as guides. The level of cooperation of the *mangi* shaped which routes explorers established. Moshi and Marangu were the settlements with the most interactions with Europeans. It was also the case that, at that time, the two chiefdoms competed to attract European attention to themselves. The *mangi* of Marangu courted European explorers better than the *mangi* of Moshi. Both Johnston and Meyer shifted from Moshi to Marangu, allegedly because the *mangi* of Moshi proved difficult to work with.

The colonial mindset of European racial and cultural superiority is evident in the way that these explorers wrote about and treated their porters. For example, they cited the simple wants and aptitudes of the porters or their complaints about the work as evidence of their racial weakness. Johnston described the variety of food he took for himself, then contrasted that with the beans and maize they packed for the porters, exclaiming, "How easily fed these Swahili porters are! What other race would be content to trudge twenty miles a day with a burden of sixty pounds, and be regaled on nothing but maize and beans?"[9]

Johnston and Meyer revealed their views of Africans in the way they wrote about crew behavior. They both deliberated on the best way to inspire discipline in the porters. Johnston recounted an incident at the beginning of his trek where he physically punished a porter, which he claimed established his authority.[10] Other local or Arab caravan commissioners and managers certainly also meted out punishments, especially if the porters were enslaved. Yet Rockel indicates that African caravan leaders took a more non-violent approach.[11] Europeans thought it important to make an example of those punished for ill-discipline because of their distrust of Africans and expectations of deviant behavior. Johnston and Meyer described porters they could trust as exceptions to what they otherwise believed to be a negative African character.

Johnston and Meyer also praised certain ethnic or regional groups over others, in line with colonial tendencies of ethnic classification. Johnston complained of the problematic Rabai porters he hired on the coast near Mombasa. Meyer's "rather crude" descriptions of Africans led Boris Michel to argue that Meyer "was constantly concerned with the self-fashioning of his own whiteness and with German civilization."[12] Meyer hired a small number of Somali porters on his way to Zanzibar because he held a racial philosophy that they had "superior characteristics" for working with Europeans and believed that having foreign managers reduced the chance of insubordination among porters.[13] Describing one of the head Zanzibari porters he obtained through his recruiting agent, Meyer wrote, "Ugly, lazy, insolent, cowardly, weak, dishonest, untruthful, he is a typical Zanzibari. Nevertheless I tolerate him, for he is personally responsible to Siwa Haji for the behavior of the rest of the caravan." Meyer also spoke of the "easy-going, contented Wanyamwezi" in contrast to others who were "constantly in need of the whip to bring them to their senses." On the same page, he praised the porters' "physical performances" which "would do credit to any respectable beast of burden"—to which, he added, "in many respects, they bear a striking resemblance."[14] He seemed to buy into what anthropologist Ter Ellingson has called "the myth of the noble savage," where Africans were the noble savages, but mostly savages, less human and more like animals.[15]

Those who attempted to climb Kilimanjaro in the 1880s preceded the establishment of scientific stations, colonial governments, and European farms that followed. They depended on several Chagga *mangi* for their supply of porters and other provisions. This relationship was reversed when German armies subjugated the Chagga and established headquarters in Moshi (today's Old Moshi) in 1890. The German government took over control of the region from the German East African company in 1895, after which they began to implement "rational development" in the form of colonial government, infrastructure, and new forestry and agriculture on Kilimanjaro, complete with scientific stations.[16] Alongside colonial infrastructure were also established networks of Lutheran and Catholic missionary stations and activities aimed at converting the Chagga to Christianity as well as introducing them to the new ways of the dawning colonial reality. Under German colonial rule, mainly Germans focused on mapping and studying the mountain. In 1909, the surveyor M. Lange made the second successful ascent of Kibo with his assistant Weigele, while Germans Fritz Klute and Edward Oehler made the first ascent of Mawenzi in 1912. A handful of other Germans subsequently climbed the mountain before World War I.[17] Thus did the climbing of Kilimanjaro for sport and tourism coincide with the region's colonial occupation.

The First Guides

The scramble for Africa followed the golden age of mountaineering by a few decades. European mountaineers were eager to explore the highest East African mountains, including Mt. Kenya and the Rwenzori. They were also keen on recording their attempts to summit Kilimanjaro. Published articles and historical synopses written by European climbers about the earliest attempts usually focus on the achievements of the Europeans. Still, they offer clues as to the role local guides and porters played in helping navigate the lower reaches of the mountain and in carrying equipment and provisions. They also depict how local men struggled with the conditions of the high altitudes, details corroborated by oral histories.

Wilhelm Methner of Stolberg (Harz), a former German district officer in Moshi, compiled a short history of the first ascents up to the 1930s, reportedly in consultation with Hans Meyer and Clement Gillman. Methner wrote that the difficulty for the first explorers was making a route from the forest edge, but credited local people in helping them overcome this challenge. The first few guides, porters, or "askaris" mentioned by Methner supposedly turned back at the higher points. When discussing a later 1898 attempt, Methner wrote that Meyer approached Kibo from the north, and "the two askaris who had accompanied them thus far returned to the intermediate camp." When District Officer Captain Johannes and Paymaster Korner made an attempt from Moshi in October 1898, they camped the fourth day in a cave on the east side of Kibo. According to Methner, "the porters, with the exception of Munifasi the askari and the cook, were sent back immediately on arrival there." Whether they sent the porters to fetch more supplies or whether their work was finished, we are left to wonder. Yet Methner wrote that "on October 8th, the two

Whites and Munifasi started at four oclock [*sic*] in the morning, but the latter only kept going for two hours." In other entries, Methner refers to "companions" accompanying other climbers. He described his own attempt in March 1907 with twelve porters (attempted during that time of year because it would not be so cold). They started their ascent of Kibo at 4:00 a.m. with "two natives," or "Wachagga," who eventually had to turn back before they entered Johannes Notch, a route through the ice wall. Other comments about porters in Methner's history include mentions of one porter getting lost completely and another group losing twenty men in a snowstorm.[18] Gertrude Benham, claimed to be the first British citizen and first woman to reach the summit in 1909, did so with a support crew of two guides, five porters, and a "cook boy." The guides led them through the forest, but apparently everyone stalled the next day when they came upon two skeletons from a previous expedition. According to Benham, she "argued, threatened, and bribed," but it was not until she picked up bags herself that the shame of having a "white woman" do the work led the "cook boy" and then two others to come.[19] She reportedly left them all at the upper camp and reached the top of the crater by herself. According to Methner, another 1914 group had porters give up after an hour.

Other guide names are mentioned by Methner and additional authors. Mountaineering historian Audrey Salkeld wrote about the American trek of Peter MacQueen and Peter Dutkewich in 1908 which employed the guide Souho and sixteen men provided by the Moshi chief Sulim.[20] W. C. West, a British man from Cape Town climbed the mountain in 1914. He hired a local crew of five porters, two of whom reached the crater with him. They made it into the crater, where a Chagga called Msamire stopped, while West and Jonathan, identified as Swahili, made their way up to the rim, and West reached the highest peak. They had a difficult time at the top. At one point, Jonathan disappeared into a small crevasse for quarter of an hour in a "terrific blizzard."[21] Methner also named Offoro as a guide who accompanied climbers G. Londt and Donald Latham to Mawenzi in the 1920s and wrote that a German film expedition in 1925 had an "old native guide" named Msamire who reached the top of the crater with three of the crew.[22]

It is likely that the three men who appeared in the records in the 1910s and 1920s—Msamire, Offoro, and Jonathan—began to act as regular guides, either appointed by a *mangi* (or chief) or hired as individuals looking for work. This is both evident in early written accounts and oral histories from elderly guides and porters from Marangu. The role of local government leaders in assembling crews shows up in Sheila MacDonald's writing. MacDonald, who claimed to be the first woman to reach the highest peak on Kibo, accompanied William West on his trip up the cone in 1927. In a description of the assembly of their support crew recounted later in her life, MacDonald remembered that they found a cook and a "boy" in Moshi and then traveled to Marangu where a "village headman, Mlanga" assembled porters. After giving them food ("eggs, milk and a fowl") and letting them "camp in front of his Council House," they asked for a dozen men to act as porters. "[Mlanga] had a large Kudu horn brought to him," she remembered, "on which the Royal Crier blew a great blast to summon the village. He then detailed off fourteen people who were to accompany us. That's how we got our porters. We started from there." Oral accounts of early guides also talk about *mangi* calling certain people to act as guides because of their knowledge of the forest and their prior work for the *mangi*.[23] In the post-WWI period, this method would have been used more generally to recruit labor for other purposes as required by the colonial government, including for road construction.

Both written and oral accounts of early mountain-climbing expeditions also highlight the difficult working conditions guides and porters faced. As in other photographs and descriptions from the early twentieth century, the photograph accompanying MacDonald's account in the Kilimanjaro Mountain Club's *Ice Cap* journal shows the porters wearing blankets and likely no shoes, making the "lava dust and little bits of pumice stone" difficult to walk on. MacDonald's account also gives us a clue as to how the Chagga in Marangu may have viewed the mountain and what that meant for the numbers of Chagga who may have spent time in the upper reaches of Kilimanjaro. The four porters not only had trouble finding Hans Meyer cave but reportedly "refused to go on any further, because to them it was a holy mountain." Thus, MacDonald, West, and another companion, Major Lennox-Browne, carried on the next morning, with West and MacDonald making it to the top. They later caught up with the porters at 10:00 p.m. at Peter's Hut, where the porters had a fire going.[24]

Despite the important work of these first guides, those who reached the crater rim considered their achievements European achievements. Sometimes they did not even name the local support crew that made their journeys possible. In 1921, Gillman wrote of his attempt with fellow officials of the Tanganyikan Territorial government—Charles Dundas, P. Nason, and F. J. Miller—believing they were the first British individuals to have reached the top of the crater and that theirs was the first serious attempt since British occupation in 1916.[25] In his private notes in the Kilimanjaro Mountain Club records, Gillman gave credit to the "brave and hardy gang of porters who spent two cold nights with us at 4700 m" allowing the rest of them to "enjoy much more warmth and comfort than would have fallen to our lot without them."[26] In a newspaper article published shortly thereafter, he wrote of "two natives" referred to as porters who accompanied them to caves at 15,390 ft and attempted to reach the crater with them the next morning. Cold wind, lack of oxygen, and exhaustion sent Miller, Dundas, "as well as the two natives" down partway, leaving Gillman and Nason to mark Gillman's point on the top of the crater. Apparently one porter, who must have been an adventurous and tenacious person, made it quite far: "cheerful to the last, only gave up at about 18,000 feet." However, when reporting on the significance of the ascent, the *Dar es-Salam Times* only reported about the four Europeans. The newspaper report reads: "The intrepid party have added another link to the chain [of] civilization, and the fact that two of them were not successful in the final accomplishment of their object does not detract from their achievement. The party have carved for themselves a niche in the history of great achievements, and to them all honour is due."[27]

Oral histories from older guides and porters from Marangu both corroborate the written records and give further clues as to the character and work of early guides, as well as how they fit in their home community. Older guides and porters likely conveyed the important aspects of the stories passed down over the years through generations of guides. Similar to written and photographic records, some interview participants emphasized the difficult work conditions the early guides faced, among them climbing without shoes and warm clothing and sleeping in caves. A few also talked about how the guides were hired. Some said they were youth who were chosen by the *mangi* because they had hunted in the forests. Others said the guides worked as messengers for the *mangi* or had some language skills that led them to obtain this work.

Although Yohane Lauwo eventually received respect from the community and recognition by the government in 1989 for his role in early Kilimanjaro climbs, there was a consensus in the oral history interviews that the community saw the few individuals who worked in the industry in the early years as either ordinary individuals or people to disdain for carrying the loads of the white Europeans.[28] Some of the older porters and guides even said that it was difficult to find a wife when they were young because the community saw them as no better than pack animals. It is possible that these community views explain why there does not seem to be a strong oral history tradition about these men beyond what is written on the commemorative plaques at the National Park gate in Marangu. Oral history has been clouded by narratives on these plaques that arose from the centennial celebrations of the first known successful ascent of 1889. This is evident in explanations about the first guides and Hans Meyer that contain chronological contradictions or mischaracterizations (e.g., that Lauwo and others met Hans Meyer at Kibo Hotel, which was not established at the time, or that Lauwo knew Hans Meyer because he was a missionary who worked in the area, or that Lauwo knew Rebmann, or that Hans Meyer came by himself the first time but returned with other visitors the second time). Those with closer familial and temporal ties to the history of the early guides shared more information similar to what we have found in the written record and have acknowledged that history has favored Lauwo.[29]

As more people beyond mountaineers came to climb Kilimanjaro in the early twentieth century, a tourism industry developed on the mountain. The birth of this industry can be attributed in large part to two hotels in Marangu and the efforts of the Kilimanjaro Mountain Club. The Lutheran missions and German colonization brought the first Europeans who made homes in Marangu. A German family built the Kibo Hotel likely in the 1880s or 1890s.[30] In the early 1900s, the German Thomas Kloss owned and managed the hotel. After the First World War, Kloss also managed the huts built on the mountain for climbers. The Marangu Hotel, built by Martin Bohdan von Lany, has operated longer than the Kibo Hotel (which collapsed in the early 2000s). Lany first went to Marangu in 1895 as a young missionary from Austro-Hungary where he helped build the Lutheran Leipzig Mission in Mamba, Marangu. Through the activities of the mission, he provided training in building and farming skills. After returning to Marangu with his wife, Emma, he left the mission in 1907. Having been granted a plot of land by *mangi* Marealle, he and Emma established a farm and embedded themselves in the community. The First World War disrupted their life, with Martin detained in Egypt and the rest of the family moving to the Usambara mountains for a time. After reuniting in Marangu and trying their hand in the coffee market, the Lany family added tourism onto their agricultural activities. Some of them had already employed local guides and porters to hike up to Kibo with visitors. The Lanys started to turn part of their farm into the Marangu Hotel and offered guided tours to Kilimanjaro beginning in the early 1930s.[31] These hotels outfitted groups of tourists with equipment, provisions, and arranged for local guides and porters.

The Kilimanjaro Mountain Club was founded in August 1929 by Mr. N. R. Rice and an indomitable missionary for the Leipzig Mission, Reverend Richard Reusch.[32] Club members consisted of Europeans living mostly in Moshi town and Marangu.[33]

Within the first six months, the club gained twenty-nine members. The club worked closely with the two hotels in Marangu to manage use of the huts on the mountain and organize trips for climbers. By 1932, the British government officially transferred control of the mountain huts from Kloss of the Kibo Hotel to the club. The club built a Kibo Hut near the final ascent of the crater later that year and took full control over hut maintenance and equipment.[34] An important leader in the club, Reusch came to love spending time on Kilimanjaro. At times, he was based at Marangu, at other times among the Maasai. He even acted as a guide himself, having ventured up to the top of Kibo multiple times and having explored Mawenzi "with some very thrilling adventures."[35] Reusch was later awarded medals for climbing Kilimanjaro fifty times over his thirty years in the region. He was also elected an honorary vice president for life of the club in recognition of all he had accomplished for the club.

The new mountain club sought to register competent guides and porters. In one of its first general meetings held in February 1930, Reusch named six possible guides and the number of porters they could each call upon to work with them: Offorro of Old Moshi (with ten porters), Jonathan of Marangu (with twelve porters), Johannes of Mamba (with eighteen porters), Mlombare of Mamba (with seventeen porters), and Somali and Eliah of Marangu (with seventeen porters).[36] Based on other records, it appears that these men were also known as Daniel Oforo, Jonathan Mtui, Yohane Lauwo, Mlombare "Thoma" Mosha, Somali son of Maruni Mahoo, and Elia Minja. A system emerged wherein local leaders, hotel owners, and the mountain club scheduled and arranged the trips and created a formalized process of registering and paying guides and porters. By the 1930s, these men emerged as the regular guides of the industry. "We have for several years had amongst the natives some who can to a certain extent be called guides," Methner wrote. He concluded, "If I have not mentioned the faithful natives who have taken part in the climbs, their efforts and good work have certainly not been underestimated or forgotten."[37]

These first guides set the tone for decades to come. We only find glimpses of their personalities and personal history in the written and oral historical record. Mountain club correspondence and meeting minutes occasionally provide important information regarding their personal particulars and work, such as their age, place of residence, family names, and maintenance or other work. Outstanding deeds are also mentioned. Some surviving reference books the guides were asked to carry and visitors' or climbers' books left in the huts and at Gillman's Point and Uhuru Peak (or Kaiser Wilhelm Spitze) from the 1930s into the 1950s are more revealing when it comes to their work on the mountain and their interactions with visitors. Oral histories mix ideas gleaned from the National Park plaques with more reliable commentary on the work and families of the guides. When analyzed critically, these sources help us reconstruct aspects of their experiences on the mountain, their expertise and services, and their contributions to mountain tourism on Kilimanjaro. The sources tell us the most about four men: Lauwo, Mlombare, Mtui, and Sambonanga.

Yohane Kinyala Rauya Lauwo (also known as Johane or Johannes by climbers) has gained the most attention over others because the Tanzanian committee in charge of the centenary celebrations of the first successful ascent of Europeans to the top determined that Lauwo, still living in Marangu in 1989, had accompanied Hans Meyer and Ludwig Purtscheller in 1889. A series of plaques at the Marangu gate celebrate Lauwo as the first "Tanzanian/African" to reach the highest peak and list his life span as 1871–1996 (which if true, would make him one of the oldest recorded persons ever to live at 125 years old). The plaques list the men who worked with Lauwo as assistant guide Jonathan Mtui and porters Elia Minja, Toma Mosha, Makelio Lyimo, and Mamba Kowera. Although early written records depict Chagga as being deterred from attempting to scale the ice-capped crater because of the weather or spiritual beliefs, it is possible that a Chagga person reached the highest point on Kibo before or around the same time as Meyer and Purtscheller. Chagga traversed the Kilimanjaro highlands as army scouts or to avoid clashing with other Chagga groups as they traveled to other regions. Yet historical records and reported oral histories cast doubt on the claim that Lauwo was at the top with Meyer and Purtscheller. Bernard Leeman, a local history enthusiast with a family relation to Lauwo, cited records of the Lutheran Church in a sentence that claimed Lauwo's birth year as 1871.[38] However, contrary to what Leeman implied, the baptismal record cited does not provide that information on Lauwo's birth. In fact, the catechist record accompanying the baptismal records for the Mamba Kotela mission station where Lauwo was baptized listed Lauwo as born in 1898, ten years after Meyer and Purscheller's ascent (which would mean he lived until age ninety-eight).[39]

Kilimanjaro Mountain Club archives offer further compelling pieces of evidence for a later birth year and later entry into guiding for Lauwo. Lists of guides and porters in the early years of the club record that "Yohane bin Rauya" was involved as a porter then guide as early as the mid-1920s. In October 1938, a list of guides and their porters included him as a guide from Mauo-Marangu with twelve years or more experience. Notes on the list indicate that Lauwo had a letter documenting his experience, which could have added more proof of a start-date for his work of at

FIGURE 4. Lauwo and Meyer plaques at Marangu Gate, 2021. PHOTO BY L. A. HADFIELD.

the latest 1926; however, this letter was not found in the archive. The list estimated Lauwo's age at "about" thirty-seven (which would have him born around 1900).[40] A 1953 entry by a Danish man in the Gillman's Point book reads "guide Yohanna is 50 years, and I am [70]." If language barriers and efforts to socially connect did not skew the information, this would have also put Lauwo born around 1900.[41] Twenty years after the 1938 lists of guides, a memo typed by the Kibo Hotel owner (then a German woman named Anne Bruehl) dated May 22, 1958, certified Lauwo's position as a guide and gave his brief curriculum vitae. The memo stated that Lauwo was born November 25, 1891, two years after the 1889 ascent. The document continues with details about Lauwo's career beginning in the 1930s: "Dr. Reusch appointed him a guide in 1932 (he has an original letter about it), and he got another letter confirming him to be a guide from the Mountain Club, in 1934. (He started 1930 as porter.) He has made at least 500 ascents (he was not only the guide for climbing safaris, but went up for many years to read the thermometers on behalf of the Meteorological Department)." While exact birthdates given about a time when African births were not immediately registered and both the written record and oral history can easily contain discrepancies about exact information, Lauwo's birth years in these written records are much closer to each other (1891, 1898, 1900) than

1871. Moreover, the dates listed in documents temporally closer to the event of his birth are likely to hold more accurate information.

Lauwo's own oral history as reported in *Tanzanian Affairs* and Meyer's writings corroborate the later dates. The *Tanzanian Affairs* article reported that Lauwo could not remember when he was born, but said he had climbed the mountain three times before World War I and remembered he and Jonathan Mtui meeting European men seeking to climb Kilimanjaro in Moshi. They asked them to accompany them to Kibo, a trip which took eight days.[42] While the centenary committee interpreted this and other documents and photos as confirming that Lauwo had met Meyer in Moshi, 1889 was twenty-five years before World War I. Lauwo still could have been in his teens or early twenties before World War I even if he had been born after 1889. Moreover, Meyer wrote that he and Purtscheller spent sixteen days in their upper camp, which would mean their trip was much longer than eight days. Furthermore, Meyer only mentioned two unnamed guides he hired from Marangu who returned without spending time near the crater. He wrote more extensively about Mwini Amani, a man from the coastal region of Pangani who maintained Meyer and Purtscheller's upper camp while they summitted.[43] The fact that Meyer did not name the two Marangu men is not a sure sign that other Chagga guides were not at the upper camp. Meyer desired to make his ascent a heroic German accomplishment in his writings and thus downplayed the contributions of local peoples.[44] However, deeper research into Lauwo's life reveals that he may not be the national hero Tanzania was hoping for in 1989.

Oral histories shared in 2021 and 2022 also give clues that Lauwo started working later than Meyer's attempts on Kilimanjaro. When asked about the history of the first guides or when asked about Lauwo directly, many interview participants repeated what the plaque at the Marangu gate said and even referred the interviewers to the gate. Even older guides and porters from Marangu, who may have known Lauwo and his family or had familial relations to him, talked about Lauwo as the one who guided Hans Meyer.[45] However, as mentioned, some of these stories of Lauwo contain chronological contradictions or mischaracterizations. There is also a range of reasons given as to why he became a guide. Some said he was close to the *mangi*, others that he was a hunter, or that the sight of snow intrigued him.[46] One said he was a carpenter or builder when he was not working on the mountain.[47] Samwel Mosha said he was a regular farmer and hunter and that he had more language skills than others, making him a good candidate for guiding foreigners. Presumably, he could communicate in Swahili, English, or German. Some older guides told stories that would more closely link Lauwo with mountaineers in the early twentieth century rather than Meyer. For example, Eliandra Minja said Lauwo worked with German missionaries when the white people came to climb the mountain, which could have been people who ran the Kibo Hotel, Reusch, or the Lany family.[48]

What might explain the discrepancies in oral histories or the lack of a stronger oral history of Lauwo's experience leading Meyer? If Lauwo was in fact with Meyer and Purtscheller, perhaps he did not fully recognize the historicity of his achievement. Becoming the first to reach the summit of major mountains was a focus of much of the European mountaineering community but may not have been a value of the Chagga or even Lauwo at the time. Lauwo and his colleagues may not have even been aware of the mountaineering fervor that existed in other parts of the world until they became wrapped up in the mountain-climbing industry that later developed on Kilimanjaro. Moreover, the community may not have viewed Lauwo as a hero until later in his life when the government celebrated him in 1989 and built him a new house. Thus, although Lauwo trained some of their fathers and uncles to be guides, subsequent guides who were interviewed later may not have been told much of his history or Lauwo may not have had fame in the community for what he did before the narrative featured on the plaque gained traction. Or, Lauwo simply may not have been there. Still, several others may have done it before him, making Lauwo's achievement more ordinary than novel.

Those with closer familial and temporal ties to the history of the early guides indicated that there is more to the story than what appears on the plaques. Lauwo did not have any sons. However, one of his brother's grandsons, Samson Lauwo, was seen as a grandson to Yohane and later became a porter, guide, and tour operator.[49] Because he was born around 1983, Samson only knew Yohane Lauwo when he was quite old and could not remember everything from his past. Still, Samson enjoyed listening to Yohane's stories as he spent time sitting with him. Samson described him as a loving, friendly person who was talkative and charming. Samson also remembered *wazungu* (foreigners, particularly white people) coming periodically to visit Yohane (when they would leave chocolates for the children). Samson remembered Yohane saying that his first guiding job came when he was a teenager and was appointed by the *mangi* because he was a hunter and knew the forest. His first client knew how to walk on the ice, using spears or axes. He also told Samson how challenging it was to work on the mountain without proper equipment, clothes, shoes, or itineraries. The foreign mountaineers brought their own food, and the Chagga guides brought their own food or found it in the forest. Furthermore, he did not know how to speak much English, so would often communicate by signaling with his hands or saying "yes, yes, yes."

Samson's oral history from Yohane Lauwo corroborates others with family ties to the first guides who sought to clarify or assert their family history in a way that affirms other written and oral records.[50] Yohane Lauwo became in-laws to his colleague Toma Mosha and trained many others. Samwel Toma Mosha, Toma Mosha or Mlombare's son, said that the plaque at the gate was wrong in listing Toma Mosha as a porter because he believed that his father was an assistant guide. This position would make more sense in comparison with Kilimanjaro Mountain Club records from the 1930s. Heavenlight Israeli Mtui and Zakaria Fataeli Mtui both said that their grandfather, Jonathan Mtui, listed on the plaques as an assistant guide, was one of the first to climb the mountain with Lauwo. Three also named Makelio as a guide and two named Elia Minja as a guide, two names that also appear on the plaques at the Marangu gate.[51] Samwel Toma Mosha's idea that his father and Lauwo were among a group of young men who did work for Mangi Mtema and knew the forest because they hunted there is also consistent with the stories Samson remembers hearing from Yohane.

Even if a local man had not been with Meyer and Purtscheller in 1889, Tanzania can still celebrate Lauwo and his fellow guides for their achievements. Perhaps even greater than being the first or accompanying Meyer and Purtscheller, these early guides spent the longest time on the mountain, gained the most intimate knowledge of it, and supported the most people in reaching the top. In that sense, they all—not just one—should be celebrated as the long-time heroes of the mountain, along with the others in the support crews.

What is certain about Lauwo's history is that he knew the lower forest regions of Kilimanjaro as a young man and became a commercial guide for at least thirty years, playing a crucial role in the development of the Kilimanjaro tourism industry. As the number of climbers increased, Lauwo became largely based at the Kibo Hotel in Marangu and was called upon by the Kilimanjaro Mountain Club.[52] Since there was more than one Yohane or Johannes in visitor's books (or other spellings of the name), it is unclear how many mentions of this name referred to Lauwo in the mountain club records; however, it is safe to say that Lauwo was likely the only Yohane working in the late 1940s and throughout the 1950s, as other possible names for those referred to as Yohane or Johannes fall out of the other records during those decades. In the hut visitor books, Lauwo is described as "indefatigable" and praised for his stamina. One visitor observed Yohane "'frolicking about' like a 'two

FIGURE 5. Yohane Kinyala Rauya Lauwo.
Photo by Edward Simango.

year old'" as they battled a headache and fatigue on the ascent to the crater rim.[53] Later that same year in October 1943, a visitor wrote that Yohane was sick (the visitor called it an attack of malaria). He went down to Peter's Hut to recover, then caught up with the party to see them on to the highest peak. Despite not feeling well, he persisted in helping his clients reach their goal. "If he had not been there to encourage party on," the visitors wrote, "it is most certain that we should never have reached K.W.S. He simply would not allow us to return until the peak was reached."[54] Lauwo likely developed his endurance and skill in difficult conditions early on. If the guide "Johannu" in Frant Paul's description of his 1930 ascent of Kibo is Lauwo, he already proved himself light on the snow and determined, with other porters, to test their strength against wind and altitude sickness.[55] For this kind of work and other heroic rescues, he received recognition from the *mangi* and the German government as well as the mountain club upon his retirement in 1959 (likely around age sixty-one).[56]

The next most prominent guide in the historical record is Mlombare Mosha bin Ndewicho, named Toma Mosha in oral histories and also known as Toma or Thoma by the mountain club and visitors. From Masia-Marangu or Mamba, Mlombare was likely born around 1905 and started working as a porter and guide around 1928 or 1929.[57] If his son is correct, Mlombare and Lawuo were likely age-mates who became guides because they hunted in the forests together or worked as messengers for the *mangi*. Like Lauwo, Mlombare spent many years on the mountain. According to his son, Mlombare worked a bit longer than Lauwo, retiring in 1966.[58] He appeared in the records as a quieter man than his colleagues, although the language barrier could have factored in to how he interacted with visitors and how they perceived him. His only son to follow him in his career on the mountain, Samwel Toma Mosha, remembered Lauwo as having greater language skills than his father. He also remembered his father as polite, slow, and gentle—never one to lose his temper with his children: "He was very polite, he was very polite; when he becomes firm, once he tells you do *shuwani*, that was his language, do *shuwani*, he leaves and goes to sleep; that he could take a stick like this and cane you, that I never saw."[59] The way that his son explained their work in the early years, these first guides would indeed need to be slow and careful. Samwel Toma Mosha said his father told them they had to make a route by following elephant trails and baboons. They carried spears for protection and used oil with a particular smell to deter lions. The oil and their experience as hunters helped them navigate in a way that no one was harmed. Samwel Toma Mosha also remembered his father telling him that they did not know the environment beyond the forest, as they had not gone there. They also went without footwear until visiting hikers gave them shoes.

Visitors described Mlombare as a steady, skilled, and perceptive person. A group of Swedish visitors in 1947 commented that he was "very silent but kind and efficient."[60] A year later, other visitors wrote about him as "quietly efficient" or noted his "tact" and "patience" and that he organized his team of porters well.[61] In 1955, another group highlighted Mlombare's leadership, writing that "Guide Thomas 'stood out' in gifts of leadership, ability, and character. His share of responsibility is obviously very highly developed, and he endeared himself to the whole party."[62] His sense of responsibility may have led him to come across as gruff to other workers. Elias Andrea Minja remembered him as rude ("*mkorofi*") because he wanted people to listen to the guides. He seemed to have been a little more outgoing in later years or with certain people, with a group of two women writing in 1951 that not only was he organized and efficient, but he "encouraged and coaxed" a member of the party to the summit—with his encouragement taking the form of "continually telling us the summit was only just a head and of [singing] little songs"—leading them to conclude, "Altogether a delightful character and the best of guides to have on a safari such as this."[63] Elias Andrea Minja said that Mlombare was the chief guide on the mountain, but history has focused on Lauwo.[64]

Sambonanga bin Ndeshingio, presumably from Marangu, started working as a registered guide in the 1930s. His unique name features in many visitor books through the 1940s but did not elicit memories from those interviewed. Also described as "indefatigable," he powered on whether he was ill, cold, or had a sprained leg.[65] He also appears to have been more outgoing, with greater language skills likely helping him converse more freely with visitors. "Sambonango [*sic*], the guide was excellent in his capacity as guide, cook, porter and general [factotum]," one group wrote, "we shall remember his 'tayari bwana?' ['ready, sir?'] for a long time to come."[66] Others even called Sambonanga their friend: "Sambonango as guide, [philosopher], friend and cook was magnificent."[67] With his mountain guiding and social and communication skills, he certainly would have been the kind of person one would want to have as a guide if five months pregnant, as was the case with one woman in 1945.[68] He worked until he died in the first part of 1951. At a committee meeting of the mountain club on April 29, 1951, "It was voted that the Secretary write on behalf of the Club a letter of sympathy to the family of one Sambonanga, one of the most efficient and well-liked guides of the Club employed by Marangu Hotel, upon his sudden death recently, and also to add a word of appreciation for faithful services rendered these many years."[69]

Referred to as the "Mzee of Mamba" (meaning the respected elder of Mamba) by Samwel Toma Mosha, and at times by others, "Nathan," oral histories shed some light on the Jonathan Mtui listed on the plaque at the Marangu gate. Those interviewed mostly provided kinship links between Mtui and his grandchildren who had worked on the mountain, rather than his character and work. This is likely because Jonathan Mtui was an older guide who may have started even before Lauwo and Mlombare. The written record indicates that Dr. Reusch often worked with Offoro and a guide named Jonathan. He listed Offoro and Jonathan as the guides in his history of successful ascents, starting in 1925, and in his account of his own first attempt in 1926. Reusch wrote that they left Marangu with ten "native porters" and "one native guide named Jonathan."[70] A 1928 newspaper article describing an adventure of British missionaries up the mountain noted that the party was accompanied by "our escort, and Jonathan, a capable native guide."[71] It is likely that the Jonathan acting as a guide for Reusch in the 1920s is the Jonathan of Marangu listed as one of the first registered guides of the mountain club. Since he worked with Lauwo and Mlombare and oral histories indicate that these early workers knew each other well, it is also likely this is the person also known as Jonathan Mtui.

It appears that this same Jonathan ended up being employed on the mountain as a caretaker before passing away. In a February 1947 letter from the mountain club to the current *mangi* Petro Itosi Marealle, the club proposed the hiring of a caretaker of Bismarck Hut to protect it from thieves. They mentioned that they had

FIGURE 6. Sambonanga and Kimatare, 1948. JIRI HANZELKA AND MIROSLAV ZIKMUND, *AFRIKA: TRAUM UND WIRKLICHKEIT*, TRANS. Adolf Langer (Berlin: Verlag Volk und Welt, 1959).

employed a caretaker before—"Jonathan an old mountain guide—who has since died."[72] He likely passed away before many of those we interviewed knew him and could explain why they had little to say about his character or work. For example, in oral histories, Daudi Mtui and Faeteli Mtui were identified as sons of Jonathan Mtui who worked on the mountain.[73] Heavenlight Israel Mtui and Zakaria Fataeli Mtui, both grandsons of Jonathan Mtui who started working on the mountain in the late 1970s, talked more about these men, their fathers. Zakaria Fateali Mtui started working on Kilimanjaro in 1979, the same year his father, Faeteli Mtui, unexpectedly died while working on the mountain in very wet weather conditions.

The prevalence of Mtuis and Moshas (relatives of Mlombare) are indicative of the importance that family connections played in mobilizing workers in the early days of the mountain-climbing industry. Many recruited their family members—brothers, sons, grandsons, nephews, and in-laws. Mountain club records of the 1930s detailed the names and ages of porters who worked in the first decade of the club. All of them are men, mostly from the same villages as the guides under which they are listed. Some even have the same father's name as the guide, indicating that guides recruited family members.[74] These men were in their mid- to late thirties, with some younger than thirty and others in their early thirties. Oral histories confirm that many in the second generation of guides were taught the work or brought into the work by their brothers, fathers, uncles, cousins, or in-laws.

For example, Sambonanga likely trained his half-brother, Kimatare (figure 6), who worked into the 1970s.[75]

Working on the mountain either drew upon family connections or led to greater family connections between the earlier guides. The older guides and porters from Marangu related to Lauwo, Mlombare, and Mtui said that Lauwo married Mlombare's sister and that Mtui married someone from the Lauwo clan.[76] Gibson Minja's uncle was Elias Minja, one of the early porters listed on the plaque at Marangu gate, his wife's uncle was Mlombare, and his great uncle was Lauwo (through his father). Gibson summed it up by saying, "therefore, we are all one clan."[77] According to interview participants, the way the community generally looked down on the early porters and guides meant that mountain workers had difficulty getting married. This may have had to do with the way that others looked down upon them carrying goods for Europeans as well as their profession entailing long times away from home when other Chagga men would have been taking care of their banana groves, in many ways the marks of success for the men and their families. As evidence that they had not achieved an elevated position in their society, Samwel Toma Mosha commented that the first guides lived like others in the village, residing in regular mud houses. This very well may have contributed to the guides marrying into other guides' families, as they presumably would have shared the same social status.

Marriage and family were important motivators for those who worked on the mountain and important aspects of their lives. In the early twentieth century, the gendered division of labor among the Chagga of Marangu meant that wage-earning, physically demanding labor like porter and guide work was seen as appropriate for men and not for women. Women were expected to work around the home in agriculture, domestic labor, small business, and childrearing. As Atanus Isack Lekule put it, "there was also the traditional belief by our fathers that women were not allowed to work for a wage or go to school."[78] For the Chagga men then, aside from female tourists (who violated some Chagga gender norms, such as when they wore pants), it was a man's world on the mountain. Even if they performed tasks usually performed by Chagga women such as cooking, this was seen as part of the grunt work of the mountain, thus a man's job.

Despite the absence of Chagga women in mountain work, the world the men occupied on the mountain was integrally connected to women and their families. Establishing and sustaining a family was an important goal for these men. While in some ways, mountain work hurt men's chances for marriage in the earlier years of the industry, the economic benefits allowed them to get married in later years.

For example, Heavenlight Mtui said he was attracted to the wage he could earn on the mountain because as a youth, he needed to have a social life and needed to go courting for a wife.[79] Getting married was important for establishing a homestead because he could not be given land to farm unless he was married. Many other interview participants expressed gratitude for the way their jobs allowed them to support their families and send their children to school. This arrangement also meant that the women married to these men assumed more responsibilities in their homesteads. Although their husbands could support them with the wages earned from their mountain jobs, the women looked after the family banana groves and took on some day-to-day roles that belonged to fathers in raising children.

Although we do not have direct thoughts and commentary by women on this time period, we have clues as to how they were connected to and impacted by the work. While some women shunned mountain workers, other women saw the occupation as something offering economic benefits. Christo Mbanda said his wife was happy when he went to the mountain.[80] Others supported their husbands by packing food for them as they began a trip or bringing them clean clothes to change into at the gate at the end of the trip. Others surely worried about their husbands, brothers, and sons. For example, Zakaria Fataeli Mtui said that after his father died on the mountain, he and his mother were nervous about him going again so his mother asked others to watch out for him.[81] Clues of this kind go a long way to show that the emerging mountaineering industry did not only affect the few Chagga men directly involved in it, but also their immediate families and the whole society around Kilimanjaro.

Although the historical record of the first porters and guides to work for European mountaineers on Kilimanjaro is incomplete, it reveals significant characteristics and achievements of these men. Evolving out of long-distance caravan work culture and then intersecting with Chagga knowledge and society, mountain support crew work on Kilimanjaro was a mixture of local, global, and European colonial characteristics. This shaped the mountain-climbing tourism industry that developed in the early twentieth century. Throughout, it is clear that the men introduced in this chapter played a crucial role in the success of the early climbs for which Europeans claimed much of the credit.

CHAPTER 4

The Kilimanjaro Climbing Tourism Industry

WORKING FROM THE 1930S THROUGH THE 1950S, LAUWO, MOSHA, AND SAMBONANGA played a key role in the development of the climbing tourism industry on Kilimanjaro along with other crucial local actors. The hotels and the Kilimanjaro Mountain Club coordinated trips on the mountain, provided information, managed infrastructure, and hired the mountain crews. Chagga political leaders and mountain crews with their expertise and valuable labor also determined access to and understanding of the mountain. Porters, cooks, and guides shaped the growing industry by establishing crew culture, negotiating pay and work expectations, developing unmatched expertise, and ensuring the success and survival of climbers. All these actors and their relationships with each other explain the evolution of the industry as they adjusted to changing conditions, regularized procedures, and professionalized mountain work.

The colonial context within which the industry developed continued to hang over all those involved, even as power over the industry was contested. Guided mountaineering or mountain tourism is not necessarily colonial in and of itself. It utilizes the knowledge and skill that guides have to offer and is part of risk-management in adventure tourism.[1] Yet the mountain tourism that developed on Kilimanjaro followed, as sports studies expert Paul Beedie wrote, the European pattern of a "rich and educated relatively elite group buying local guiding services in the pursuit of personal glory." Beedie argued that this pattern spread to other parts of the world in the twentieth century with the "expansionist agenda" of "'opening up' wild and remote mountain areas, often in relatively poorer countries."[2] As the industry on Kilimanjaro matured, it echoed colonial practices of serving the foreign visitor's agenda with little regard to local interests, particularly with respect to porter work. Porters, cooks, and guides still exercised some power as they pushed for their desired compensation.

The Kilimanjaro Mountain Club, Hotels, and the Mangi of Marangu

Europeans engaged in mountaineering in the late nineteenth century formed mountain clubs to support their activities and provide infrastructure. This trend spread to eastern and southern Africa as well.[3] As interest in scaling Kibo grew around the turn of the twentieth century, mountain clubs formed and built huts on Kilimanjaro. German interest in climbing Kilimanjaro led to the establishment of a Kilimanjaro Mountain Society by a Dr. Förster, living in Moshi. Assisted by the Hannover Section of the Alpenverein (the German Mountain Club) this group built the Bismarck Hut (about 9.5 mi/15 km from Marangu, about 9,000 ft/2,743 m), the Johannes Hut (about 15 mi/24 km from mission station at Old Moshi, about 9,000 ft/2,743 m), and Peter's Hut (about 12,000 ft/3,656 m). In 1912, the Hannover Section planned to build a structure between Kibo and Mawenzi. The First World War "thwarted the plans," however. The building materials were repurposed to construct a military hospital, even after they had been transported to 16,000 ft/4,900 m on the mountain, and Hannover Section member Dr. Arning, who traveled to East Africa to participate in the opening celebrations, was captured by the English and became a prisoner of war.[4] The German club came to an end in 1914. After the war, the Tanganyikan territory was taken over by the British under a League of Nations mandate. It was the new colonial government that turned the German mountain huts over to the Kibo Hotel until the Kilimanjaro Mountain Club gained control of them in 1932.[5]

The mountaineering industry grew steadily in size and sophistication and required greater collaboration. The Kilimanjaro Mountain Club that had been established within the new colonial setting kept pace with the industry. Yet, while controlling the huts on the mountain since 1932, it had to work closely with the women who managed the Marangu and Kibo Hotels. Men did the guiding and porter work, and mostly men filled positions in the Kilimanjaro Mountain Club. Some (European) women climbed the mountain while others managed the home base, such as the wives of guides and porters and the women managers of the hotels. Throughout the early years, the club worked on coordinating bookings and passing along the hut keys between the hotels. Anne Bruehl continued to manage the Kibo Hotel for many years. Martin Bohdan von Lany and his son, Ludwig, directed the reconfiguration of parts of the family farm to the Marangu Hotel while Emma von Lany and daughter Erica looked after guests. After Martin Bohdan passed away unexpectedly in 1941, Emma and Erica continued to manage the farm and hotel, with Erica taking the lead into the 1950s and beyond (Emma passed away in 1964) with the help of her sister Ruth and husband John Salt between 1958 and 1963.[6] A friend of the Lany family, Frank Brice-Bennett, who had been a British district officer in the Kilimanjaro region in the 1920s and 1930s, brought his family from Nigeria in 1951. Frank's wife, Margaret, known as Peggy, became business partners with Erica into the 1990s. Relationships between the Kibo and Marangu Hotels could be strained as they worked out misunderstandings and adjusted protocol to avoid visitors to the mountain finding huts in disrepair or negotiating double bookings. The mountain club also worked with hotel owners in setting prices; establishing pay rates for porters, cooks, and guides; and regulating crew registration. Some of the guides ended up working primarily with one hotel or the other.

The mountain club and hotel owners also worked with the *mangi* of Marangu, whose influence continued to shape the industry. The first huts were built on the way from both Marangu and Old Moshi. The industry shifted, however, when the *mangi* of Marangu and his people were more amenable to participating. For example, in 1938, the club found it difficult to obtain porters from Moshi to repair the Johannes Hut because they apparently did not like the work and it was difficult to cooperate with the *mangi*. Mountain club records refer to a misunderstanding between the guide Oforo and the *mangi* of Moshi in July 1938. The club ended up hiring porters from Marangu through *mangi* Petro Itosi Maraelle, who offered to be responsible for the porters and guides of the club from then on and to open up the Bismarck trail.[7] Seeing the opportunity for influence, favor by the British, or employment for his people, the *mangi* of Marangu stepped in to divert traffic through his settlement. Indeed, in September 1938, the club secretary and treasurer wrote to the *mangi*, "The Mountain Club will not be unmindful of this voluntary effort and will see that Marangu obtains a good share of the safaris which go up the mountain in the future," for which the *mangi* later thanked the club on behalf of his people.[8] Moreover, the route from Marangu was shorter, making this the more attractive route.

The mountain club thus focused on the Marangu route, setting about refurbishing the Bismarck and Peter's Huts in August of 1938. At first, the club worked in cooperation with the *mangi*. The *mangi* managed the porters and guides, and his men maintained the Bismarck trail while the Marangu and Kibo Hotels played prominent roles as keeper of the hut keys.[9] The club oversaw scheduling and maintenance and liaised with forestry officers. Soon, however, the *mangi* of Marangu found the work to be too much and by March of 1939, declined to manage the guides, porters, and provisions for journeys. A tipping point may have been the trouble the *mangi* encountered securing reimbursement for meat he had bought for one journey.[10] By that time, however, the club had established itself in Marangu. Eight years later, the guide from the Old Moshi route reported to the mountain club that porters from Old Moshi were still not willing to work unless they were paid two shillings a day (about twice the amount they were offering at the time), so the club did not pursue that route any longer.[11]

Although the *mangi* of Marangu recused himself from the management of guides and porters, he still made recommendations to the club about who could be registered. The club made it a point in its first decade or so to ensure that those working on the mountain were registered and had some qualifications. Not everyone who climbed utilized mountain club resources or porters and guides. (Some people started from the northern side, at the Rongai ranger station, but the club did not deal with them.[12]) In 1942, the club still found it necessary to insist that guides and porters be registered with the club and advised that amateurs not attempt the climb without a guide.[13] The club wanted to be apprised of issues with the huts and other equipment and required climbers to fill out a form. They also issued books to the guides to serve as personal reference books and maintained visitors' books in each of the huts where visitors were asked to record their challenges and successes and provide advice.

Guides

On the mountain, it was important that the guide and his crew all worked together to ensure a smooth and enjoyable trek for the visitors and to successfully deal with difficult circumstances that might arise. On February 16, 1944, a party of people visited Kilimanjaro to learn about "movements of game on the mountain" at the higher altitudes. Their brief but complimentary entry in the Peter's Hut book encapsulates the different considerations of climbers and crews: "The guide Johannes lived up to his reputation of many years and took my wife to the top, he is a grand safari companion and is well liked and respected by the porters; the cook Alimeleki was a great asset and an extremely good cook. The weather was perfect."[14] Guides like Johannes (likely Lauwo) focused on getting their clients to the top. This included managing logistics, watching the weather, and providing important leadership for the crew and visiting climbers. Safety was paramount. If things went well, they also succeeded in acting as "grand" companions. On the trail and back in Marangu, guides served as intermediaries between the visitors, the crew, the hotel owners, and the mountain club.

Certified and employed by the mountain club (for which they carried their own reference books), Lauwo, Mtui, Mlombare, and Sambonanga also affiliated with one of the two hotels in Marangu and rotated trips between themselves. Their main work was to guide visitors to Kibo and Mawenzi. This required varied expertise as well as arranging provisions and leading the support crew. As more and more visitors came to the mountain, especially after WWII, they would take multiple trips per month. These guides were invaluable. As entries in books on the mountain attest, many visitors could not have done it without them. Indeed, some who did not employ a guide got lost or ran into other trouble, moving the mountain club to push for regulations requiring guides.[15] "Unless climbers are absolutely confident of their ability to stand high altitudes," a club pamphlet read, "they are strongly advised to take a guide. A few porters are essential since only climbers of exceptional stamina can carry their own food and equipment."[16] The custom emerged to have a guide and three to four porters for one climber and two to three additional porters for every extra person. Larger groups employed more guides.

Mostly based in Marangu, the men hired as guides knew the region already, but their work made them the experts on the mountain as well as how the mountain interacted with the visitors—they advised on weather conditions, knew altitude levels, set the pace for hiking, and ensured climbers had adequate food, acting as cooks themselves at times. Wise visitors learned to follow the guide's advice to keep a slow but steady pace and listen to their warnings about snow or weather conditions. In 1945, one visitor wrote about their ascent up the scree: "The guide, Johannes, who throughout was very helpful and foreseeing, went up the snow covered scree in reverse and hammered out footholds." Because of Lauwo's trailblazing, they made it to Gillman's Point, but "on the advice of Guide Johannes, no attempt was made on KWS [the highest point] because of the deep, soft snow."[17] "Mlombare proved an excellent guide throughout," one British visitor wrote in the guide's book in March 1936, "his experience and confidence on the snow beyond Gillman's Point being especially valuable."[18] A few years later, a visitor commented that Mlombare "guided us through snow often knee deep, without making a false step."[19] Another wrote that Mlombare "has a thorough knowledge of that mountain and one has a great feeling of confidence in him."[20] Jack Grover of the American Embassy in Cairo wrote that "[Mlombare] of course knows every part of the route."[21] In 1948 and 1949, visitors described Mlombare's "remarkable understanding of the needs of climbers; their pace and the special requirements at high altitudes." Mlombare and his colleagues not only knew how to expertly guide people to the top of Kibo, but knew Mawenzi and the technical abilities needed there.[22] An entry in the Mawenzi Hut book in 1953 claimed that "Toma and Seria" (Mlombare and Syara) were the first two Africans to reach the Mawenzi col.[23] Mlombare and Syara often show up in the Mawenzi Hut book in the 1950s, but Lawuo, Effata, Fuateli, and Daudi also appear there, with one entry writing how Lauwo described a particular route to a group in September 1955.[24]

The guides were attentive and encouraging to their clients. A representative entry from a party of six in February 1940 reads: "We all thought Mlombare was an excellent guide and most thoughtful for the comfort of those members of the party in his care. The last climb was made as easy as possible by his patience and consideration in taking us up in easy stages, waiting whilst we rested and seeing that we did not over-exert ourselves."[25] One wrote of Mlombare in January 1941, "I could not speak the language and yet he understood what I wanted almost by instinct."[26] Similarly, a group wrote of Lauwo: "very cheery and helpful and fully understands one's needs."[27] Another group of visiting climbers noted in January 1942, "We were very impressed and most grateful to the Guide Thoma, cook, and porters. They looked after us very well and we felt, took an interest in our welfare."[28] The guides would even have to deal with climbers vomiting on the trail. One, in 1950, wrote that he had eight attacks before reaching Gillman's point. "Thomas was most sympathetic and helpful during each of these attacks. If it hadn't been for his encouragement I think I would never have made it," he concluded.[29] "I was greatly helped by the example of Thoma the guide," another wrote in 1946. The entry continued to describe Mlombare's help, "He actually came down about ten feet one time on the scree to give me a hand and after that I just had to get to the top. He also produced two oranges which I found very helpful."[30] Sambonanga similarly descended to help climbers up the last bit of the way. In July 1941, a climber wrote in the hut book: "The excellence of Sambonanga's guidance and [efficiency] surpasses anything that I know. I should never have reached Gillman's point without his help. He produced a rope and almost dragged me up."[31] This was not the only time Sambonanga, Mlombare, or Lauwo offered a rope to climbers.[32] Pep talks and persistence helped other clients reach their goals. "If he had not been there to encourage party on," a group wrote about Lauwo in 1943, "it is most certain that we should never have reached K.W.S. He simply would not allow us to return until the peak was reached."[33] Kimatare started as an assistant guide and then worked as a full guide beginning in the early 1940s. He also earned praise from visitors along with the other men as "excellent" and for ensuring the success of climbers: "Guide Kimataru [*sic*] invaluable and gave me great encouragement to carry on."[34] A 1946 entry sums up the critical encouragement guides provided: "Only the cheerful . . . [disposition] of our guide Sanbonanga [*sic*] kept us going at times when mountain sickness brought us to our knees."[35]

Into the 1950s, tourism grew exponentially, necessitating bringing more guides into the industry. Some started as assistant guides and then moved into a lead guide position. Visitors gave less and less commentary in the books into the 1960s. Rather, they thanked or just named the guides and signed their names, especially when hundreds of names left little room in the books. It could also be the case that increased commercialization of the industry minimized personal encounters, causing interactions to be viewed purely as commercial exchanges. Yet comments and other records indicate that the guides who joined the profession followed similar old practices. They were joined by Sambonanga's brother, Kimatare (figure 6), who often worked alongside his brother in the 1940s and into the 1950s. Assistant guides mentioned include Maletto and Kimadammy as well as others who became guides in the 1950s. Syara Kisaka, Daudi, Samueli, Effata Nathaniel, Fuateli, Sadikieli, and Safari Kisaka (stepbrother to Syara) appear in the books on the mountain in the 1950s into the 1960s with comments showing they also encouraged climbers affected by mountain sickness and gained admiration for their expertise and attentiveness. For example, expressions such as making it to Gillman's Point "by the grace of Kimitare" are repeated in various ways for Syara, Daudi, and Effata. Another described Syara Kisaka as "an able, helpful, persuasive guide" in 1957, and one thanked Samueli for dragging him up to Gillman's Point in 1961. Other guides named in the 1960s include Alexi, Fernandez, Thomas, Christofe or Christoforo, Obedi, Herman, and Geoffrey.

Oral histories from the second and third generation of guides and porters show that the first guides trained their successors to provide similar service to their guests. It is also possible that mountain club leaders and hotel managers also had an influence on setting protocol which the first guides passed down.[36] Anasen Ndenimfoo talked about the responsibility of guides to lead guests from the gate to the top and answer every question they had about the mountain along the way.[37] David Sifueli Mtui and Emmanuel Mongi talked about the importance of providing attentive help to tourists. Heavenlight Israel Mtui remarked that singing made tourists happy. Good service resulted in good tips and referrals, but the guides were not just concerned about money. George Eliapenda Kimaro, who worked starting in the 1970s, said he had fond memories of reaching the top and then later sitting in the bar to share drinks with his clients. Guides also prioritized the safety of their clients. One challenge guides talked about was working with visitors who concealed a negative physical condition that the guide needed to know about to keep their client safe. They also highlighted the difficulty of convincing some hikers that they needed to descend before reaching the summit for their own safety.[38] Oral histories indicate that it was traumatic and devastating for a guide to lose a guest or a crew member to death. Elias Andrea Minja told of a guest he had trouble communicating with because of the language barrier. Minja told the person they needed more water, but the person seemed to say they had enough. Unfortunately, the client and Minja both ran out of water, and Minja felt the person ended up dying because of a lack of water. Others talked of times when people died when asked about memorable moments on the mountain, although they mostly talked about crew members.[39] These were scary incidents and a blow to those who lost fellow workers or even family members.

A significant part of a guide's work was to provide first aid and rescues of various types to prevent catastrophes. Some oral history interview participants detailed rescue procedures or counted rescue equipment among the improvements in the industry over the years, showing the prominence of rescues in their work.[40] Samwel Toma Mosha understood that as a guide, he was supposed to put the lives of the visitors first. It is quite possible he gained this view from his own father and his colleagues. In February 1945, a member of a party got lost between Kibo and Peter's Huts during the night. Even though they were not part of the group, Mlombare and two porters made an impression by immediately searching for and finding the person.[41] Later, Mlombare and his porters took turns carrying a sick climber on a stretcher between Peter's and Bismarck Huts.[42] A February 1943 entry wrote that someone overtaken by the cold "had to be brought down by Lauwo from half way up to Gillman's Point."[43] A less mentioned guide but one listed with Lauwo on the Marangu gate plaques, Timoteo bin Makelio, was celebrated on Chagga

Day in 1954 for nursing a priest who "fell seriously ill" on the way back from Kibo (although the priest eventually "died through cold").[44] In 1959, club minutes read that "Guide Johannes had received the Queen's Certificate and Badge of Honour for his magnificent effort in bringing to Marangu an injured climber in record time and also, for continued service to climbers in the past thirty years."[45] (Rescues sometimes even included fetching equipment that had fallen out of hand. Although one man complained that Mlombare had left snowshoes behind, he also wrote of how he "courageously climbed back about 400 yards of that appalling scree" to rescue his camera after the strap had broken. This was not the only time Mlombare performed such a service.[46] Kimatare reportedly did the same in 1943.[47])

The guides also struggled with the elements and suffered injuries and illness; however, like Sambonanga, records indicate these men went to great lengths to ensure their clients had a safe and successful experience on the mountain. In December 1941, the "indefatigable" Sambonanga showed his strength and commitment when on December 23, he fell at twelve thousand feet "and badly sprained his left leg." He was carried to Peter's Hut. Despite the pain, he "insisted on doing the cooking for the party." The party continued on to Kibo Hut and, although he initially thought he could not make it with them, he "crippled in" shortly after the rest of the party had arrived. He even accompanied them on their "final assault" on Christmas day, "crippling along in great pain" with help from the visiting climbers. The visitors concluded, "All honours in this trip go to the guide Sambonanga who would not give in."[48] A few months later, Sambonanga tried again to guide a party even though he felt ill and successfully led another party with "badly frostbitten" feet.[49] In 1943, he had a bad earache when the group reached the top of the crater, but he still took them to the summit. "Sabomango [*sic*] should certainly be praised as being a fine guide. He was as keen to get us to K.W.S. as we were ourselves," the party wrote when back at Peter's Hut.[50] There was a time in October 1943 that Lauwo was sick—the visitor called it an attack of malaria. He went back to Peter's Hut to recover, then caught up with the party to ensure they went on to reach the highest peak.[51] On another climb, Lauwo was praised for helping one member of the party who set off on his own and got lost. The lone climber had told those left behind at Kibo Hut that he was going out for an hour's stroll and ended up making it to Gillman's point. Lawuo spent "many hours" looking for him.[52] An accident in December 1957 involving a solo German climber serves as a final poignant example. The man fell just below Gillman's Point and "went quarter of a mile on the iced scree before stopping." He injured his head and was "badly cut up." Luckily, another party with a guide, presumably Lauwo, was climbing nearby and attended to him, although this meant that he had to leave his other clients to take the injured man down the mountain.[53]

The guides likely performed to such a degree because it earned them a good reputation and thus further employment. They enjoyed the work, or at least the pay was enough to continue with such difficult and risky work for many years. Most of these men also had the physical strength to continue. The guides and porters in the second and third generations who were interviewed said they rarely or never had any health problems because of their work. They often commented on how the work strengthened them physically, although they would acknowledge how others could be negatively affected by the cold or rainy conditions. The written record held only a few mentions of the guides being exhausted or sick. Mostly, visitors praised the guides for their performances and help at those high altitudes. After struggling up the daunting scree of lava dust and pebbles or collapsing with exhaustion or mountain sickness, many wrote they were glad they climbed Kilimanjaro but would join others in saying "never again." Yet the guides and porters went up again and again, year after year.

In down times or at times when maintenance was needed, the Kilimanjaro Mountain Club often turned to the guides to organize labor to do the work. When the club searched for a caretaker for Bismarck Hut to help prevent thefts or break-ins, they turned to Jonathan, by that time "an old mountain guide," who stayed there into the 1940s.[54] Mlombare took "*shamba* [farm] boys," perhaps men who were not registered with the club but occasional laborers, to clean and maintain huts and clear the path to and around the first hut on the Marangu route after the rains for 120 or 125 shillings total in the 1940s.[55] Lauwo also did work for the Meteorological Department (often with a fellow named Mleki or Muleki), evidenced by his stamps in the books on the mountain and the 1958 Kibo Hotel memo.

Cooks

Cooks played a special role in the support crew and earned praise for providing much-needed nourishment. This could not have been easy, as some hikers lost their appetites because of the high altitude. They were also often responsible for waking the climbers so they could get a good start on their ascents to the crater rim. In early years, guides acted as cooks as well. In September 1941, a climber wrote that

"Sambonango [*sic*] made an excellent breakfast of porridge, two eggs, bacon and tomatoes. I am very struck by Sambonango's cheerfulness and thoughtfulness."[56] In 1943, a visitor wrote about Kimatare's invaluable help and added, "And he cooks—how he cooks!"[57] As the years progressed, it became practice to have a designated cook among the crew. Cooks who feature in the records—some of whom became guides—include Syara, Fuateli, Sadikieli, Samueli, and Lucas, who often worked with Mlombare and guides referred to as Yohanne. "Special commendation due to Fuataeli, the cook, the hardest working member of the party who turned out excellent meals all the time," one visitor wrote in 1944.[58] In 1939, cook Satali was praised as a "very good cook. Intelligent, willing." He woke up the visitors and also worked as their interpreter. "Worth having on any trip," the visitors concluded.[59] One man in 1945 insisted on staying the night at Kibo Hut, as he was feeling ill after his ascent to Gillman's Point. "Cook Lucas, assistant Simoneli and porter returned and produced meal" for him, although they had already moved their crew to Peter's Hut as they had planned to sleep there that night.[60] Other cooks named in mountain books include Asmani, Petro, Isaac or Esaka, Maletoo or Maletto, Lumie/Ayumi and Nicholas, Alimeleki, Eliangaringa, Rafaldi, Kish, Kayiyoo, Aliali, Safari, and Pratasi. Stanley Mosha's father, Rumisha Mosha, also worked as a cook. Atanus Isak's father cooked for Effata Jonathan's crews.

The food the visitors and support crew ate on the mountain included local food as well as food prepared for a more European taste. It is possible that guides and cooks learned from people like Emma von Lany how to cook more European cuisine. The Marangu Hotel was known for its excellent meals and even sent visitors on the mountain with tablecloths and cloth napkins.[61] Visitors mentioned porridge, eggs, bacon, and tomatoes as well as Bovril (British beef paste) and cakes. A few also talked about the importance of drinking enough tea. Cooks often woke the visitors with tea or coffee already prepared. In the late 1950s, daily rations for a support crew member included: Maize meal (1 lb), rice (½ lb), meat (½ lb), ghee (2 oz), sugar (3 oz), salt (½ oz), tea (½ oz), and two cigarettes.[62] Guides and cooks were responsible for buying the food and arranging for the provisions. This became a problem when the cost of providing a "plush" experience for the average tourist climber cut into the provisions for porters.[63]

The crew usually lined up with their containers to receive their food after the guests were fed. Older porters and guides from Marangu gave some insight into the diet of these men. According to the oral history interviews, they mostly started off with tea in the morning, perhaps with some bread or maize meal porridge. If they were prepared as an individual and wanted it, they could have something small to carry in their pockets on the way to the next camp, such as *maandazi*, *chapati*, or peanuts. In the evening, they would have dinner of *ugali* and some vegetable or meat. David Sifueli Mtui said they would not feel the cold as much if they were not hungry, and yet Gibson Minja commented that they did not want to eat too much lunch in case the combination of the high altitude and a full stomach would make them vomit. There were not many complaints about the food among the older interview participants; however, Samwel Toma Mosha said he felt they did not eat enough, and Kamili Lyatonga Mtui remarked, in reference to the food, that the past was no joke.

Porters

As oral history interview participants observed, if the guides are like the steering wheel of the work on the mountain, the porters are the engine.[64] Because porters provided a load-bearing service that only humans could perform at high altitude, they were an important part of the industry from the beginning. They engaged in this difficult work because it offered opportunities when they needed to diversify their economic activities. Sources provide a window into how they worked together to sustain themselves and provide quality service. We also see how they pushed for certain terms of remuneration. This all shaped the experience people had on the mountain and the dynamics of the industry.

Although there were no tsetse flies on Kilimanjaro, the already existing porter labor industry and the high altitude's effects on pack animals meant that it was still preferable to use human labor to transport gear and provisions on those mountain-climbing treks. The mountain club complained about Kloss housing animals in the climbers' huts, and an entry in Mlombare's guidebook in 1937 mentioned that the party that made it to Kibo Hut consisted of two English travelers, one "Native Guide," one cook, five porters, and three donkeys.[65] Yet donkeys had trouble in the higher elevations and would not be taken beyond Kibo Hut. A newspaper article recounting an expedition by Safari (Africa) Limited in 1935 wrote that the company had "an ass, a mule and a horse, as well as native bearers." The animals did not make it, with the horse collapsing at 12,000 ft/3,658 m, the mule at 15,000 ft/4,572 m, and the ass at 17,000 ft/5,182 m. The local Chagga men proved more resilient, although they still suffered from the elements. The article read, "The natives, shivering under their blankets, took the loads."[66] Moreover, if climbers wanted to succeed in reaching the highest point on Kibo, it was best they hiked the whole way themselves. A request for a donkey for a climber's wife in 1938 elicited this response from the mountain club: "I regret that there are no donkeys available on this side of the mountain [Moshi] but frankly I do not consider that your wife would find one of very much use. The effect of the exercise in climbing in the early stages is most valuable on the third day when the final attempt is made and the use of a donkey is apt to cause stiffness."[67]

Porters were brought into the formalization of the industry on the mountain early on, with the mountain club requiring them to be recommended by the *mangi* and guides and then registered with the club. Once a guide received a job, he would work with people in his locale as well as the *mangi* to assemble his crew. Oral history interview participants remembered the practice of guides recruiting porters continuing into the mid-twentieth century. Some went to the streets, others, as noted, recruited family members and neighbors. For the most part, guides and crews, especially crews of men from the same locale or families, could work well together. Thus, it is likely that the guide Johannes mentioned in the February 16, 1944, Peter's Hut book entry was likely truly well-liked and respected by his porters.

In the 1920s and 1930s, the number of climbers or hikers was not as steady, making it difficult for guiding and porterage to become a constant form of work. The work was also seasonal, with visitors coming to the mountain when they would find the best weather conditions and when it was holiday season in Europe and America. Thus, men who worked as porters had different forms of occupation or subsistence. Porters, mainly in their thirties in age, engaged in this work for similar reasons as long-distance porters in the past—to invest in their homes and families (especially for the young men building a foundation for their future), supplement other economic activities, or sustain themselves through hard times.

The growth in the mountain tourism industry in the mid-twentieth century coincided with an increase in pressure on the land. Porter work opened opportunities for some Chagga men to earn a wage in a more monetized economy when their access to land declined as the population grew and forest reserves and European agriculture limited expansion.[68] Interviews of the second and third generations to work on the mountain give us a sense that people worked on the mountain more out of necessity or because it was a good economic opportunity for their families. Many went to do the work once they finished grade seven and their families could not afford more education. Heavenlight Mtui, grandson of Jonathan Mtui, said his

II.

No	MAJINA / NAMES	UMRI WAO / Approx: AGE	MTAA / LOCATION	Kuingia kazini / when entered service
1	Toma Mlambare bin Ndewicho	Kiasi / about:- 33 yrs.	Masia - Marangu	Yapata miaka 9½ anao ushahidi barua zake.
2	Christoforo " Nderingo	" 29 "	Masia - Marangu	Yapata miaka 8.
3	Absai " Nderingo	" 36 "	Masia - Marangu	" 9
4	Anaseli " Manzewa	" 33 "	" "	9½
5	Dawidi " Mika	" 28 "	" "	7.
6	Elinaja " Kiwerei	" 32 "	" "	11.
7	Zerubabel " Yeremia	36 "	" "	8
8	Nikereme " Nderingo	" 34 "	" "	7
9	Fataeli " Muru	" 33 "	" "	9
10	Aunisa " Ndewicho	" 30 "	Mamba —	10
11	NgasaniaMui " Ndesingo	22 "	" —	8
12	Nderingo " Malata	35 "	" —	6
13	Augustino " Slayo	35 "	" —	8
14	Anaseli " Mallombo	29 "	" —	6
15	Oforo " Kirasi	25 "	Masia - Marangu	4
16	Mangalili " Kiranga	29 "	Arisi - Marangu	4

FIGURE 7. List of guides and porters. BOX 4, KILIMANJARO MOUNTAIN CLUB ARCHIVES.

father worked on the mountain as a porter, but then focused on farming coffee because of the difficult work conditions. When his son expressed interest in working on the mountain, his father tried to explain how hard the work was. Yet Heavenlight felt there was no other way to earn money. Samwel Toma Mosha was the only son from his father to work on the mountain. His mother attempted to keep him out of the industry by persuading him to train as a tailor. He did this for a brief time but returned to work on the mountain for greater pay.[69]

Porters performed hard labor, carrying 40-lb loads or more for four- to five-day trips, and doing it in difficult conditions at times. Interview participants remembered that long before the Tanzanian government instituted weight limits, the guide would work with the porters to distribute the loads, getting a feel for the weight just by lifting each load by hand. Depending on the size of the crew and the relationships between the guide and the porters, porters could carry more than 50 lbs, or around 30 kg.[70] In a letter to the president of the Kenya Mountain Club in 1957, Bruehl explained: "The porters carry 40 lbs. each plus their own personal kit and including the weight of containers, but they consume about 2 ½ lbs. of food per day and this must be allowed for when working out the number of porters required. The guide carries nothing other than his blankets. Loads are normally packed in wooden boxes, but kit bags are quite satisfactory. Containers should be waterproof." A paragraph crossed out below gave some added insight into how they started a trip, especially as they walked through familiar territory on the first day: "The porters often haggle a lot at Marangu and one gets the impression that they won't last long. However, once on the march they are reliable, and although they may vanish to their huts en route the loads are quite safe and always get there."[71]

Carrying the large loads to higher and higher altitudes was difficult work on its own. Czech Franta Paul, who climbed with members of the Lany family, described the scene as they arrived at the last cave before the summit attempt in 1930: exhausted porters arrived one by one, then found a sheltered spot to cover themselves in their blankets and rest.[72] Oral history interview participants stressed that inadequate clothing in inclement weather was an additional major challenge. Their fathers and grandfathers often went without shoes and socks. Samson Lauwo remembered Yohane Lauwo telling him that they took animal skin shoes or depended upon their clients to gift them shoes. Along with accounts of initial ascents in the late nineteenth and early twentieth century, photographs hanging on the wall in the dining room of the Marangu Hotel, some likely taken by Franta Paul (figure 8), show a party of Europeans dressed in khakis with Chagga men wearing only blankets, no shoes.

FIGURE 8. "On the Saddle of Kilimanjaro," 1931, with Ludwig von Lany standing with foot on boulder. Franta Paul, *V Rovníkové Africe* (Praha Orbis, 1931), Plate XVII.

Porters appear to have worked with no shoes and little extra gear for decades. In 1939, a visitor included a postscript in an entry that reads, "p.s. If intended take porters up crater, essential see they have shoes or boots."[73] Hiking without boots would make it very difficult to proceed when the snow was deep. Gibson Minja said his father told them the snow could reach as high as their chests. It is no wonder that Sambonanga was "badly frostbitten in both feet" in 1942.[74] One visitor commented in 1942 that "Poor Johannes seemed to have few nails in his [boots] and was sliding about all over the place" in the snow, but insisted he accompany the climber to the highest point.[75] An entry in 1945 detailed another incident when inadequate gear interfered with the guide's work. The party ended up ascending with another group "and their guide [Oforo], Somali having discovered at the last moment that he couldn't get his boots on."[76]

Even if guides had boots, they may not have worn socks. Visitors from Sweden wrote in Mlombare's guidebook in July 1947 that "Thoma . . . should be supplied with socks, we had to give him [some]."[77] Later that year, a party from Cape Town wrote, "Thoma, however, was quite game to set out at 3 am from KIBO HUT and face really bad conditions—dense clouds, snow, and bitterly cold wind. But I lent him my . . . [cardigan]. He wore boots . . . I gave him some socks and . . . [sandals]. But why are these stout-hearted natives—tropical . . . allowed to set out on these safaris in more or less rags? Could they not be furnished with old army [kit] and boots?" The following entry agreed, writing that porters and guides needed much warmer clothing in the higher elevations and "the guides should not be expected to make that last 3 am safari from Kibo Hut to the summit in anything less than the clothing worn by the other climbers." Yet the following year, Mlombare "even lent his coat to one of the party whom he considered incompletely equipped for a snow storm."[78] In 1951, visitors also commented on Mlombare's clothing: "We were appalled at the very inadequate clothing worn by our guides on the bitterly cold morning that we set off for Gilman's point. We gave Thoma a pair of socks and discovered that he was wearing them as gloves. Surely something can be done about this?"[79]

Porters had different access to and use of clothing and footwear than guides who would have been given gear by visitors. Porters appear to have hiked without adequate shoes for decades. Some interview participants said they would instead use what they called Maasai sandals (rubber-soled sandals), although this may have been more so in the mid- to late twentieth century. One can imagine the pain shoeless porters would have likely experienced when attempting to carry loads up the scree for a geologist, Mr. Richard, in 1942, and understand why they had to give up.[80] Even a 1950 letter regarding a dispute about payment for a trip cut short by bad weather indicated that at that time, porters did not wear shoes. Although they had marched through much rain in the lower regions, the porters "refused to walk to Kibo Hut, as there was much snow on the path and they had no shoes." Without the provisions and equipment the porters carried, the party returned a day early.[81] Still, an entry from 1960 read: "Reached Gillmans Point at 6:45 this morning. Saddle and slopes of Kibo covered with 2 to 3 [in] snow. A pleasant exhilarating climb culminating in a marvelous view. I wish to express my admiration for my guide Syara and porters Safari (a most able cook), Raphaeli, Israeli (who climbed in bare feet) and [Layrenie?] without whose help I could not have ascended."[82]

The rain could also lead to hypothermia. The cold was biting and even fatal, especially if the crew did not have adequate shelter at night. They took blankets to sleep under or to use to take cover. Blankets were a key item for the Chagga, offering some protection against the elements. An account of an ascent in 1929 described one unnamed guide from Marangu as "wrapped up in a huge blanket from head to foot," and wearing "a big ugly cap, stripped clear down over his face, with big round [holes] for his eyes."[83] The mountain club built huts for porters, but before the huts were established or if the number of tourists filled the huts (a common situation as the numbers of tourists grew), the mountain crew had to sleep in caves. Porters would gather grass and leaves to make a bed for themselves and huddle in the caves, which could be crowded and smoked-filled by a fire. Although porters were more accustomed to the altitude of the foothills of Kilimanjaro than visitors from outside the region who usually came only once to make the trek, they still were susceptible to the high-altitude mountain conditions and did not live with snow in the lower elevations. On January 29, 1941, in the Peter's Hut book, a visitor noted "all fit except one or two porters suffering from minor ailments." An entry in 1956 took more notice of how the porters fared: "The porters have done their tasks cheerfully and well," someone wrote, "except that firewood has sometimes been rather short. Obedi and Kasiomaka are obviously well-experienced; the others Joram, Jacob, and Balimaba seem to be less used to the work, but have played their part. Jacob and Balimaba seemed to suffer from the cold due to inadequate clothing."[84] That suffering could be minimal or have dire consequences. Stanley Mosha remembers people who had to have parts of their legs amputated because of the cold. Zakari Fataeli Mtui's father died on the mountain during excess rain, and Kimili Lyatonga Mtui told about a porter who similarly died during an especially rainy trip.[85]

Another challenge highlighted in oral history interviews was the work required of porters once they delivered their loads at the destination for the day. In addition to carrying supplies and bedding for the tourists (which could include heavy mattresses in the early twentieth century), the crew had to arrive before the climbers to set up camp.[86] For many years, the Marangu route was the only route used. Since it had huts, the crew could focus on fetching water and firewood for the cook and then preparing a place to sleep. As the next chapter details, as more and more firewood was consumed, searching for this firewood became a more difficult chore. Porters could also be sent ahead or behind to prepare or replenish supplies. For example, it was necessary to carry firewood and water ahead to Kibo Hut where those natural resources could not be found. When provisions ran short, a few porters would be sent down to Marangu to obtain further supplies. Others would be sent back to Marangu to accompany those needing to go down as well. For example, one entry in the Peter's Hut book noted in January 1941 that porters carried wood and water to Kibo, another went back to Bismarck Hut when the visitor's personal servant fell ill and needed to go down, and then two porters went to Marangu to get four more days' food. The author regretted not leaving more firewood at Kibo Hut, but a porter had also fallen ill at Peter's Hut, and they had to leave him there with another porter, so they were "shorthanded."[87]

FIGURE 9. Porters for Czech travelers Jiri Hanzelka and Miroslav Zigmund, 1948. Jiri Hanzelka and Miroslav Zikmund, *Afrika: Traum und Wirklichkeit*, translated by Adolf Langer (Berlin: Verlag Volk und Welt), 1959.

Some visitors expressed not only appreciation for the porters' work but acknowledged their strength and stamina. For example, a 1943 entry in the Peter's Hut book described the porters as a "bunch of sports." "I wouldn't, nay couldn't, yank the burdens they do for a mile, let alone all the way up Kilimanjaro!" the climber disclosed.[88] Another particular porter named Bariki made a significant impression with his physical strength, leading to one of the rare comments about individual porters in the hut books. "One porter, Bariki, who on a previous occasion carried some 30 lbs up to Gilman's Pt. has put up an excellent show today," the visitors wrote in January 1944, "He left Bismarck at 0800 to return to Marangu for further supplies, and made the journey Bismarck-Marangu-Peter's in seven hours twenty minutes—most of the return journey having made through rain and severe hail."[89] Emmanuel Mongi remarked that perhaps they did not seem to have as many problems in the past because they started young.[90]

Porters were also called upon at times when work needed to be done on scientific expeditions or for mountain club work repairing huts and clearing paths. In September 1937, 130 men transported materials and built a porters' hut at the Johannes Hut site and continue on to do the same at Peter's Hut.[91] Sometimes, even as they carried loads they had to clear the path, as in May 1945 when Lauwo and Fataeli's crew led the first party of the season and the porters "had to do a fair amount of panga work to clear the way."[92]

Visitors' books give insight into porter culture as well. With years of experience and apparently good relationships among at least some crews, they worked efficiently. Interview participants stressed the importance of a crew working together as a team. David Sifueli Mtui said that in the past, guides treated the porters carefully because without the porter, the loads would not make it, and a late load would cause problems for the tourists. If porters were overcome, he continued, the guide would help them until they made it.[93] Aside from David Sifueli Mtui, interview participants did not elaborate much on this topic. It seems they generally enjoyed good relationships, especially among porters. Some summed it up by saying that they worked together as a family. Working as a team was especially important when facing difficult weather conditions. In 1942, a visitor who made it to Gilman's Point commented: "Otherwise, the organization and efficiency of the safari has my highest admirations. The boys work like clock-work, the food is excellent and they contribute no small part to the success of the adventure."[94] One visitor wrote that they made it to the saddle, despite the difficult weather conditions. They described the weather as "vile, wet and foggy and no visibility," but Mlombare "did his job well and the porters were cheery and good."[95] Stanley Mosha commented that even if the porters would have wanted to go home because of the rain, they could not because the tourist had already paid for the trip.[96]

At the same time, although the work was hard, it did not take all day and porters found ways to entertain themselves as they rested in the evenings. In 1941, visitors expressed appreciation for Sambonanga's "excellent and courteous service" as well as "the 'choir' of Christian porters who furnished us with music in four parts every evening."[97] Czech travelers Jirí Hanzelka and Miroslav Zikmund wrote about the celebratory dancing and singing of the porters at Bismark Hut on their way down from their successful ascent of Kibo in 1948.[98] One can imagine a few especially musically inclined men with strong lungs among the porters instigating the singing. Even though the tourists had separate quarters from the porters, the sound of a group of men singing would have carried easily to their quarters. Two climbers devoid of other company with whom they could communicate fluently were grateful for the singing, with one thanking "Johannes, Lucas and the 4 hymn-singing porters who helped me not to feel quite so lonely on the trip."[99] Another group that same year connected with the porters for religious services at Peter's Hut. After describing how the porters took seven loads of firewood to Kibo, they wrote that it was Monday, but they treated the day "as Sunday and had service with porters."[100] Likewise, porters participated when a group of reverends, all of UMCA (Universities' Mission to Central Africa), Masai, Southern Province, held communion on the mountain in February 1942.[101]

Very few visitors who signed the books at the huts, the books at the peaks, or the guides' books named the porters. The larger number of porters versus the fewer number of guides and cooks as well as the social separation on the trail likely contributed to people naming guides and cooks more than porters. The language barrier likely played a role in separating visitors from the porters, as well as the social distance of the colonial period. The loneliness solo visitors experienced or comments about not being able to speak the local languages reveal that there were at times difficulties connecting socially. Yet some entries highlight memorable porters and give the impression that visitors who named the porters made an effort to get to know them. In August 1936, an L. Robertson, climbing to Kibo after a previous trip in 1932, named Affitta, Alinaja, Isaiah, Desanjo, Awnissa, and Christoforo. In the margin next to his entry, he wrote that he had employed Mlombare previously and had "a high opinion of his work and of that of his porters." Two people from a school in Arusha shortly after listed Kimatare, [Awinia], Amanli, [Kunidasani], and Sufaeli.[102] Another named a particular porter, Kibo, and in 1947, the following porters were listed in Mlombare's guidebook: Dowdie, Bariti (or Bariki?), Duneddi, Orbedi and [Erichilea], Seria, and [Firiedi].[103] Often, in the early years, the porters were described as "cheerful," and "willing." Others were described as well-behaved and "in good spirits all the way."[104] The personalities of other porters came out in a 1941 entry in the Peter's Hut book. "It has been a most enjoyable safari," the visitor wrote. He described Sambonanga as a "wonderful guide" and praised his cooking along with that of Maletto. He continued to comment about the porters, giving the sense that the jovial interactions with the crew played an important role in making the safari "most enjoyable": "The porters, Maletto, Danielle, etc. were a very cheery and willing crew. They're tough. They gave us a concert every evening and the wit of the party who nicknamed himself 'Masai' (His only resemblance to a Masai being a blanket flung over his shoulder. He is a little fellow) always kept us amused on the way."[105] Another comment on Sambonanga's assistant being nicknamed "stoogie" after calling Sambonanga a friend gives a similar impression.[106] Sianga was thanked for paying close attention to someone's steps.[107] Jack Grover of the American Embassy in Cairo described the cook Samuel and porters Abmarry, Hairmas and Chilia (notes as attempts at phonetic spelling) as "all jolly, good chaps."[108]

Provisions and Pay

A significant part of all of this work was the pay and provisions guides, cooks, and porters earned. Remuneration became an important site of negotiation, especially with porters. It shaped the industry in critical ways in the first half of the twentieth century. It influenced the routes Europeans established in the late 1930s, as when men in Old Moshi refused to work for less, and determined the overall cost of trips, which had an impact on who participated in the industry. Climbers paid for the use of the huts and provisions. Guides, cooks, and porters were paid per day, given provisions, and expected a form of a tip or final payment at the end of the journey. Guides were paid twice as much as the porters and cooks slightly more than the porters. In the 1930s as the club standardized and formalized the process, they started paying guides three shillings a day, assistant guides two shillings, and porters one shilling, plus "full rations and blankets."[109] Although it was understood that tips depended on the good will of the tourists, they were established early on as part of the culture of payment in the industry.

At times, porters used their collective power to obtain pay increases. The hardships of World War II and the increase in costs after the war strained labor relations. Supplies of blankets were restricted during the war, so the hotels and club started offering payment of three shillings instead of blankets and started keeping "a stock of superior cotton blankets" to be used and returned by porters.[110] An incident in 1943 demonstrates the power that porters and guides had in the industry during this time of limitations. An accusation that a porter stole a ring from a patron led to the patron withholding pay for everyone. This action raised concerns among the hotel owners and club leaders that porters would strike, "which would be bad for everyone, hotels included."[111] After the war, pressure from the porters and guides to increase pay relative to the increase in the costs of living popped up periodically with porters striking in 1945, leading the Kibo Hotel to hire a new group of porters and the club to reach out to Old Moshi.[112] In 1947, Anne Bruehl of Kibo Hotel urged the club to settle the matter so that she did not have to continue to have unpleasant discussions, even in front of visitors. Bruehl eventually advocated for an increase in pay in 1949.[113] The club had printed information pamphlets in 1946 and did not want to change the rates because they had already advertised otherwise. Although some compromises had been reached and tips covered some of the demands, it was becoming more and more difficult to manage in 1949. At this point, guides were paid three shillings, assistant guides three shillings, cooks two shillings, and porters one and a half shillings per day, plus five shillings each in cash instead of a blanket for each safari of five days. Provisions were costing more, putting a strain on the food they carried. Since the club and hotels wanted to present only the finest to the patrons, the food for the support crew was affected. Bruehl concluded, "The Natives are always asking for higher pay and would not do the job if they would not be sure to get a good Baksheesh [tip] from the climbers on top of their pay."[114]

Negotiations continued into the 1950s. In 1951, porters and guides asked to be paid in blankets instead of the five shillings because the blankets had become more valuable (and thus could be sold for more money). Trouble with a geological visitor also highlighted tensions over pay.[115] In November of that year, the district commissioner and vice president of the mountain club decided it would be best to amend the fees so as to ensure that the club prospered and built up a "loyal and keen gang of guides and porters." They suggested raising the rates per day (in old British shillings) for guides or assistant guides from three shillings and fifty pence to five shillings, cooks from two shillings and fifty pence to three shillings and fifty pence, and porters from two shillings to three shillings. The five-shilling blanket fee would remain the same, but a major change was the suggestion of a ten shilling per month regular salary paid by the mountain club to all regular guides.[116] It appears they hoped the regular pay would keep the guides loyal and would then negotiate with the porters or keep them in line (although there is no evidence that a monthly salary was adopted). In July 1952, negotiations continued regarding rice, with porters demanding more but the authorities restricting rice and scoffing at their claims that "posho" [ugali] was bad for the stomach at the higher altitudes.[117] However, some club leadership acknowledged the necessity of answering porter demands, with Hughes writing to Bruehl in 1953, "it is a waste of time to climb unless the porters are willing and I am afraid that there is no alternative but to pay higher wages."[118]

Things came to a head in 1954. The trouble started at the beginning of the year after some holiday climbers based in Kenya paid over the customary amount, and coffee-harvesting work offered Chagga workers better wages. As at many other times in the history of the industry, up to this time, the guides and porters did mountain work on top of working their own fields.[119] Coffee prices were on the rise in the 1950s, making plantations as well as small holders on the lower slopes profitable. Anne Bruehl of the Kibo Hotel wrote to mountain club officers and the district commissioner in February about the "greatest difficulties" she was having getting porters to work for visiting climbers. "Some extra pay, the porters have got from outside climbers during the Christmas time, and especially the enormous money they receive now for the coffee, the high wages, they are paying one another for picking the coffee, made the porters discontent with the present wages for the safaris," Bruehl explained. They asked for fifteen more shillings total for each porter per safari. Although this would cause difficulties in adjusting charges made to clients or reducing the number of porters they could hire, Bruehl had to support the requests, "as it is at present nearly impossible to get the necessary number of porters for the safaris." According to Bruehl, the guides were willing to work and often took on extra loads to make sure a safari happened.[120] Soon, however, it was not enough for the guides either. Mountain club correspondence in April reported that "Miss" Lany (likely Erica) from the Marangu Hotel said guides were asking her for "exorbitant rates" and guides and porters refused to carry out some maintenance work unless they were paid ten old British shillings a day per guide, five per porter, and cooks five and a half plus rations and ten shillings for a blanket.[121]

After "long, long discussions" with the "mountain people," "Mrs." Lany (the mother), and mountain club secretary P. Ungerer , Bruehl reported in May that they had reached the point where the guides and porters would not work for less than ten British shillings per day per guide, five and a half shillings per day per cook, and five shillings per day per porter, plus ten shillings for the blanket for each trip. The club recommended that climbers plan a four- to five-day journey to acclimatize and allow for a long hike up the cone. Added to costs for provisions, the new charges for a five-day trip amounted to (in old British shillings): "1 person: Shs. 400; 2 persons 375 each; 3 persons 350 each; Extra day Shs. 75 each person." Aware that this was not what the club and the Marangu Hotel would have wanted, Bruehl wrote that she was "still trying to get the charges down," but that did not seem possible or even a long-lasting solution as her people were "hardheaded as anything," and she was afraid "if we would succeed to persuade them to be cheaper, the old trouble would start very soon again."[122] Because of the economics and labor demand, the porters had the upper hand. The accepted pay lasted for the next few years, at least as the official pay (tips and other negotiations happened as well).[123] Thus, in the mid-1950s, the porters and guides exercised their labor power to increase their pay by over 200 percent for guides and 400 percent for porters from twenty years earlier, reminding the hotel and club managers how much they relied on the consent and collaboration of the Chagga men who made it all possible.

Interview participants who started to work on the mountain the earliest started mostly in the 1970s after these negotiations, with two starting earlier. Only one, Samwel Toma Mosha, talked about pay negotiations in the earlier period. Even then, he mentioned that Lauwo stopped working at Kibo Hotel because he asked for greater pay instead of talking about porters going on strike or negotiating their salaries. Oral history interviews give the impression that the pay into the 1970s was relatively good, with a number of interview participants remarking that they could do more with the pay they received when they began working than in more recent times. Of course, the larger context was slightly different in the 1970s, as discussed in the next chapter.

A final important aspect of the labor arrangements that emerged at the beginning of the industry and that persisted well beyond was viewing mountain work as contingent work. At first, porters and guides were viewed almost as servants. In the latter part of 1953, a question as to whether or not guides and porters qualified for workman's compensation insurance arose from the labor officer in Moshi, revealing the way the government viewed mountain labor. In a letter to the mountain club, the officer debated whether or not the guides and porters fit the definitions of laborers needing that insurance and questioned who was responsible for reporting accidents. "There is doubt as to whether a Guide is a servant, though almost certainly a Porter is," he wrote. And yet, "Some argument seems available to those who would deny that they are masters of these possible servants." Were the guides considered the porters' employer, or the hotel, or the mountain club? He concluded that insurance was not "compulsory" but thought it "wise for the position of Guides and Porters to be clearly defined so that they themselves can insure, or so that their employers may take out Workmen's Compensation Policies."[124] The question of insurance for mountain workers continues to this day. The raising of the issue in the 1950s gives insights into how porters and guides fit into the colonial economy and labor relations of the time.

Colonial Relations

While many visitors described the mountain workers with great affection, the written and oral records illuminate the dynamics of the colonial context within which they worked. This had an impact on social relations on the mountain as well as the economics of the industry. Oral history gives some clues as to how the Chagga people and the mountain workers viewed the relationship over time. As discussed in the previous chapter, in the first decades of the industry, the Chagga communities looked down on those who worked on the mountain because they saw them as acting as servants of white Europeans who had come to colonize their land. It did not help that they came back from the mountain covered in dirt and soot with eyes red from smoke or the burning glare of the sun coming off the snow. The mountain crews may have also felt the hierarchy of this labor arrangement. Current expectations that porters should keep their distance from visitors feels reminiscent of colonial master-servant relations (although the hierarchy between the guides and porters has changed over time, particularly with shifting roles of companies in the industry). At the same time, the fact that mountain workers asserted their autonomy when demanding better pay in the 1950s shows some defiance of any feeling of inferiority. However, oral history interviews did not elaborate on this much. A few interview participants talked about how they came to see *wazungu* as ordinary people. As they learned more about their lives and personalities while spending time with them on the mountain, they did not see them as exotic, untouchable, or colonizers. They also talked about the way that the community began to recognize the job opportunities they brought.

The written record is more revealing of European and American perspectives. Colonial social hierarchies pop up in many of the mountain club records and visitor books. As in the writings of earlier explorers, some European visitors expressed patronizing views of Africans in general while comments about their service or pay revealed prejudices or stereotypes they held. While some made clear comments about racial differences or the need for racial segregation, others erased the humanity of the porters as they enacted the "romantic lonely white man in the wilds of Africa" trope.

Patronizing views of porters and guides showed up in mountain club records, as both visitors and club leadership wrote about porters as "boys" even though they were grown men in their thirties. This was the same way they spoke about and to personal servants. Comments about porters being "cheerful" could have been genuinely complimentary or may also reflect a view of Chagga porters as simple people like noble savages.[125] The language barrier may have played into this—either creating more of a social separation or making some view those who spoke little English as simple people. There was also a concern in the earlier years about the discipline and cleanliness of the porters, as if porters were naturally some unruly lot that needed to be controlled. Perhaps the preface to the guides' reference books drew these comments out more than they would have naturally appeared. Clients were asked to comment on the "condition of the huts, the behavior of the guide and the porters," as well as the particulars of the size and journey of their party. In 1949, a visitor complained that the cleanliness of the Bismarck Hut was not to European standards. Signed, "G.L. Boedeker, O.F.C. Box 30 Kongwa," this visitor was likely an employee of the Overseas Food Corporation (OFC), a British colonial development agency that led the infamous groundnut scheme.[126] "I regret that my knowledge of Swahili is not yet advanced enough to explain 'ideals' to the guide nor have I time to do anything this trip," the visitor wrote.[127] Possibly in response to this, the manager of Kibo Hotel wanted to send a "lady-climber" (most certainly a European) to supervise a crew of porters to clean the huts.[128] In an information pamphlet of the mountain club, visitors were warned about the lack of cleanliness of the guides and porters and the need to ensure orders to clean were carried out. "The guides and porters do not mind the filth and will do nothing about it unless directed to do so," it read, informing readers that "Any guide or porter who refuses to carry out a reasonable order to clean will be suspended if he is reported."[129]

Oral histories show that the crew did not like the dirtiness of the work. Samwel Toma Mosha thought perhaps the way they looked after working on the mountain led people to disdain their work. The default was to blame Africans, but there were many actors involved. Other correspondence from the club to a visitor with a complaint about vandalism in the area around Peter's Hut in 1951 reveal how expectations that Europeans kept a certain level of cleanliness over Africans may have skewed the club's understanding of who was causing messes at times. In this case, David L. Sampson, with the Department of Geological Survey in Dodoma, wrote to District Officer and mountain club vice chairman, J. F. Millard, that he trusted the African who was in charge of his group's expedition—"I have enquired into the matter and find that one of the Africans who spent most of the time of the safari in charge of that camp was responsible. I am certain, however, that he intended to commit *no* act of vandalism . . . I shall strongly oppose any attempt to penalise this man for his action as I feel that the responsibility is my own." He was "rather humiliatingly forced to admit that the European behavior in this respect is even worse," and recalled all too many examples" of Europeans doing similar deeds at other times.[130] Still, there is some indication that some people in the mountain club felt guides also needed to be dealt with sternly. "The guides can be made to toe the line quite early by evoking their licenses," a club leader wrote.[131] Hughes wrote to Bruehl in 1954, "The guide and porters will be paid the normal wage for [said day washed]. I [fail] to see why we should pay them more per day for cleaning than for portering . . . all they are only cleaning up the mess they themselves are responsible for and should have been dealt with on previous safaris. If they do not like these terms their license to work for the Club will be cancelled."[132]

There were some outright complaints and derisive comments. A lonely climber in 1929 complained about the pay his guide earned, not recognizing the difficult and valuable role he played: "By the way this guide was getting two shillings a day to carry a load of 40 lbs, up to 15,000 feet, and then if he succeeded in getting you up to the top he was to get ten shillings extra. We all think him frightfully cheeky for demanding so much money for so little work."[133] Before learning to respect the mountain and the need to acclimatize, an American wrote in the Peter's Hut book of his boredom:

> Left Kloss' Hotel 9.15 a.m. 11th July 1940 with the guide Johann, one cook and three porters. . . . To date I am bored stiff—with one donkey to carry provisions, etc. I could have sauntered up this far in one day on my own easily and the cooking would have kept me amused. This is not mountain climbing at all—it is just typical African laziness. Unfortunately I am unable to speak Swahili and cannot, therefore, do much about it.[134]

This particular author evidenced a change in views. His next entries talked about how difficult it was to breathe near the first glacier and how he learned to respect the mountain and not be overconfident. Europeans of a higher socio-economic class or colonial position wrote particularly strong disparaging remarks about Africans. Those accustomed to having personal servants almost always accompanying them and attending to their personal needs transferred expectations and even affections to porters who stepped into that position for them. For example, one man on holiday from his colonial duties in Nigeria brought his Nigerian "boy" with him. When his "boy" had to return to Marangu because he fell sick, the man named and described the work of a porter, Kibo, who looked after him. Perhaps he highlighted the work of Kibo because he was not used to being without a personal servant.[135] Although two clients based in Kitale Kenya wrote in 1949 that Mlombare was a very good guide and had effective control over the porters, they also felt "His manners however seem to need improvement and it is suggested that he be instructed in the correct standard of manners and politeness that he should adopt towards his temporary employers." The problem, it seemed to them, had to do with the system of changing "masters" for these supposed servants. They continued, "The look and personal [boy] service has now reached a very low standard presumably owing to many masters and lack of supervision. The present standard bears no relation to what Africans are [capable] of under similar conditions."[136]

Not everyone held the same views. Some explicitly countered negative remarks. Immediately following Boedeker's 1949 complaint about the lack of European standards of cleanliness, a Miss Hauga from Switzerland wrote, "Sorry but I think we should be glad that there is a hut here at all. These remarks are quite unnecessary."[137] The Czech visitors Franta Paul in 1930, Jiří Baum and Frank V. Foit in 1931, and Hanzelka and Zikmund in 1948 wrote about their crews more like teammates. Paul, for example, named and kept track of his porter Msumba, described the careful work of their guide, "Johannu," and talked about the porters and guides' desires to test their strength.[138] Naturalist Jiří Baum noted the shabby sleeping quarters for porters and also chronicled their physical conditions along with the rest of his party.[139] Hanzelka and Zikmund similarly tracked every person's physical condition and recognized that without the mountain crew's help, the "white man" could not make it to the top.[140] Others described the personal service they enjoyed. The *Alpine Journal* writer and mountaineer American D. L. Busk wrote in 1955 about the breakfast on the morning of his summit: "A shout aroused my 'cook-porter' and tea was served to me in my sleeping bag from the petrol primus, a luxury I have never enjoyed in a hut before. I then deigned to rise for porridge and bacon and eggs, served on a table cloth with a napkin placed neatly beside my plate."[141] Yet even some of the complimentary entries came with arrogance, such as these comments in Mlombare's first guidebook: "The Guide behaved very well—was most helpful and encouraging—one of the few remaining respectful Africans—an excellent fellow for a Safari of any sort. He had very good control over the porters and Cook, all of whom worked well in particular the Cook."[142] Two subsequent entries mentioned that these Africans were the best they had met, also working off of stereotypes or classifications.

Sometimes the snubs came when visitors viewed themselves as the lone European or white adventurer and seemingly considered porters and guides as part of the landscape or listed them alongside animals.[143] A climber in 1929 described himself heading up "all alone except for the native guide."[144] An entry in Mlombare's guidebook in 1939 mentioned the fact that the European visitor had a Kikuyu "boy" with him as well, almost as an afterthought. After listing his accomplishment of reaching the top of the crater, he wrote, "My [dog?] and my cook, a Kikuyu, also reached G.s point."[145] In an account titled "Planting the Jewel on the Snowy Crown of Africa: The Bible on the Empire's Summit," published in the mountain club's 1932 *Ice Cap*, the author dramatically described how he reached the top of the crater after falling and hitting his head. Although four Africans, including a personal servant, hoisted him up the last five hundred yards or so, he felt he was the loneliest white man on the continent at the top.[146] A man from London viewed the last ascent to the top of the cone as the part of the climb left to the white man. Having a guide up Skiddaw, a mountain in England of no more than 3,000 ft/914 m, looked like a joke compared to tackling Kilimanjaro. Still, although he praised Kimatare as his guide, he was looking to prove himself as a white man. "I shall see in two days time [*sic*] where I can do the only part of the climb that is (partly) left to the white man—wapi [where is the] scree?" he wrote on June 20, 1944. Two days later, he reported that "the white man" had made it to the highest peak and concluded, "Kimatare was very great indeed. (Never Again)."[147] As Reusch prepared to leave the area in 1938, the club meeting minutes read that "His record of ascents of Kilimanjaro and Mawenzi was not likely to be surpassed."[148] The club awarded him a gold medal after his twenty-fifth climb and said that he had trained three guides and arranged for ninety-six porters at the beginning of the club's operations.[149] By 1953 he had climbed the mountain sixty-five times.[150] These are great accomplishments and contributions, and yet obviously the guides who took multiple people to the top had already done so, some of them probably many more times.

The mountain club accommodated colonial racial segregation at times, although this does not come through very much in the records. As they refurbished the huts in the 1930s, the club built separate quarters for "native guides and porters."[151] The prospect of having a mixed-race group of schoolboys from Kenya in 1951 revealed the way that the mountain club and other Europeans visiting the mountain viewed the social distance that should be maintained on the mountain. It was not that the support crew was a different class or that those who lived in the region were necessarily squeamish about mixing with other races. They worried about how other Europeans would react or the "confusion and resentment on the part of many European climbers to sleep in a hut occupied by Africans or Asians the previous night."[152] When Mr. R. A. Lake sent information to an interested party, he noted that the Marangu and Kibo hotels handled reservations for guides and porters and warned him of a possible conflict of dates. "I say 'conflict of dates'" he explained, "because there is a possibility of being unable to stagger reservations for huts in case of climbers being of mixed races."[153]

Racial sensibilities remained prominent throughout most of the period extending from the 1930s to the 1950s. However, this was also the period in which there was a gradual evolution of the identity of porters and guides as distinctly separate from both the *mangi* who mediated their hiring and the hotels and tour operators that hired them. With this distinction emerged greater specialization of the roles of guides and porters. These roles being played exclusively by Africans who were almost all Chagga had considerable impact on the mountaineering industry. Politics around Kilimanjaro and across Tanganyika directed fresh attention on the mountain. In Kilimanjaro, the native administration was greatly centralized, culminating in the election of a *mangi mkuu* (paramount chief) in 1952. The *mangi mkuu* would go on to advocate for Chagga control of at least some of the mountaineering activities. Yet even the *mangi mkuu*'s advocacy appeared to have come too late. The pre-independence nationalist movement that swept Tanganyika in the 1950s saw Africans canvassing for better working conditions and ultimately for independence, measures that had serious implications to the working conditions and self-perception of guides and porters on Kilimanjaro. Additionally, as independence approached, the mountain was also claimed as a natural national monument not to be controlled entirely by the Chagga people.

CHAPTER 5

Wagumu in Post-Independence Tanzania

ALTHOUGH THE HIGH ALTITUDES AND EXTREME TEMPERATURES RESTRICTED WHO would attempt the climb, Kilimanjaro became more open to amateurs in the latter part of the twentieth century. Post-war tourism brought a growth in the interest in Kilimanjaro, along with a receding snow line and the opening up of less technical routes to the top of Kibo. In 1939, the club reported that fifty-eight people had reached Peter's Hut during the year and that five reached Kaiser Wilhelm's Point.[1] In 1950, the club had record of 116 total climbers and expected many more the following year, with sixty already having climbed by the end of May 1951.[2] In 1958, the club noted that between four hundred and five hundred people booked accommodations during the previous year, and those using the huts were mostly not members of the club.[3] The *Alpine Journal* later reported that more than seven hundred people attempted to summit the highest peak in 1959. Only about half reached the top. Yet a mere 50 percent success rate did not deter other adventurers. The journal wrote that climbing Kilimanjaro had become a "popular business" by the 1960s.[4]

This popular business of climbing Kilimanjaro challenged the system that had been in place at the same time that a wave of African nationalism brought in new claims on the mountain. As the industry outgrew the Kilimanjaro Mountain Club, the club sought at first to implement new regulations, then to turn management over to a public parks system. Local Chagga political leaders attempted to gain control of the industry, but the new independent Tanzanian government eventually took control and emerged as an important player. The mountain was no longer the main stewardship of the Chagga but became the mountain of the new nation of Tanzania. The nation worked to harness Kilimanjaro and other national parks for conservation and tourism development but had to adjust its socialist approach in the mid-1980s. Near the turn of the century, the stage was set for the mushrooming of private companies and an expansion in who engaged in Kilimanjaro mountain work.

A New Era

As more and more people with less money sought to scale Kibo, more people wanted to climb Kilimanjaro on the cheap. Some people also wanted to prove their own strength. This led to more people attempting the climb without a support crew or mountain club services. One person wrote in the book at Gilman's Point on December 14, 1959, "Carried my own 50 lb pack no guide or porters . . . came up like a man."[5] The following entry in the same book by an Englishman expressed the same sentiment and an entry four pages prior wrote that they had made it and "No porters either!" The *mangi* of Marangu became involved when tourists requested help in outfitting their treks when they wanted to arrange their own trips without hotel fees, to which he said he could arrange for someone to help, though he did not have time himself.[6] Those who went on their own at times would break into the huts, get lost at the top, or run into trouble with the weather. One of the major problems with people going without guides was the susceptibility to accidents. Most of the visitors to Kilimanjaro in the 1950s and 1960s were amateurs who had never been to the mountain before.

The number of accidents and injuries with those hiking without guides led the mountain club to push for more regulations in 1957 so that climbers would not attempt the ascent alone. The club first instituted (or reinforced) a rule that people could not use the huts without a guide and at least one porter.[7] They then sought to bring climbing activities under the forest ordinance to have formal government backing and to establish protocols for involving porters and guides as well as the local police in rescue operations.[8] An accident in December 1957 involving a German solo climber served as a poignant example. The man fell just below Gilman's Point and "went quarter of a mile on the iced scree before stopping." He injured his head and was "badly cut up." Luckily, another party with a guide, presumably Lauwo, was climbing nearby and attended to him, although this meant that Lauwo had to leave his other clients to take the injured man down the mountain.[9]

While the Kilimanjaro Mountain Club grappled with this burgeoning clientele on Kilimanjaro, forces across the continent were changing the broader context. Kwame Nkrumah, president of Ghana, one of the first African nations to gain independence from Great Britain in 1957, declared the 1960s the decade of Africa. Tanganyika's Julius Nyerere became a prominent pan-Africanist figure alongside Nkrumah and contributed not only to the nationalization of Kilimanjaro, but also to its continentalization and globalization. In 1959, even before his country's independence, Nyerere made one of his most popular declarations, saying, "we, the people of Tanganyika, would like to light a candle and put it on top of Mount Kilimanjaro, which would shine beyond our borders giving hope where there was despair, love where there was hate and dignity where before there was only humiliation."[10]

With political independence on the horizon, Chagga leaders became more interested in the future of the mountain tourism industry. One big question was what was going to happen with the club's huts and the new national parks administration. In 1958, the *mangi mkuu* of the Chagga, Thomas Maraelle II, wrote to the mountain club and to the Tanganyika National Parks Committee, informing them that they had formed a Chagga Trust that would like to take a more active role in the mountain tourism industry. Of course, the Chagga had already played an integral part in the industry as the crucial support crews for climbers, and the club was already working toward making support crews mandatory. However, in his appeal to the national parks committee, the *mangi mkuu* explained it was important to the Chagga to be intimately involved in the management because of their relationship to the mountain. "For, to us," he wrote, "the Mountain is not only a Continent-wide landmark and tourist attraction, but a most benevolent grandpa for untold generations." He understood the club held the leases on the huts and proposed that the Chagga Trust take over responsibility for them and establish an information office and provide other services at Marangu. On the eve of independence, Maraelle hoped to assert influence over the Chagga and sought to regain control of the land that had shaped their lives as well as an industry that drew visitors from around the world and wherein their people provided key labor. The formation of the Chagga Trust meant they had funds to buy the property and assert their position.

Discussions had already started on naming Mawenzi and Kibo a national park. Maraelle thus proposed the club and the national parks all meet to discuss questions as to the preservation of the peaks, upkeep of the huts, the organization of guides and climbing parties, and the construction of a road leading to Peter's Hut. (He also raised the issue of people trying to take parts of the leopard which had frozen in the upper snows of the mountain, made famous by author Earnest Hemingway, and which was now an important symbol of the Chagga flag.[11]) The parks authority responded that a lack of funding would likely prevent the establishment of a national park, but they were open to discussing improving cooperation for managing the facilities and considering the idea of a national park.[12] Maraelle thought the club would respond favorably to his request; however, the club saw things differently. The following year, club members discussed the proposal at length. "It was the feeling of the members that the interests of the climbers should remain paramount," the meeting minutes concluded. Apparently, they did not think having the Chagga Trust in charge would do that, although the meeting minutes did not elaborate why. Club members also did not want to jeopardize their arrangements with the Kenyan Mountain Club by giving up their control over Kilimanjaro.[13] They were not quite ready to concede to Chagga control.

The idea was tabled but could not be put off long with Tanganyika gaining its independence in 1961 and then joining with Zanzibar to become Tanzania in 1964. The shift in political control was marked with symbolic name changes on the mountain. The new government gave new names to the huts and the highest peaks. Bismarck Hut became Horombo, Peter's became Mandara, and Kaiser Wilhelm Spitze became Uhuru Peak, the word for "freedom" in Swahili. In 1961, Lt. Alexander Nyirenda of the Tanganyika African Rifles hiked to the top of Kibo to place the new Tanganyikan flag on the freshly minted Uhuru Peak, signifying that Africans had conquered the former colonists and taken back the land.[14] In December 1962, two mountain club members, A. Nelson and the only African member of the club, Kirilo Japhet, along with a schoolboy, carried a heavy Uhuru commemoration plaque to the top to contribute to the celebration of Tanganyikan independence.[15]

Although it would take a few more years, the stage was set for the national government to supersede both the mountain club and the Chagga Trust in managing mountain tourism. By 1967, the mountain club secretary estimated that nearly three thousand people climbed the mountain every year. The club longed for the government to form a Kilimanjaro National Park to handle the growing industry.[16] The club also no longer had a monopoly on climbing routes. Club members had developed new routes such as the steeper and shorter Umbwe Route by 1961. The

FIGURE 10. Lieutenant Alexander Nyirenda hoisting the Tanganyikan flag on Uhuru Peak (fifty-cent stamp). Govenment of the Republic of Tanganyika.

new College of African Wildlife Management built in the foothills of Kilimanjaro at Mweka had also established a route from their campus by 1966.[17] The college at Mweka was partially the outcome of the Arusha Manifesto held September 5–12, 1961, on the "Conservation of Nature and Natural Resources in Modern African States," which acknowledged the necessity for Tanganyika to have personnel who were sufficiently trained to assume the solemn responsibility of managing the African wildlife heritage. The state continued to move in this direction throughout the 1970s. In April 1970, the Tanzania Tourist Corporation took over the administration of the tourist routes on the mountain in anticipation of the formation of the Kilimanjaro National Park.[18] In 1973, the corporation had secured enough resources to create the Kilimanjaro National Park Authority (KINAPA) to manage the mountain as a national park open to the public.

Establishing KINAPA granted the state new authority. It began to require that each group entering the park to climb the mountain be accompanied by a registered tour company with trained guides. It also issued guide licenses and began

FIGURE 11. Peter von Lany and two friends from school ready to set off from Marangu Hotel to climb Kibo, 1969. Photo courtesy of Peter von Lany.

to administer guide training. The government further passed regulations to force tourist agencies taking visitors up the mountain to return to Tanzania instead of diverting tourist business to Kenya.[19] Recognizing the pull of main attractions to the northeast of the country, the Tanzanian government also built the Kilimanjaro airport halfway between Arusha and Moshi in the 1970s to facilitate tourist visits to Kilimanjaro and the country's most famous national parks in the region. Throughout all these changes, the Marangu hotels managed to maintain their role in arranging treks up the mountain and employing mountain crews. When Nyerere's Arusha Declaration was adopted, Erica von Lany (who had taken Tanzanian citizenship) successfully petitioned the government to let the Marangu Hotel remain privatized. She and Peggy Brice-Bennett worked to continue their community of porters, cooks, and guides associated with the hotel until their passing in the 1990s, when the hotel management was passed down to the second generation of the Brice-Bennett family.[20] However, the industry was about to experience further major changes.

Persistent Difficult Working Conditions

As the new country established itself into the 1980s and 1990s, many of the same working conditions that mountain workers experienced previously persisted as detailed in oral history interviews. However, with the increase of tourists and pressure on the mountain's resources, some of these conditions worsened. For example, the sleeping conditions that the crews, especially the porters, dealt with, could be quite difficult with more people on the mountain. Forty-six of the sixty-three oral history interview participants spoke about sleeping on the mountain. Those who worked in the late 1970s through the 1980s and 1990s talked about sleeping in caves while tourists slept in the huts or tents. Many first used sheets, then blankets, and slept on top of grass or leaves before they acquired a sleeping bag and a mattress. Caves could be small or crowded, leaving only room enough for part of one's body to be covered or a cave may be occupied by another group already. On the Machame route, at Barranco camp, Shisauya Nkya said there was only one hut and only small caves, meaning that the crew only had room to put their head in the cave. Caves might also leak water, some feared the cave might drop on them, and another said they might attract lice from the grass. They also had to sleep in very cold or snowy and icy conditions. For Joel Nkya, sleeping in caves was the most difficult part of the work. Anasen Ndenimfoo, who started working in 1975, said that he almost died on his second trip because he slept in the cold without adequate clothing. The cold and wet conditions from the rain caused people to die, James Nkya from Machame explained. For Coletha Abel Shirima, these harsh conditions contributed to porters being called *wagumu*—the toughers. Other colloquial names for porters include *mborokwai* (downtrodden), *nyoka* (the snake, implying someone without a portfolio), and *mburuta* (the luggage).[21]

Similar to sleeping conditions, having the right clothing was critical, and inadequate clothing could cost someone their life. The development of more sophisticated clothing and gear facilitated more mountain tourism on Kilimanjaro; at the same time, porters, those most in need of good gear, had limited access to it. There was no local market for cold weather or mountaineering gear. What might be available for purchase was very expensive. Many struggled to afford the kind of gear needed to work in those conditions. Many talked about the difficulty of supplying their own adequate clothing for the cold and rain, as most were required to provide their own, although the Marangu Hotel was known for outfitting its workers.[22] Some hiked in gumboots or rubber work boots, which could easily be pierced by the ice or damage feet when cold. Hiking boots were important, but many also used *mandala* or Maasai sandals on certain parts of the mountain because of the availability as well as the flexibility they offered hikers. Fredy Solomon Mtui said the boots were for guides while porters wore sandals. Shisauya Nkya said one man thought having an open shoe gave the toes room to move and allowed them to dry quickly. Stanley

Mosha talked about how some greatly struggled with their shoes, even with frozen feet. Some started off with little gear and would buy or obtain what they needed bit by bit as they earned money. Some borrowed from friends as they started out and obtained advice from fellow workers on key items of clothing. Some received gear from visitors. Eventually, as the supply of clothing built up with more and more workers and tourists on the mountain, a secondhand market emerged for mountain clothing. This made buying adequate gear a little easier. Still, Samson Lauwo said that in 2023 there was no local market for new mountain clothing and gear. In addition to the right type of clothing, it could also be difficult for mountain workers to obtain adequate bags for their belongings. Fredy Solomon Mtui mentioned that at one time they used bags from a local sugar company to carry their clothes until they later had more access to proper packs.[23]

A particular task that increased in difficulty as resources depleted was fetching firewood. Thirty-five participants mentioned looking for firewood as part of the work of porters and at least twenty-six talked about it in a negative way. Firewood was important for cooking and for warming those sleeping outside or in caves during the night. Once they arrived at camp, porters would lay down their loads and cooks like Anasen Ndenimfoo would start cutting vegetables and preparing the food to be cooked. Porters assigned to fetch firewood would venture out, even if it was already dark. Once the fire was going, it could take some time for the food to cook, and porters or the cook would need help tending to the fire. If fetching water sent porters half a mile away, fetching dry wood could send them twice as far.[24] As the years went on, the porters had to search farther and farther away. Fredy Solomon Mtui said a porter may have had to walk 2 km to find wood, and Steven Matero said it could be up to 3 km. Already tired, they would walk those long distances and, since they did not carry axes, may even have to break the wood into smaller pieces by hand. They preferred dry wood and not cutting green living trees.[25] As David Munguatosha pointed out, rain would make the task that much harder.[26] Moreover, in earlier times when more animals lived on the mountain, if one had to walk far, one ran the risk of running into animals such as a leopard, wild dog, or elephant, especially by Mandara Hut.[27] For Zakaria Fataeli Mtui, the animals were not so much a problem as was people getting lost.[28] As detailed by Shisauya Nkya, fetching firewood at certain camps was worse than others. At Barranco, for example, porters hiked down to the junction with the Umbwe route to search for wood along what Shisauya Nkya called a bad road because of the canyon and frequent fog. Then at the base camp, Barafu, there was no firewood or water. They had to cook for everyone—the tourists and the workers—but could not eat until they had gone to fetch the water and wood. George Kimaro summed it up: "in the past we had to use firewood and it was very bad."[29]

Other challenges workers faced included the weight of the loads and inadequate nutrition on the trail. As regulations about weight limits came in only in the early 2000s, it was up to the guides to distribute the loads in an even manner or in a way they chose. Many interview participants remembered guides lifting loads with their hands to determine the weight of the loads compared to others. That may have helped guides ensure loads were relatively equal but did not necessarily serve as a function of checking to see if the loads were too heavy. Interview participants estimated that they could carry as much as 30 to even 50 kg. When he first started working, fresh from high school and desperate for work, Samson Lauwo remembered waiting at the Marangu gate, then running to grab any load available when the guide needed extra porters. As a beggar for work, Samson could not stop and check the weight but tried to prove he could take any load.[30] Overweight loads would become more challenging if porters did not eat properly. Most interview participants who worked from the late 1970s through the 1990s said that in the morning, they would receive *chai* (tea), with perhaps some porridge and some type of bread (such as *chapati* or *mandazi*). Fourteen said that they would work straight through lunch and only expected one meal in the evening. Others remembered having to wait for the cook to finish the food for the tourists before they would have their evening meal of *ugali* and *mboga*. And when the food supply got tight, workers might have mixed peanuts with water or toughed it out without food for a day or two until they could descend.[31] Otherwise, they might have been forced to beg other crews for food.

Those who entered the mountain work in the 1970s through the 1990s often did so for the economic benefits. They could make anywhere from $2 to later $5 to $10 a day, more than other opportunities at the time. The job brought quick money. According to Remsi William Nkya, more people started working on the mountain in the 1990s because of the better pay.[32] Tanzania as a country had suffered economically beginning in the 1970s, like many African countries hit hard by the worldwide economic downturn spurred by the 1970s oil crisis. The failed hopes of *ujamaa*, repeated droughts in the 1970s and 1980s, and sending troops to fight against Idi Amin in 1978 left Tanzania in a difficult position. Whereas Nyerere had resisted accepting foreign aid and promoted self-reliance (even making it difficult for mountain workers to exchange USD to Tanzanian shillings), the country was forced to turn to the international community for aid. This meant that government jobs and other public sector employment did not hold the promise it did before.

Moreover, structural adjustment programs imposed by the International Monetary Fund and the World Bank led to the privatization of a number of sectors.

Many mountain workers had limited education, having finished only primary school. Yet they would say the job did not require education, only one's physical strength. Thus, someone without a high school certificate could make as much money as a teacher—or a welder, tailor, farmer, or typist (different professions interview participants tried). Tips given by the tourists continued to play an important role in supplementing the income. There was consensus that in the past (before the 2020s), the money they were paid stretched further than it did in the present, as it covered school fees, household needs, and investment in livestock or building a home. Some saw it as a steppingstone to reach other financial goals they may have had. Others aspired to become guides to increase their earning power and advance in their profession. Emmanuel Makule found his personal progress in the industry and making tourists happy motivating.[33] Other porters, guides, and cooks enjoyed walking in the forest, appreciated the different climates, found the exercise beneficial, and delighted in meeting people from different walks of life (both from Tanzania and around the world). Almost all expressed satisfaction in providing for their families and paying for their children's education.

Nonetheless, mountain workers still faced many frustrations regarding pay. Steven Matero, who started working in 1990 said, laughing, "So, if you see that we are there putting up tents quickly, it is so that at least you can get some relief from life." Similarly, Ezron Samuel Nkya said that people chose to do this difficult work because life was difficult.[34] A few said they felt there was no other way to earn money. The seasonal aspect of the work meant that mountain workers had to learn to budget or plan ahead for the low season. A number complained of guides who would steal porters' tips, have ghost porters (reporting more porters than actually worked so they could pocket the supposed porters' salary while making those that worked carry more weight), or who accepted bribes or "soda" in exchange for giving porters a job opportunity. Others experienced difficulty obtaining their salaries from tour operators. These aspects gained more attention at the turn of the century when there was a shift in the way tourists viewed their relationship with porters.

Tanzania Is for Everyone

By the beginning of the twenty-first century, thirty thousand to forty thousand people were visiting the mountain every year, and an estimated ten thousand porters, five hundred cooks, and four hundred guides worked on the mountain in 2009.[35] In fact, porters constituted the majority of people on Mt. Kilimanjaro, with at least three porters per tourist, and at least one cook and one guide per team. The increase in the number of people on Kilimanjaro facilitated an expansion in who worked on the mountain, in number and in origin. The years surrounding the turn of the century brought some significant changes in the ethnicity and gender of mountain crews.

Although it is widely accepted now that people from anywhere in Tanzania can work on Kilimanjaro, non-Chagga workers had to push through some discrimination to be fully accepted. Before the mid-1990s, the vast majority of mountain crew members came from the villages in close proximity to the start of the main routes, especially in Marangu and Machame, followed by the Kibosho and Moshi area. The porters located in West Kilimanjaro are least represented on Mt. Kilimanjaro. Maasai are numerically the largest group in West Kilimanjaro. Maasai are mainly pastoralists and are more involved in cultural tourism than in climbing tourism. Other small ethnic groups found in the western and northern parts of the mountain but involved in small-scale farming are the Wasafa, Wapare, and Wameru.

Although Arusha was a growing center of commerce and tourism, even guides from the Arusha region were few in number and found it difficult to be accepted on the mountain. When Alex Lemunge started working in 1993, he remembered only about five guides, including himself, coming from Arusha. Those from around the base of Kilimanjaro wondered why they were working there, saying things such as "This mountain is for Chaggas." Others from different regions remembered the Chagga using the term *kyasaka* (a derogatory term for outsiders or foreigners) to refer to them, showing they did not view them as belonging on the mountain. Even Chagga from other areas beyond Marangu faced discrimination. Matthew Laurent, a Chagga from Himo, remembered Chagga sending those who were not born in their area or even on the route's side to go fetch firewood to keep them away. Batchi said some may have reserved huts or sleeping places for certain groups. Hassan Sakweli Buga remembered Chagga and non-Chagga groups restricting each other from the kitchen or from eating the leftover food from the tourists and singing songs against each other. Aratas Syril Massawe remarked that he did not like tribalism or when guides hired only their own people.[36]

It was the "hard-core" guides from Arusha and people like Joshua Mwakalinga who persisted and opened up work on the mountain to other ethnic groups.[37] Lemunge remembered that his fellow Arusha guides did not care what the Chagga guides said to them but continued their work. At times, they replied that Kilimanjaro was Tanzania's mountain and God did not just give the mountain to the Chagga. At about the same time Lemunge and his Arusha colleagues started in the early 1990s, Joshua Mwakalinga moved to the area from Mbeya in southern Tanzania. Joshua Mwakalinga was drawn to the mountain, which he had only seen before in schoolbooks. As he searched for a new way to make a living while residing in the town of Himo, he decided he wanted to summit Kibo. He learned that he had to pay money to do so. Then, he discovered he could try to work as porter and earn money while also achieving his personal goal. As an outsider, the only way he could obtain a position as a porter was through a connection with someone who worked at the gate and who came from his own ethnic group. He summited on his first trip up the mountain. Soon after, he qualified as a guide. The first time he brought his own crew made up of people who did not live near the gate, it took him an hour to convince the park rangers to admit them.[38] When he became a guide, Kapanya Kitaba, originally from Mbeya but based in Arusha, also pressed the company he worked for to hire people from Arusha. According to Batchi, as people like Joshua Mwakalinga challenged these barriers, even national park officials began to promote ethnic inclusivity. He asserted that almost every ethnic group in Tanzania is now represented among those who work on the mountain and observed that KINAPA intentionally stationed officials from various parts of the country in the park and encouraged crews to speak Swahili to be more inclusive.[39]

Eight out of the sixty-three oral history interview participants expressed some dislike or concern over people from other regions working on the mountain. They either commented on it as a negative development or wondered about the ability of others to do the work effectively. Those with stronger negative feelings came from older generations, although not all from older generations felt that way. Some feared those who had traditionally been the backbone of the industry would lose out. For example, Samwel Toma Mosha felt people from Marangu lost job opportunities to people from outside their area. He said that people from the city had taken over the mountain with companies established in Arusha and Moshi not hiring people from Marangu. He did not believe they knew the way but would go to the mountain anyway and have the money to pay for the new guiding licenses. Three others, along with Samwel Toma Mosha, also talked about the role that education began to play in securing job opportunities. Mosha saw those with greater education and language abilities coming from outside the region and interacting well with tourists, thus giving them more justification for earning greater salaries. He also felt at a disadvantage with his class seven education when trying to meet the new requirements to pay for and earn a license at the College of African Wildlife Management at Mweka.[40] Heavenlight Israeli Mtui said that Chagga in the past disparaged others as *kyasaka*, and asserted "this mountain is in our land." Yet the Chagga lost their special claim to working on the mountain because those from outside went to school and thus could fulfill positions that the Chagga no longer qualified to hold.[41]

Most interview participants seem to have now accepted the ethnic diversity among those who work on Kilimanjaro, including many Chagga, or more specifically, people from Marangu and Machame. Eight even declared that all were welcome to work there or that there was no tribalism in mountain work. Another eight repeated the idea that the mountain belonged to the nation, not just the Chagga. For example, Frank Leonard Nnko observed that Marangu people were the first to climb the mountain because of their location, but he said the mountain really belongs to Tanzania. Similar to Lemunge, Laurine Shuwa said the Chagga could not claim the mountain because it was national land. Steven Matero marked the change from using *kyasaka* in the past to the idea that "Tanzania is for everyone." Nuru Samson liked that working on the mountain introduced him to different ethnic groups from across the country. Five more argued that Tanzanians are allowed to work anywhere in the country, with David Munguatosha saying that people go where there is an income. He further made his point by asking, "Are you not from Tanzania if you come from Mbeya?" Fredy Solomon Mtui from Marangu said the Chagga cannot complain because Chagga people are welcome to work elsewhere in the country. Finally, questions about what they thought of the diversity of people working on the mountain led some interview participants to comment on the lack of interest in the work by Chagga or problems with Marangu and Machame youth being more interested in alcohol or drugs. David Sifueli Mtui remarked that if Chagga do not do the work, others will.[42]

Although women have historically stayed away from porter work, the gender composition of mountaineers also started to change in later years. The low representation of women in mountain tourism reflects the perception that nature-based tourism is an activity of men because women lack physical strength, assertiveness, and mental endurance to accomplish major peaks in mountaineering. Nambeke, a surveyed female porter, agreed and stated, "people underestimate and downplay women" due to preconceived notions of women as passive, soft, dependent, and maternal. In addition, the early narratives about mountain climbing capture much of the heroic, brave, and physically fit men, such as Lauwo or Nyirenda who raised the Tanganyika flag on top of Kilimanjaro. Therefore, women grew up hearing stories of their men counterparts, not women. The burden of reproductive roles and cultural and religious barriers limited women's engagement in outdoor activities such as portering. Gender-based traditions and beliefs have contributed to women's low education and inflexible domestic responsibilities. Women also still find themselves expected to attend to household responsibilities such as cooking, fetching water and firewood, and caring for children, gardens, and animals.

However, more and more women are engaging in porter work on Kilimanjaro, especially in the twenty-first century. A few women tried to work on the mountain in the 1970s. Emmaline N. Swai from Machame was one of the first women to work on the mountain around 1974 or 1976. Swai was the daughter of Daniel Swai, a guide from Machame who was prominent in oral history as one of the first guides from the Machame community. Perhaps this exposure to the mountain led her to disregard gender norms of the time and try mountain work. Or perhaps it was her familial connection that led a guide, Kiungai, to tell her she could go work on the mountain. She had graduated from primary school and was living with her parents, tending to the cows. She desired to make her own way in the world and support herself. When she heard there was work on the mountain, she wanted to try it. She took her first trip with another woman from the community named Masho and also often worked with a woman named Kyara. It appears that these three women were the first women who worked as porters on Kilimanjaro. Swai worked on the mountain twice that first year and continued intermittently over the following years when she needed money to reach her goals. It was a way she could get a quick injection of cash that covered many of her needs.

When she was interviewed in 2021, Swai was proud of the life she built and the way she could educate her child. When her child was secure in school, she decided to farm and keep livestock. Again, going against the grain of gender norms of the time, Swai's father gave her a farm from which she could earn money. When her father died, she inherited the land, cleared it, and started cultivating it. At over sixty years old, when asked what she thought when she looked at the mountain, she replied, "I clap my hands when I see the mountain . . . [because] it gave me the hope to live . . . I went there and received the money to develop myself . . . children went to school [and] others did well in life."[43]

Eunice A. Kimario said there may have been women who started working on the mountain in the 1990s.[44] However, more women started working as porters around 2010 and after, and attention to their working conditions has risen, although it has lagged behind the general efforts to help porters. More of these women came from Machame and Tarakea rather than Marangu, where there seemed to be stronger feelings from both men and women that mountain work was not for women. Like Swai, most women interview participants entered into mountain work for many of the same reasons men did—the job offered a quick way to earn money, and they were looking for a way to remain self-reliant and educate their children when life difficulties hit them hard. Once they reached their economic goals, some stopped and only returned to mountain work out of necessity. However, women crew members have had significantly different experiences on the mountain since they were entering a predominantly man's world. Working with crews that did not cater to separate genders led to problems with maintaining female hygiene, obtaining privacy, and resisting sexual harassment.

Nine out of the sixty-three oral history interview participants were women, making up 14 percent of the participants. Thirteen of the thirty-two porters surveyed for the tourism research were women, making up 40 percent. This was a little more than the gendered ratio of men to women in the industry (with men making up 95 percent of the workers) but the oral history interviews included historically significant women. Like Swai, eight of the nine women interviewed for the oral history were single, including two widows, two divorcées, and others whose previous marital status was unclear but who had children to raise alone. Although some had more positive feelings about the work than others, over half did the job more out of necessity to support themselves and their children economically. As Mary Pallanjo put it, it was the "difficulties of life" that drove many women to engage in such physically demanding mountain work.[45] For example, Coletha Abel Shirima sought out mountain work after her husband died, leaving her with five children from the age of thirteen down to two months. She had no way of paying for their education. After her youngest one was nearing two years old, she went to a gate of the Kilimanjaro National Park to seek work as a porter. When asked what she liked about the work, she remarked, "Really, you can't say that you love it. It's not because you get the salary, because this work is difficult . . . it's just difficult. Because of our ability, you do this work, and like it [to some degree], but you are also forced because of your limited abilities. . . . If I had other skills, I would not do this work."[46] On the other hand, Lightness Filex said she loved working as a porter because it gave her strength and the ability to fulfill her needs. She had two children from different men. She lived with the father of her son for some time, but when he stopped supporting her while he worked far away, she described living with his parents as a form of slavery. Porter work allowed her to become independent and care for her children on her own.[47] Being away from family, the harsh cold weather, the rough terrains, and the lack of proper equipment to ensure safety and comfort all keep women from participating in Kilimanjaro tourism. At the same time, for some, the lack of amenities made portering an alluring escape from mundane life. For women, the revenue earned from hiking elevated women's status in the community and granted them the power to contribute economically to family income. Women made money to buy livestock, join savings and credit cooperative societies, and give tithes or *sadaka* as offerings in church.

In one sense, crews made little or no special accommodations for women workers. In principle, aside from Jacqueline Shuma, whose companies acted more sensitively toward women, women porters were expected to carry the same weight as men. There was also no indication in oral history interviews that women were paid less than men just because they were women. Male crew members also generally did not seem to change their behavior because of the presence of women. Lightness Filex remarked that she heard a lot of swearing on the mountain between men of all positions, and Mary Pallanjo said that men did not realize how insulting they could be with the stories they told. Women were also expected to share tents with the other workers regardless of their gender. Swai was the only one who remembered that she and her female colleagues were given their own tent or place to sleep. This lack of privacy caused problems for women seeking a place to change their clothes or wash themselves alone. They would resort to dirty latrines or bushes or ask for a few minutes of privacy in a shared tent. They also struggled at times to have their female hygiene needs met. Jacqueline Shuma talked about the need for women to pack for their own sanitation, including wipes. In an emergency, a woman could ask the cook for some hot water to wash, but with water a scarce commodity at certain places on the mountain, that could be a difficult ask and might have been turned down. Lightness Filex mentioned the same difficulty in asking for water when she also talked about how working while one was menstruating made the job more difficult.[48]

Mary Pallanjo represented the struggles of women porters well when she said:

> My challenges as a female porter are many . . . really, we say that when sleeping, we are many in the tent, and you can't be given your own tent because you are a woman, you have to gather both male and female. So this is how challenges arise, especially when you have to change clothes. During your period, you have to

> maybe clean yourself and it becomes difficult with the toilets there which are not [good]. So you really get big problems, and you have to go in the bush with your clothes and take them off there and finish and then return—or ask them, if they are people you know a little, you ask them . . . "Hey, please can I have just three minutes and I'll finish?" and indeed you go in there, but it is very cold there so you can't tell someone to wait for three minutes outside. Others you don't know, again they must come in. So you must go in the bush because the toilets are dirty and also not appropriate. But also, another challenge is with the loads. Truly, a woman is just a woman and that load is not normal, every day is new, even if you climb for twenty years [*all laugh*], you are not used to that load even to this day . . . other many challenges, you can climb . . . you climb but you meet this, I don't know how to say, it's the body is sick . . . you are shocked, I don't know what it is, you are surprised you have started the first day or second day of your period and now you bleed, now you have carried the load, now it's the weather, now there's no food . . . now the food itself is tea, and you are given tea in the morning, and the tea is filled with leaves and a little sugar, so it is like there is nothing, and the journey must continue and still your strength is decreasing rapidly, your ability is becoming small, but because you have problems that brought you there, you can't give up. You continue. These are the challenges.[49]

In another sense, women received a great deal of different treatment from the men on the mountain. Unfortunately, some attracted a great deal of unwanted attention. Women found that a few unsavory guides and other workers would try to seduce them or trade help with their load for sexual favors. As Ritha Marandu, a surveyed porter said, "Females [porters] are badly treated by male guides and society in general; they receive unsolicited [relationship] proposals and face other kinds of mistreatments, especially when they refuse to give in to advances of sexual nature." This put women in a difficult position. They may have really needed or wanted help as they struggled with a load, yet they did not want to sell their bodies. If they refused a man or raised a complaint against him, they may have been treated harshly or denied a job in the future.

Eunice A. Kimario was driven to work as a porter to support her four children after a painful divorce. She lived with her parents when her children were small. Mountain work helped the whole family economically. She became emotional as she spoke of her divorce and the struggles she faced obtaining work at the gate. The challenge was that she needed to know someone to help her find work or she was afraid her body would be used for the sake of finding a job. She lamented, "A man is one bad person in the world. He is happy to lie to you and tell you that you are beautiful, I don't know why . . . he just needs to take advantage of your body for his use at that time, but tomorrow doesn't come." But, she concluded, the women of Tarakea were fighters.[50] Joice Baktalemo said that the women who went to the mountain for the wrong reasons, such as having relationships with men, were few in number, but they made it difficult for other women. Because mountain work had for so long been performed by men and seen as improper for women, people in the community had the idea that women went to the mountain not to work, but to "have a good time" with the men. Those that caved into seduction perpetuated those harmful perceptions. On the other hand, Jacqueline Shuma indicated that perhaps some women deliberately led men on without intentions of following through. She said that prostitution did not happen as much as people may think. She herself said she refused men but had at one time accepted help, then blocked the man's number once they came off the mountain.[51]

Some found ways to draw boundaries, keep their head down, and do their work. Emmaline Swai mused that maybe people laughed at them because it was only men going to the mountain at the time she started, but she was too busy to pay attention. Lightness Filex asserted that she went to the mountain strictly for work. Lightness Dominick said she just kept to herself, performed her duties, and went to bed early. She refused to do any favors for guides and would remind other women why they were there in the first place to help them focus. Laurine Shuwa's final words in her interview were to thank Mama Samia Suluhu Hassan, then the current and first female president of Tanzania, for showing that women could work in different sectors and that the book that would come from the oral histories the research assistants were conducting should convince women to have self-respect. Mary Pallanjo remarked that people may believe women are weak and will need help, but a woman who knew she could do it would go to work and be fine if she carried her 20 kg the whole time.[52]

Others had better experiences, with some saying they had friends who would help them get a job or help them with their load on the trail without any expectation of favors in return. Mary Pallanjo said some men encouraged her in part by telling her about other women who succeeded. Coletha Shirima took a more assertive approach, saying that one must speak out against those that treat women badly. Similarly, Kimario said that women had to stick up for themselves. According to her, Lutheran priests in Tarakea helped advocate for the women to be accepted as mountain workers, in addition to the women of Tarakea being fighters.

Some felt that creating all-female crews and unions could reduce problems women faced on the mountain. Some female guides have created all-female crews and some have started to work with global groups to bring awareness and changes to the conditions under which women work (such as Kilimanjaro Women, created by Ekeney Njau in Machame, and Women who Hike Africa Ltd, both part of the Mountain Women of the World organization[53]). Trekking companies are said to be unwilling to place female porters in positions of authority over their male counterparts; yet some women have succeeded in becoming guides. Batchi remembered seeing a group on the mountain in 2017 led by female guides and with almost 80 percent female porters. Perhaps this predominantly female crew was put together in an attempt to cut out gender friction. While some interview participants wondered if a women's union would help make things better for women, Mary Pallanjo and Coletha Shirima did not feel the women were united with each other. Lightness Dominick said she was often the only woman on the crew, whereas Jacqueline Shuma had experience sometimes working with nine or ten other women. Perhaps working with other women more frequently would help some unify.

The male oral history interview participants who were asked about their view of women working on the mountain generally had a similar range of ideas across generations, although those who had more opportunities to work with women talked more about the challenges women faced (such as sleeping arrangements, maintaining hygiene, and some disrespect or sexual misconduct from men). Overall, the men observed changes in opportunities and expectations for women in the new millennium. In this new era, it was more acceptable for women to do the same work as men. For example, Christo Amani Fataeli Mbando remarked that nowadays, women wear pants, and thinking has changed about what they can do. The oral history interviews were conducted in the context of the first two years of the presidency of Samia Suluhu Hassan. At least two male interview participants explicitly cited the fact that they had a woman president as evidence of the opening of opportunities for Tanzanian women. "Don't we have a woman president?" Lamerck Samwel Minja asked when talking about the absence of the gendered division of labor. Although they did not speak of President Hassan, twenty other male interview participants acknowledged that women had the ability to perform the work and six said they could even do the work better than men. Alex Lemunge spoke particularly positively about women, saying he was proud of them and encouraged them. He had even trained a group of women organized by a local organization. A few others recognized that like many men, women also worked on the mountain to answer economic hardships or family problems. Alberto Jonas

Haramba commented that if one knew the reasons a woman was performing this kind of work, one would be more understanding. Christo Amani Fataeli Mbando observed that men could leave their wives nowadays, so women have to depend on themselves and can get money quickly with mountain work.[54]

In addition to those who spoke more positively about women working in Kilimanjaro, about eleven men simply acknowledged that women worked in the industry without judgement on their value. However, twelve said women would ask or need help to perform the work, implying that women would have difficulties with the work. Women interview participants talked more of the sexual misconduct and pressures they faced than the men did, although some men discussed their strong feelings about both men and women who may go to the mountain for the wrong reasons or men who treated women badly. Only three male interview participants explicitly said that women caused problems or should not be involved; however, the fact that the Marangu Hotel had a policy of only hiring men showed that a significant player in the industry felt for some time that mixed-gendered crews caused too many problems. This also contributed to the geographic distribution of women working more on the northeast side of the mountain than in Marangu.

New Working Conditions and Regulations

At about the same time that the diversity of Tanzanians who worked on Kilimanjaro was expanding, the world was paying more attention to the mountain. The United Nations Education, Culture and Science Organization (UNESCO) declared Mt. Kilimanjaro a world heritage site in 1987, for it was "an outstanding example of a superlative natural phenomenon."[55] As the number of tourists heading to Tanzania to climb Kilimanjaro continued to grow, more people attempted to climb Kilimanjaro on a lower budget. At the same time, the world was seeing a growing trend toward more responsible tourism.[56] Organizations and activists started to whittle away at some of the unequal aspects of a system rooted in past customs while competing with economic forces influencing tourist decisions and cost-saving practices of companies, guides, and porters. A more competitive job market for porters exacerbated some of these aspects. International and local groups, plus the Tanzanian government, established a basis of regulations and advocacy networks; however, not all these regulations were followed, especially for temporary or occasional porters.

Changes in difficult working conditions began both with the private sector and non-governmental organizations (NGOs), with people from the places where most tourists originated, Europe and America. Samson Lauwo began working in 2000. When he first started, he remembered dealing with similar challenges that others before him described. Although his great uncle had worked as a guide and had told him a few stories in his old age, when Samson began working as a porter, his uncle had passed away. Samson was not well prepared for his first journey. He remembered wearing his school shoes, carrying his provisions in his school bag, and bringing bed sheets to sleep with. He carried heavy loads (once so heavy a guide intervened to reduce the load) and struggled to eat enough with some companies.

In Samson Lauwo's experience, Jimmy Forster, and his colleague named Richard—tour operators from America (and the United Kingdom) first working for Exodus and then founding African Walking—were the first to bring big changes to porter working conditions on Kilimanjaro. Forster brought equipment such as tents and sleeping bags to improve sleeping conditions. Forster and Richard also would either bring food or check food at the gate and give warm clothing to some men to wear up to the summit. There was a high demand for guides to meet the growing number of tourists at the time. Samson felt drawn to the work and wanted to become a guide. However, some of the older guides who had less education and thus struggled to communicate with tourists did not like how Samson could interact well with the foreigners with his high school education, which led them to try to exclude him from becoming a guide. Samson additionally credited Forster and Richard with introducing the position of summit porter: a porter who would assist the guides in taking tourists to the summit. This gave porters experience to help them progress into becoming a guide. Then, Samson remembered the National Park offered guide training in 2003. This training entailed seven days in the classroom, then a successful climb up to Uhuru peak in a proscribed amount of time, and finally, an exam. In Samson's view, this made a big difference in improving the quality of guides. His summit porter experience and official guide training propelled him to working as a guide and eventually establishing his own company, Kilimanjaro Bound.

Samson Lauwo remembered the Kilimanjaro's Porters Assistance Project (KPAP) arriving after the changes he saw while working for African Walking. KPAP was part of a wave of organizations founded to improve conditions for porters in the late 1990s and early 2000s. Two international organizations formed in the late 1990s: the International Mountain Explorers' Connection (IMEC) based in Colorado, founded in 1996; and the United Kingdom-based International Porter Protection Group (IPPG), founded in 1997 in part by a British doctor and mountaineer. Organizations focused more specifically on Kilimanjaro soon followed. The IMEC supported KPAP, which was established in 2003. The Mt. Kilimanjaro Porters Society (MKPS) was formed in 2005. Local associations and unions run by Tanzanians subsequently formed, including the Kilimanjaro Porters' Association, Mt. Meru and Arusha Associations, the Kilimanjaro Guides and Porters Union, Kilimanjaro Porters Assistance, and finally, the Tanzania Porters Organization, founded in 2013.[57] These organizations registered porters and endorsed teams and companies that followed their recommended guidelines (which are meant to entice tourists seeking to engage in responsible tourism).[58] They also handle complaints lodged by mountain workers. Some local organizations provide free educational programs and training for porters and some, such as the MKPS, even offer some financial assistance and engage in environmental conservation activities.[59] Eventually, the Tanzanian parks' authority required all porters to belong to a recognized porters' association, evidenced by an identification card, to keep track of those working on the mountain.

Regulations and changes in porter working conditions have related to the weight porters carry, equipment and clothing, sleeping conditions, food, the health and safety of the porters, and wages. KINAPA's adoption of recommended policies as well as other conservation-oriented regulations has also improved working conditions. Interview participants talked mostly about five changes that affected them positively: weight limits, the prohibition of fire, the prohibition of cigarettes or smoking, trash management, and gear checks (including clothing and sleeping equipment). Interview participants also talked about the food and pay they received; however, efforts to regulate these two aspects of porter work have yielded a mixed bag of results. While a number mentioned an improvement in food especially, the quality of both food and salaries given to porters seemed to depend more on the companies they worked for.

A majority of interview participants talked about the weight of the loads they had to carry as a significant determinant of the difficulty of porter work. Thirty-four cited new regulations that porters may carry only up to 25 kg/55 lbs (20 kg for the tourist and 5 kg for the porter's own necessities) as an improvement from the past. This was also one of the main issues porters' organizations have addressed. Park officials enforce this by weighing loads on scales at park gates and other points along the way (particularly at the first camp). However, evidence confirms that corruption at park gates and guides trying to save money may mean that porters are still often given overweight loads, whether from the start or as the team progresses to camps where rangers may not have scales. Porters desperate for jobs may not resist this but resign themselves to carrying loads that are too heavy.

FIGURE 12. Porters on the first day of the Northern Circuit, 2018. Photo by L. A. Hadfield.

Twenty-three of the interview participants named the prohibition of fires as a positive development. Since going to fetch firewood in the past had been a dreaded part of porter work, the switch to using gas stoves in the early 2000s was a welcome change. Joshua Clement Ruhimbi was very happy when they announced he would not be using wood to cook. He even said it was an answer to prayer.[60] Yet this change was not just welcome because it made work easier. Many also recognized the damage that fires did on the mountain. Eleven others named the prohibition of cigarettes or smoking on the mountain as another positive regulation (alcohol has also been banned on the mountain and was mentioned by six interview participants). Indeed, there are mountain workers who view the mountain as a heritage and a resource to take care of, which also led KINAPA to adopt trash-in, trash-out regulations, meaning that crews must not leave any of their trash on the mountain. As Simon Mtuy looked to establish his own business and distinguish the work he did on Kilimanjaro, he was urged by mentors to focus on his passion. He decided to concentrate on environmental sustainability. According to Simon Mtuy, this led to him learning about and introducing "Leave No Trace" principles that TANAPA and other companies also adopted.[61] The new management of trash regulations significantly impacted the work of porters. Although they may have seen this as good for the mountain's ecosystem, the eighteen who talked about it may have also focused on it because having to keep track of and weigh the whole group's garbage changed their work. Some rangers strictly enforced these policies, placing it at the forefront of the minds of porters and guides.

Sleeping arrangements and the clothing and gear of mountain workers was also a prominent improvement over the years. Fourteen interview participants mentioned how gear checks performed by park rangers at the gate helped ensure that workers were properly prepared for their upcoming trip. Many also talked about the widespread use of tents improving working conditions (Samson Lauwo crediting Forster and African Walking with providing tents, sleeping bags, and warm clothing to their crews). Indeed, certain companies and porters' organizations have worked to ensure porters obtain adequate clothing. Some companies may even provide gear for their crews, though this is not a standard practice across the industry. The IMEC and KPAP established a clothing and gear bank where porters could borrow clothing for free to help those who had difficulty obtaining their own. Porters' organizations also lobbied to ensure that porters had tents to sleep in.

There have been efforts to improve the crew's food and increase the wages of porters with some success, but there are continued challenges, especially for temporary workers. While eighteen interview participants mentioned that the food they ate on the mountain was better than when they began working, either because they had more meals or better kinds of food, many said the quantity and quality of food also depended on the company one worked for. As Samson Lauwo described, some companies took the initiative to work with the guides and cooks to provide enough food. Porters' organizations also advocated for three meals a day, a practice of their affiliated companies or teams. Interview participants reported that some companies did very well with this, while others skimped on food in order to save money.

Interview participants were more ambivalent about their pay, with some talking about an improvement over time, yet more mentioning the variation of pay between companies, indicating a need for more enforcement. Some indicated that inflation and increased park fees cut into the value of their salary, while others were attracted to the work because of the quick money they earned. In 2010, the Tanzanian National Parks Authority (TANAPA) set the minimum daily wage for porters at $10 per day (or around 10,000 TZS), with some receiving a portion of wages before the job. Tanzania is one of the world's poorest countries.[62] Porters do not receive lucrative pay; yet, in comparison with farmers and teachers, they are seen as having profitable jobs. On the other hand, they also are frequently hit by waves of climate change.[63] In 2010, a World Bank publication reported that guides received an average annual income of $1,830, porters $842, and cooks $771, while scholar David Peaty reported that the average annual income for Tanzanians was $300 per person.[64] Thus, some guides, cooks, and porters who manage their money well can make a secure living, even putting their children through school. Many also benefit from their connections with tourists who may pay for their porter's further study or offer other types of sponsorships. Tips also play a big role in the money workers receive, although this is much more dependent upon the gratitude and generosity of tourists. This prospect attracts some temporary or standby porters; however, they are more easily exploited. Standby or temporary porters who wait at park entrances for jobs may not receive the same amount. They may even only receive half the amount and be given inferior gear because of their disadvantaged position.[65] The pay is also seasonable and arguably still not commensurate with the risk of this difficult work.

The classification of mountain workers from the 1950s as contingent laborers has followed decisions or perceptions about the mountain-climbing industry labor into the twenty-first century. A few interview participants pointed out that mountain workers do not have pensions and health insurance. Most tourists come with health care and extra provisions for emergency care, whereas the porters have not always had such resources. KINAPA and some companies promise help if someone dies or is injured on the mountain, and companies are expected to pay someone if they fall ill while working on the mountain and have to descend before the trip has concluded. Requiring each crew member to register with an association and carry an ID aids KINAPA and companies in providing health care services. A few companies provide some health care, and some companies and associations provide first-aid training to their members.[66] Still, some end up pushing themselves to work while sick or injured because of the possibility of losing wages if they descend early, while others are sent down alone without care if they are unable to continue.[67] Porter associations have advocated for health insurance or access to health care and first aid training for porters.

In Batchi's view, overall, more respect has developed between the guides and porters than when he started working on the mountain because of these regulations. Seven other interview participants said the associations look out for the rights of porters, their safety, and their health. At the same time, many interview participants (twenty-three) did not see a big positive role played by the associations. While a few were actively engaged in porter associations, some felt the associations' only role was to provide the IDs, and they wondered what the associations did with all the money they collected from the annual dues. Interview participants asked for more transparency and hoped for greater security and better treatment for the future, an indication of the continued work left to do in securing porter well-being in the Mt. Kilimanjaro tourism industry.

CHAPTER 6

The Present and Future of the Kilimanjaro Climbing Industry

The current Kilimanjaro mountain-climbing industry consists of various layers of social, political, economic, and environmental elements that have developed throughout its history and have given rise to pressing contemporary challenges. Customs and relationships rooted in the past continue to shape the experiences of porters, cooks, guides, and their clients on the mountain, even as new actors and forces emerge. Focusing on the present reality, this chapter highlights relevant continuities from the past while uncovering some of the challenges faced by the porters currently working on Mt. Kilimanjaro. The chapter illustrates that, just as the mountain was once primarily a geographical monument for the Chagga people and has become increasingly nationalized and globalized, the everyday lives of the Chagga around Kilimanjaro have also been more profoundly influenced by realities originating from far beyond the mountain.

Porters take on various roles at different times. Occasionally, they serve as guides; at other times, they entertain by singing or sharing laughter. They may also act as cooks and representatives for hiking companies. In fulfilling these roles, porters interact with influential Kilimanjaro stakeholders, including guides, tourists, climbing companies, KINAPA, and porters' unions. Some porters have even been recruited as environmental stewards, particularly as the industry has become increasingly focused on sustainability. Beyond their duties on the mountain, porters are heads of families and community members, where they fulfill additional social roles. These roles are influenced by their experiences on the mountain. Some stakeholders they encounter in their work are allies, while others can be challenging clients or colleagues who behave more like adversaries than partners in the climbing experience. Furthermore, harsh working conditions can lead to negative emotions that may affect the quality of life for porters' families. By sharing these realities, we aim to encourage initiatives that enhance porter welfare, promote more environmentally sustainable practices, and foster better relationships among all parties involved on the mountain.

Profile of Present-Day Porters

Today, mountain crews on Kilimanjaro engage in work for reasons similar to those in the past. Many low-income individuals with limited formal education are drawn to work as porters as a way to enhance their livelihoods. In addition to agricultural activities such as growing coffee, cereals, bananas, and various fruits and vegetables as well as raising dairy cattle, tourism has become the second most lucrative source of income for the Chagga community. Mountain crews have turned tourism on Mt. Kilimanjaro into an effective vehicle for local development. Porters face both figurative and literal uphill battles due to their challenging socio-economic conditions. For instance, the United Nations Development Program (UNDP) ranked Tanzania 167 out of 193 countries on its Human Development Index in its 2022/23 report. While Tanzania has transitioned from a low-income to a lower-middle-income country, a significant portion of its population continues to live among the poorest in the world. According to the same UNDP report, in 2022 Tanzania's gross national income per capita was $2,578 (based on a 2017 constant) and the average life expectancy at birth was 66.8 years.[1] However, people living around Mt. Kilimanjaro enjoyed a standard above these national averages. Using natural resources from the mountain, the Chagga people have a reputation in Tanzania for being entrepreneurial, well educated, and politically active.[2] For porters, tourism offers a way to earn a living wage without the need for extensive formal education, as they can make at least $5 to $10 a day—comparable to the typical daily wage of a farmer in Tanzania. These earnings provide enough for a dignified living, allow for their children's primary education, and enable improvements in farming practices that continue to operate in the background thanks to the labor of women and youth.

In addition to low income and limited education, age and gender may also be significant factors influencing participation in mountain climbing. Physical fitness is undoubtedly crucial, as mountain climbing is a demanding physical activity. Furthermore, porters must carry 20 kg or more on their backs or heads while navigating cold, steep, rocky but walkable terrain. Typically, porters on Mt. Kilimanjaro are young, able-bodied men aged eighteen to forty years. After the age of forty, the number of porters significantly declines, although there are occasionally porters who are over fifty. Connected to age are notions of patriarchal masculinity and a desire for adventure. Additionally, gaining firsthand experience of Africa's highest point—a mountain they have studied and admired since childhood—serves as another motivation for individuals to engage in portering on Mt. Kilimanjaro.

With this social role in mind, portering offers an opportunity to demonstrate physical fitness and can also provide additional income for families. Among the surveyed porters, six were married, with family sizes ranging from one to three children. The average family size among porters is notably lower than the national average household size of 4.3, although it is comparable to the Kilimanjaro regional average of 3.7.[3] While porters can support their families within their regional context, married porters often face challenges in maintaining close relationships with their spouses and children.

Today, the qualifications for hiring porters have evolved. Individuals must be members of a legally registered porter union and must demonstrate qualities such as honesty, discipline, and trustworthiness. Membership in these formal unions promotes active citizenship within the Mt. Kilimanjaro region. These unions maintain records of porter profiles and contact information, ensuring that members are healthy, physically fit, and abstain from harmful substances like alcohol during hikes.[4] In cases of misconduct, the unions impose appropriate penalties. Moreover, these unions advocate for the concerns of porters. Hiring porters from a registered union indicates that the hiring entity recognizes the potential for these porters to seek fair treatment, including a safe working environment and equitable compensation.

Mountain Crews and Tourists

The relationship between visitors and the mountain crews is the pinnacle of interactions in the Kilimanjaro mountain-climbing industry. The visitors' desire to hike the mountain brings the crew to the mountain, and the crew facilitates the visitors' relationship with the mountain. Similar to the visitors' books of the early twentieth century, visitors' books from 2013–19 provide insight into who comes to the mountain and why. In 2024, 2.2 million international tourists visited Tanzania. With an average of 58,575 people climbing Mt. Kilimanjaro annually between 2018 and 2023, it can be safely projected that about 2.7 percent of all the tourists who visited the country in 2024 actually climbed the mountain.[5] Most trekkers come from the United States, northwestern Europe (France, Germany, Great Britain, Poland, Spain, and the Netherlands), the Russian Federation, Africa (i.e., Tanzania, Kenya, South Africa, and Uganda), and more recently, China. Statistics indicate that 40 percent of ascents take the Machame route, 31.7 percent go through Marangu, 14.6 percent through Londorosi, and 11 percent through Rongai. The Umbwe route, by far the most challenging because of a sharp ascent, is the least preferred.[6]

Similar to mountaineers of the past, ascending to Uhuru Peak is the ultimate goal that one can strive for. However, while past climbers tended to be experienced or career mountaineers, a majority of the people currently climbing Kilimanjaro are ordinary people with a variety of motives for doing so. Many have sought to make records or climb to commemorate a significant personal achievement such as graduation, retirement, marriage, or divorce. For example, on September 21, 2014, an American couple exchanged wedding vows on Uhuru Peak, and on September 24, 2014, a group of international cricketers played in the flat area of the crater at a height of 18,799 ft/5,730 m. Some also climb to draw attention to a worthy cause or charity: to raise money to cure cancer or bring attention to a condition such as autism. Individuals with disabilities have scaled the mountain to show that with courage and perseverance, a disability does not have to be an absolute limitation. The success rate of eight out of ten lung-transplanted patients and twenty-four accompanying medical personnel in 2017 for a seven-day climb as well as the success of the oldest persons—some at the age of eighty-six and without oxygen support—probably attest to Kilimanjaro's "coca-colaness"; that is, ease of access. Some hikers, including young (Ognjen Živković from Serbia at five) and old (Anne Lorimor from the United States at eighty-seven) have made records climbing the mountain. Karl Egloff, a Swiss mountain runner, completed the trail in four hours and fifty-six minutes, and Simon Mtuy, a Tanzanian from Marangu, completed the fastest unsupported round trip in nine hours and nineteen minutes.[7]

For many, personal challenge and adventure lead them to Kilimanjaro. It is estimated that only about 40 percent of hikers who attempt to reach Uhuru Peak actually succeed. For various reasons, most people give up and return to the base of the mountain before reaching its summit. Many trekkers have expressed concern over reports of cold and threatening weather conditions. These unfavorable conditions can hinder both the ascent and photographic opportunities, characterized by extremely cold and windy nights on one hand and intense, unfiltered sun on the other, along with cloudy, misty weather. A contemporary barrier to successful summits is hypothermia and altitude sickness (also known as acute mountain sickness, or AMS). Increased reports of altitude sickness likely reflect the unpreparedness or inexperience of many modern climbers. Common symptoms of altitude sickness include nausea, dizziness, shortness of breath, headaches, difficulty concentrating, confusion, lack of coordination, and insomnia. Most trekkers reach the summit when the weather is favorable—warmer, sunny, and marked by variable cumulus clouds. Climbers often experience a sense of awakening when the clouds part, revealing a breathtaking view of Moshi town, the plain, Mt. Meru, and the Shira range. For climbers, Uhuru Point represents a place of vision, inspiration, renewal, and new beginnings. In Eddie Frank's words, "reaching Kilimanjaro's summit was one of the most incredible personal accomplishments . . . it's a feeling of empowerment, a sense that you can accomplish anything."[8] The journey to the top teaches people that nothing is impossible if they remain positive and persistent, step by step, despite physical and mental exhaustion. Many who reach the summit are overcome by feelings of disbelief. Some people cry and are stunned.

Along with the visitors, moving through their challenges and triumphs on the mountain are the cooks, porters, and guides. As the caliber of climbers became more ordinary, the role of the mountain crew evolved to be more professional. Climbers increasingly relied on the experience and expertise of the local workers who accompany them on their journeys. For this more professionalized crew, Kilimanjaro serves as both an office and a backyard. Some individuals have grown up on the slopes of the mountain, gaining native knowledge of the Kilimanjaro environment. When additional information is needed, it becomes easier to build upon the expertise the crew already possesses and share it with the wider community on Kilimanjaro. Ultimately, they become the central focus of a tourist trekker's adventure. They bring a wealth of knowledge, experience, and training that is critical to the success and safety of a Kilimanjaro climb. They offer insights into the ecology of the surrounding landscape, as well as the politics, geography, culture, and daily life in Tanzania. They share mountaineering stories and ensure that climbers are prepared to face the journey with determination and commitment.

They act as a support system for climbers all the way to the summit, ensuring they remain healthy, strong, and successful. They provide comfort and encouragement to thousands of climbers. Visitors' books, oral history interviews, and surveys of porters provide instructive information about the relationships that develop as visitors and mountain crews share these experiences. In the visitors' books from 2013–20, visitors often commented on the support of the mountain crews, particularly guides and porters. Expressions of gratitude and praise included:

> I can't praise the guides, chefs and porters enough. Everything was perfect.
>
> We really did not know what to expect, but we were blown away by the care and attention each member of the mountain staff and every . . . employee we came across throughout the trip, and leading up to it.
>
> I always felt like I was in good hands. The guides were highly motivational. On summit day, there were times when I thought I couldn't carry on—I know that the guides' positive attitude and encouraging words kept me going.
>
> Although I have nothing to compare it to, I thought Abraham and the other guides were informed, professional, available for questions, kind and supportive. I was very impressed by them and feel they were an integral part in my ability to reach the summit. I am very grateful to them all.
>
> The guide and assistant guides were all excellent. Highly skilled and each capable of being a lead guide. All were fun, professional and knowledgeable. They made the climb enjoyable and safe.[9]

On the other hand, participants in the oral history interviews shared various ideas and stories about their relationships with visitors in more recent times. The crew's experiences and perspectives on tourists often varied based on their position within the crew and their language skills. A prevalent theme—though not shared by quite half of the interviewees—was the sense of social distance they felt from the visitors. Twelve participants mentioned that many companies and guides instructed porters to avoid approaching or interacting with guests. For example, Aratas Syril Massawe, a porter and camp crew leader, said only those authorized could interact with the guests.[10]

Estomi Nkya, a porter and waiter, explained that it would not be beneficial for porters to engage in conversation with guests. He questioned the necessity of approaching them in the first place, wondering if it was merely "to ask for things."[11] Others may have the opportunity to interact but are hindered by a language barrier. Given the significant linguistic diversity among recent climbers, there is no single crew member capable of addressing all needs competently. Among those interviewed, twelve indicated that their ability or inability to speak the visitor's language significantly influenced their relationships with tourists. Since English is widely regarded as a global lingua franca, some level of English proficiency and mountain experience is essential for effective interaction with visitors and for accessing enhanced opportunities. This proficiency could also serve as a pathway to becoming a head guide, even without additional certification from KINAPA. Most porters are literate in Swahili, while a small number are literate in both Swahili and English. Many porters believe that portering provides them with opportunities to connect with affluent tourists, a belief that has motivated them to learn the languages spoken by those visitors. The connection between porters and tourists has resulted in some porters relocating to the tourists' countries of origin and establishing and operating trekking companies, tourist lodges, curio shops, and numerous coffee-tea shops in the Moshi and Marangu areas. They have also engaged in joint-venture projects or received academic scholarship opportunities.

Despite the social distance often mentioned, another theme that emerged in the interviews was how the crew members perceived *wazungu* as ordinary people. Some of the seventeen individuals who commented on the issue noted that their views of *wazungu* shifted after working closely with them. For instance, guide Sifuel G. Moshi initially regarded them as "pearls" or "important people." He might have believed that they were the ones who brought money and bought homes for the guides, just like other members of the community. However, after witnessing guides with only a seventh-grade education leading clients who were lawyers or PhD holders, as well as one woman who had saved for thirty-five years to climb Kilimanjaro, he recognized them as just other people. Moreover, he began to view his work as a "big opportunity" to make their dreams come true.[12] Allen Godfrey had the unique experience of working as a porter and waiter when his crew led Black Americans. He reported having a very positive experience with one named Mike, who he easily became friends with and felt close to. This experience may have led to Godfrey to say that Tanzanians who see *wazungu* as natural bosses or better than Africans have a colonized mind.[13]

Aside from a handful of interview participants talking about times they had some friction with clients, explaining the procedures for reporting a difficult client or describing the challenge of visitors concealing health problems, most of their other comments indicated they viewed visitors positively. As Aseri Aiwinjia Mosha put it, good relationships with the visitors came naturally because they depended on each other on the mountain—the visitors depended on the crew for their success and the crew depended on the visitors for their work.[14] Thirteen interviewees expressed the happiness that gifts, tips, or other forms of help from visitors brought them. Five said they saw them as people who brought jobs. Others talked about feeling that the tourists were impressed with their work and mentioned how much they enjoyed talking with tourists along the way.

Some of the interview participants also talked about what working on the mountain taught them about life. As they did so, they showed the impact their mountain experiences had on their social and economic life more generally. Simon Mtuy viewed Kilimanjaro as a great heritage that connected his people to the world: "I look at the mountain as an opportunity for connecting Tanzania to the world, I look at Mt. Kilimanjaro as an archive for the continent of Africa . . . the mountain is in Africa. I don't know what the continent would be without Kilimanjaro." Simon concluded, "So really, Kilimanjaro is very important for the continent and for Tanzania . . . Kilimanjaro connects us to the world."[15] Indeed, some of the interview participants appreciated learning to interact with people from different cultures, both those coming from other countries and those from Tanzania with whom they worked. Enock Mwakalinga called the mountain his classroom partly for that reason. Explaining further, he said, "when I met with you, talking with you is . . . education for me. I can learn something which I didn't know. . . . Because you have your own culture, I have my own culture." This, he said, helped him also learn how to manage his crews: "I can manage even to control my life in general. Even in my [little way] I can control people. Even [if] someone comes in the aggressive way and wants to beat me, I can handle him. I know how to handle people and how to live with people . . . I can learn something from porters. I can learn something anywhere from anyone who [is] around me, yeah. So, I like so much this job."[16] Enock's cousin, Hudson Mwakalinga, agreed, saying, "When you meet with someone [from] different places, different continents, and different culture, if you can manage to stay with them in six, seven days without any conflicts and then just say goodbye with them in [a] very good way, that's something else." Hudson further said he picked up characteristics he wanted to adopt as he observed different families of visitors interacting with each other.[17] Similar to Enock and Hudson Mwakalinga who talked about how much they gained interacting with people from different cultures and backgrounds, Aratas Syril Massawe said that from visitors he learned the "culture of love," which included doing chores like cooking and washing clothes for his wife.[18] Sifuel G. Moshi also commented on learning to have "a good commitment" from the example of the client he worked with who saved her money for over thirty years to climb Kilimanjaro.[19]

Some expressed concern for the visitors' safety. A guide's worst nightmare is having a client die under their watch. The story of Joshua Clement Ruhimbi, who experienced a client heart attack under his watch, illustrates the risks that guides face. It also highlights the importance of maintaining good relationships with tourists, as these relationships ultimately saved him from professional ruin. The group consisted of five guests: two women in their fifties, an older man aged sixty-nine, another older man aged seventy, and his daughter in her twenties. At the start of their summit attempt, everyone appeared to be in good health with no visible symptoms. While Ruhimbi stayed behind with a slower client, the others reached the summit and passed him on their way back down. Soon after, he heard there was a problem below. Upon arriving at the camp, he discovered that the older man had fallen and already died. This was a devastating blow for Ruhimbi; he never imagined he would face such a situation. Upon returning to the office, he was treated as an outcast by others who believed he was responsible for the client's death and should no longer work as a guide. However, as Ruhimbi recounted the events, the other guests came to his aid. They provided witness statements affirming his appropriate actions during the climb. What is more, the postmortem results revealed that the man had died of a heart attack.[20]

The relationships formed between tourists and the mountain crew can be quite fulfilling. Many tourists leave the mountain feeling as though they had become a team or even a family during the five to eight days spent together. However, the economic aspects of this relationship can lead to awkward and unsatisfactory interactions, particularly regarding tips. Tipping has been a part of the industry since it began in the early twentieth century. Tourists must pay for their trek in advance, and mountain crews hope the service will inspire them to tip at the conclusion to add significantly to their wages. The 2014 Tanzanian Tour Guides Regulation prohibits frontline service providers from requesting gratuities from

FIGURE 13. Crew singing on the final day celebration at Mweka camp, 2019. PHOTO BY L. A. HADFIELD.

tourists. Guidebooks, preparation instructions from companies, and advice from fellow travelers offer suggested tip amounts, but the final amount a tourist decides to give often depends on their personal feelings about the service, making the custom somewhat ambiguous.

On the last day of the hike, there is typically a tipping ceremony where the crew and tourists make speeches, tourists present their tips, and members of the crew express their gratitude while celebrating their successful journey with songs. It can be an opportunity to have final positive interactions with the crew, some of whom visitors may not have interacted with much during the hike. Tourists are encouraged to bear in mind that other transactions and agreements regarding porter payment may happen out of sight, as discussed in the next section. Therefore, it is recommended that tourists distribute tips one by one and announce the amounts designated for each crew member to minimize the chance of guides or others taking payments not meant for them (see further recommendations listed after this chapter). If tourists are unprepared to pay tips at all, or if they are uncertain about the appropriate amount, or if they are dissatisfied with the service for any reason, this moment can become fraught with tension and disappointment. On the contrary, if everything goes smoothly, tips can be distributed positively, allowing the entire group to leave the mountain with positive feelings.

Porters, Guides, and Hierarchies of Power and Authority

Much of how porters feel about the tipping process depends on the interaction between porters and guides. The relationships among members of the mountain crew are the second most important after those between the crew and the clients. In most cases, the expedition company hands over the recruitment and payment of porters to the head guide. The head guide is responsible for overseeing the expedition and guiding the trekkers up the correct route to the mountain summit. The head guide is also the trustees of trekkers' safety. As such, hiring porters is seen to be a head guide's primary responsibility so the guide can put together a good team that the guide also connects well with. Directly or indirectly, the guide decides the porters' hire and determines payment rates as well as the weight of the load.

Although a porter must be registered with a porters' union and be physically fit to qualify as a porter, adherence to these two criteria in recruiting a porter by a guide is not always followed. In many cases, the porter would be hired based on *undugu* and *urafiki* (ethnic solidarity, or fellow villagers, friends, relatives, and family members). About 80 percent of the guides claimed they would pick someone they previously knew because such a favor would make a porter less noisy against the deeds of the guide. For prospective porters who are looking for portering work, sometimes they are forced to pay *jembe* (a hoe), a euphemism for an upfront payment to have their name registered. Negotiation could also be made that a guide will receive some money or another favor following the offer.

The porters are even happy to bend or break the set rules on the payment of porters and carry heavy luggage to win the favor of guides. Guides may "force" a porter to carry loads exceeding 20 kg (44-plus lbs), receive less than 20,000 TZS ($8–$10) per day, contend with one meal instead of three per day, and wait for the remittance of the living wage after the descent of a climb. Carrying an extra load does not bring extra cash to a porter. A guide may deny a porter an opportunity to mingle with tourists even if they speak English. English language abilities could permit a porter to brief visitors or interpret a resource along the walking trail. Porters believe that their interactions with tourists brighten their mood, provide an emotional lift, foster friendships, and are likely to inspire the creation of business ideas, educational opportunities, and scholarships that may surpass those offered to guides. As discussed earlier, female porters face additional challenges. Some female porters have alleged that certain guides request sexual favors, while also

FIGURE 14. A mountain crew distributing loads, Marangu Gate, 2019. PHOTO BY L. A. HADFIELD.

expecting them to demonstrate confidence, stamina, and ambition to be viewed as competent enough to secure load-carrying jobs.

We spoke with porters who preferred giving tips directly to the crew, bypassing the guides. Unfortunately, they admitted that some tourists would pass their tips through the head guides, who might take a significant portion for themselves and give porters bills in Tanzanian shillings instead of USD. For instance, if a guest offered a porter $10, the guide might only provide 10,000 TZS, which is not the exact equivalent, but rather $4–$5. Even when visitors attempt to tip the crew individually, some guides might create "ghost porters" to receive tips at the closing ceremony—a practice where a porter who did not actually work on the climb could falsely appear to receive a tip. This practice is known as *kirunje* (plural: *virunje*) or "watu hewa" (ghost people). *Kirunje* occurs in situations where trekkers do not take the time to learn the number of porters supporting their climb. Guides may also conceal portions of tips intended for porters and shift the blame onto tourists for under-tipping or onto tour operators for suggesting minimal amounts. Moreover, guides often take kickbacks from tips meant for their porters, sometimes doing so because of pre-arranged unfair agreements. For example, some guides may hire a porter but still deny them essential rights associated with the job, such as a fair salary or a portion of the tip. Additionally, some guides may not compensate a porter who is unable to complete the trek due to mountain sickness or other emergencies. In fact, if a porter leaves a trekking safari early, they might find it difficult to secure work in the future. In this context, pursuing future climbing opportunities and financial rewards may compromise a porter's health and other rights.

Regarding food distribution, porters may receive their share only after all members of the party—trekkers, guides, and cooks—have finished eating. Porters not only receive their food rations last, but they may also receive them in insufficient quantity and quality. Several porters surveyed noted that, in most cases, the head cook would prepare less varied, cheaper, or inadequate food for the mountain crew. Due to the cold weather that makes cooking difficult, high-energy carbohydrate foods such as ugali, rice, potatoes, pasta, and rice served with vegetables remain the staple diet fueling the crew as they traverse the mountain. These food items are easy to prepare, provide a beneficial mix of nutrients, are relatively inexpensive, weigh less, and still taste satisfactory. In most cases, the food served to clients differs significantly from what the crew eats. At every meal, clients are provided with food such as tea, coffee, hot chocolate, vegetable soup, bread, biscuits or pancakes with jam, peanut butter, honey, chicken curry, rice, chapati, and green beans. They also enjoy various snacks, including peanuts, popcorn, cakes, and cookies. Additionally, clients can indulge in a fresh salad made with tomatoes, cucumbers, onions, carrots, and green peppers. All these are seen as luxuries too expensive to be supplied to the porters. Moreover, while there is always enough water to keep tourists hydrated, porters often struggle to access it. These observations suggest that guides can contribute to the poverty and hardship faced by porters.

Porters have expressed concerns that guides frequently use them as scapegoats, blaming them for the guides' own mistakes or shortcomings. For instance, if a guide has a poor attitude toward the porters, the blame is often placed on the porters for being irresponsible. Many porters perceive themselves as powerless to express their grievances against the guide. They endure emotional strain and bear the burden of their guides' actions. In the words of Eliakim Mshanga, a porter who spoke to Melubo, "We see cruelty and poverty because guides abuse us. . . . We pretend to the tourists that we appreciate and glorify [Kilimanjaro], but it holds no beauty at all for me. I climb solely for money to support my family."

Porters and Trekking Companies

Behind the scenes on the mountain are trekking companies. These companies establish key terms for the trips, which affect porters' pay, working conditions, and the interactions among crew members as well as between the crew and the visitors. As of 2024, there are over 150 active registered outfitting businesses on Mt. Kilimanjaro. These businesses serve as ground handlers, managing logistics such as lodging reservations, transportation, and payment of park fees in addition to organizing necessary equipment and staffing for a successful climb. They also function as information centers for tourists contemplating Mt. Kilimanjaro as a travel destination. The companies create regulations and guidelines for recruiting and retaining mountain crews, including guides, porters, and cooks. They also implement incentives to attract the best guides, such as setting a minimum salary scale and tipping regulations. Each trekking company determines the health insurance, sleeping arrangements, and transportation for porters.

Visitors have praised the trekking operators for their ability to "answer all questions without a hitch," being "easy to communicate with," "responding to emails promptly and thoroughly," and "providing relevant information," which aided in making informed travel decisions and planning logistics. This information helped tourists identify the best routes based on time, required equipment, physical fitness, and budget. In their opinions, the companies were described as "extremely professional," "caring," "a top-notch outfitter," "an excellent company with the best staff on and off the mountain," "a truly five-star operation on the mountain," and "having a good standard of employees." Some visitors commended the operators for showcasing the best of Tanzanian culture by serving Tanzanian dishes, employing a fully Tanzanian team, and singing the Tanzanian national anthem at the summit, "Kili-Mungu ibariki Tanzania." Others recognized the operators for prioritizing the welfare of porters and treating them with dignity and fairness.[21]

There is variation in the treatment of mountain crews between higher-priced trekking operators and locally owned budget climbing operators. The Tanzania Tourist Act of 2008 allowed only locally owned operators to take visitors to Mt. Kilimanjaro. Typically, these locally owned operators cater to young budget-minded travelers, particularly backpackers and volunteers who prefer low-cost accommodations and tend to tip less. It also follows that these locally owned operators do not make large profits out of the clientele they serve. Moreover, almost all of these supposedly local operators are partially foreign owned, meaning they are registered under a Tanzanian owner who operates in partnership with a foreign shareholder who has a claim on some of the profit made.

On the contrary, large operators cater to more financially endowed trekkers who tend to be more advanced in age and sometimes come in family groups. Around 70 percent of large operators are foreigners, primarily from the United Kingdom, South Africa, Canada, and the United States. As a result, much of the tourism revenue generated from the Kilimanjaro climb does not go to local operators and suppliers but instead is funneled back to the trekkers' home countries. This is a problem that affects not only Kilimanjaro but the entire tourism industry in Tanzania, as is the case in other countries like Botswana, Namibia, and Kenya that depend on high numbers of foreign tourists. "Approximately 80 percent of tourists in Tanzania arrive from either Europe or the US, with about 64 percent subscribing to package tours organized through travel agencies located abroad," observed the World Bank Group in 2015, an observation that meant that "only a portion of the spending [remained] in the host country."[22] Unsurprisingly, the better financed foreign-owned companies are praised for their fair treatment of porters, including paying the minimum wages, providing on-time payments, implementing a transparent tipping procedure, offering three meals a day of adequate portions and quality, and adhering to all local and national government standards and regulations. In contrast, the cash-stricken locally owned operators are seen as the companies most likely to trample the rights of porters. They often resist initiatives to empower porters. For example, none of the locally owned operators is a member of KPAP, which seeks to improve the working conditions of the porters on Kilimanjaro. By 2020, there were 156 KPAP partner companies (i.e., those companies committed to fair pay, treatment, and conditions for their porters), all of them fully or partially foreign owned.[23]

Similarly, to enhance the quality of service provided to tourists, porters require training in several areas, including hygiene, language skills, trekking etiquette, environmental education, altitude awareness, interpersonal skills, and customer care. This training is typically conducted during the low season. However, only a limited number of companies are willing to send their porters for training or to provide in-house training. Porters have expressed dissatisfaction with locally owned companies for their reluctance to invest in such training. They have pointed out that training enables porters to leave low-paying jobs for better-paying opportunities, which some companies see as a reason to withhold training. Additionally, many locally owned companies view training as the individual responsibility of each porter, believing that their only obligation is to pay the porters' salaries. Porters who are well-informed and better trained are more likely to advance within the organization and become guides, a progression that some companies may wish to discourage. Typically, it takes about eight years of experience for an unsponsored porter to gain the skills and knowledge necessary to become a guide.

Surveyed porters indicated that trekking companies could create difficult working conditions. Tour operators have a duty to provide breakfast, lunch, and dinner to each porter—three meals a day necessary for their health and strength. However, porters reported receiving small portions of food or only one meal per day, which seems unjustified given the heavy loads they carry. Additionally, tour operators are expected to supply appropriate clothing for porters, including hats, gloves, proper footwear, warm layers, mountaineering glasses, and waterproof and windproof rain gear. To keep porters warm and dry, companies are also expected to provide sleeping arrangements such as tents. Accounts from porters have shown that most guiding companies supply little or no sleeping gear. Since mountain equipment can be expensive to purchase or rent, porters are often found sleeping under the canvas that covers their personal belongings.

On Kilimanjaro, trekking porters face significant occupational hazards that threaten their physical and mental well-being. Common issues include respiratory infections, high-altitude illnesses, joint pain, and chronic disabilities that arise from years of carrying heavy loads across challenging terrain. As the experience in the Nepal Himalaya suggests, porters suffer from a greater variety and severity of health problems than other high-altitude workers such as guides.[24] This global problem can also be observed locally on Kilimanjaro. Each year, Mt. Kilimanjaro sees approximately one thousand evacuations, with an average of ten fatalities due to high-altitude pulmonary and cerebral edema.[25] Factors such as poor health, inadequate clothing, and high evacuation costs contribute to the unfortunate reality that a small number of porters die on the mountain each year. Tour operators are expected to safeguard the health of porters by providing proper and specialized equipment as well as health insurance. This insurance should include support for health check-ups and the provision of climbing gear. However, many porters do not have access to these essential resources. In this scenario, health often takes a back seat to profit.

To save money, some companies skip a night in a previously scheduled and prepaid hut by encouraging visitors to sleep at the next hut instead. For example, instead of spending the night at Karanga Camp (13,106 ft/3,995 m) after scrambling up from Barranco Camp (13,044 ft/3,976 m), trekkers are compelled to trek for six hours to reach Barafu Camp (15,331 ft/4,673 m), the final point before the summit. This "theft" forces porters to work for longer hours without a break while also denying visitors an opportunity to acclimatize and let the body adjust to the higher altitudes. It also scares off tourists and damages Kilimanjaro's reputation abroad as a tourist destination. There have also been incidences of actual theft of items and money from clients, which often ends up being blamed on porters. Fortunately, such incidents of theft have sharply declined in the last couple of years following the introduction of policy by KINAPA requiring tourists not to carry items of portable wealth more than $200 during the climb, as it may tempt unscrupulous people to steal. Nevertheless, disagreements on the fair treatment of porters remain a prominent feature in the industry, which has given birth to various unions that seek to protect and promote porters' rights and benefits.

Porters' Unions and Rights

Some trekking companies on Mt. Kilimanjaro overlook the human rights of the mountain support crew, exposing them to precarious working conditions. Various international and local initiatives that emerged around the turn of the twenty-first century aimed to closely monitor improvements in the working conditions of Kilimanjaro porters. Recognized official workers' unions include the Mt. Kilimanjaro Porters Society (MKPS) and the Tanzania Porters Organization (TPO). The Kilimanjaro Meru Mountain Porters (Kilimeru) and Ngurdoto Crater Porters Group serve only members from Mt. Meru. Porters are currently required to be affiliated with one of these unions. By 2021, the Kilimanjaro Porters Association (KPA) had ten thousand members but faced criticism for not holding annual meetings and for having leaders who refused to step down after completing their terms. As one surveyed porter stated, "KPA was the mother of other unions, but things started going bad when leaders began to mix their personal interests with those of the union. They disregarded the union constitutions and the laws governing union tenure. They made KPA a family project." For its part, TPO had five thousand members by 2021. Both KPA and TPO are based in Moshi and have members who serve on Mt. Kilimanjaro and Mt. Meru. When grievances arise, the unions often resort to boycotts. This strategy has yielded some positive results for porters. For instance, the government has been calling for dialogue on critical issues affecting working conditions for porters, fearing that boycotts could disrupt tourism activities and harm the image, reputation, and relationships of Mt. Kilimanjaro and trekking companies.

Membership in a porters' union is currently mandatory. However, the decision regarding which union to join is left to the individual porter and typically depends on factors such as the proximity to the union office, expected benefits, and the leadership's ability to address members' concerns. Affordable subscription fees and the provision of free educational programs, training, or financial assistance for porters are other considerations. For example, TPO, which has seen its membership decline from sixteen thousand to five thousand following COVID-19, claims to be preferred due to its quality care for members and its effective diplomatic approach when engaging with the Diplomatic and Tourist Police Unit to resolve porter-employer conflicts. Established in 2014, the Diplomatic and Tourist Police Unit was a recent initiative aimed at improving the industry. Among other responsibilities, it handles inquiries, claims, and complaints from tourists and tourism service providers, including porters. Local stakeholders have commended the unit for reducing tourism-related crimes and ensuring that porters receive their fair compensation promptly. The identity card of a TPO member includes office contact information, encouraging members to report unethical practices, particularly underpayment. Upon receiving reports of a problematic guide, TPO dispatches a text message to the accused, insisting on immediate payment to the porter. These efforts have made TPO the preferred union among porters in Kilimanjaro and Arusha.

The unions face challenges and criticisms from porters. Many porters believe that certain unions fail to hold annual meetings to update members on their progress, successes, and expenditures. Additionally, these unions often lack effective advocacy and communication skills, mobilization capabilities for a shared goal, and sufficient financial resources. They also suffer from corrupt leadership. During the COVID-19 pandemic, many porters lost their jobs and were unable to pay their membership fees. Porters also feel that these unions are not truly independent from the climbing companies, as most have only internal monitoring programs and are incapable of intervening when porters face challenges outside of the union. For example, the independence of unions, particularly that of the MKPS, was questioned by a number of the porters interviewed, who alleged that the union was in fact an initiative of a tour company called Zara Tanzania Adventures. Established in 1986, Zara is the largest outfitter for Mt. Kilimanjaro climbs in Tanzania. Being closely associated with Zara renders MKPS a weak union, as porters may hesitate to voice their concerns if Zara is their source of employment. If the allegations are true, then MKPS would appear to function more as a charity to collect gifts from tourists, which serves to protect Zara from criticism regarding its treatment of porters.

Established in 2004 by Karen Valenti, the Kilimanjaro Porters Assistance Project (KPAP) is an initiative of the International Mountain Explorers Connection (IMEC), a 501(c)(3) nonprofit organization based in Boulder, Colorado. Its mission is to support an ethical mountain trekking culture by promoting social, economic, and environmental responsibility. Unlike KPA and TPO, KPAP is neither a porter membership organization nor a tour operating business. Instead, KPAP focuses on improving the working conditions of porters on Kilimanjaro by promoting socially responsible climbing practices. KPAP receives donations and grants from the United States, making it the most powerful and resourceful agency supporting porters on Kilimanjaro.

KPAP plays an oversight and monitoring role of "telling uncomfortable truths" on the mistreatment of porters. Playing the accreditation role, KPAP publishes a list of companies dedicated to ethical travel and encourages tourists to join partner companies that meet the proper treatment related to the crew when trekking on Mt. Kilimanjaro. Being a partner with KPAP is sought to reinforce the company's reputation for fair labor practices and thus elevate the market exposure of the company among ethically conscious clients. Adherence to minimum fair porter treatment standards is primary to becoming a KPAP partner. Moreover, because most tourists to Mt. Kilimanjaro originate from the United States and Europe (Germany, the United Kingdom, France, and Spain) and their travel to Tanzania is mediated by KPAP partners based in those places, those KPAP partner companies end up bringing in the most responsible trekkers. For example, in 2021, out of 149 KPAP partners, 32 had head offices in the United States, 22 in Britain, 49 in Tanzania, 5 in Canada, and 3 in Australia. The partner informs KPAP of the routes, starts and ends of the climbs, as well as the number of people in every climb. In turn, KPAP collects seasonal data on porter treatment by placing their representatives among the crew of a partner company or by random spontaneous checks.

At times, KPAP has labeled certain Kilimanjaro operators as irresponsible regarding improvements in porter treatment. Budget climbing outfits, who are often at fault, have not received this stance well. These budget operators accuse KPAP of persuading conscientious travelers to choose ethical companies, most of which are foreign owned and foreign managed. Furthermore, trekking operators allege that KPAP secretly supported the formation of the TPO by providing initial funding for early meetings and seminars as well as covering rental costs for the organization's office. With offices in Arusha, Machame, Marangu, and Rongai, TPO has developed into a powerful union, but it faces accusations of undermining KPA and MKPS.

Since its establishment in 2003, KPAP has proudly reported several achievements that positively impact porters' experiences. According to its records, the project has lent mountain-climbing gear at no cost to 36,706 porters. It has also partnered with responsible trekking companies that ensure fair and ethical treatment for seven thousand porters. As a result, KPAP has ensured that 7,500 porters working with its approved partners receive at least 20,000 TZS ($8–$10) per day, transparent gratuities, three hot meals each day, quality tents with adequate sleeping space, and carry bags that comply with the 20 kg weight regulation. Additionally, KPAP has conducted educational and training programs to empower porters with non-technical knowledge and skills. For example, over the same period, the project has provided classes in English, HIV/AIDS awareness, and financial management to sixteen thousand porters; offered budgeting and money management training to 1,614 porters; and conducted organic farming workshops for 231 porters during the COVID-19 pandemic. Beyond directly enhancing porters' experiences, KPAP's educational and training initiatives also aim to enrich the mountain experience for both crew and clients. To this effect, it provided "Leave No Trace" certification in environmental care of Mt. Kilimanjaro to 205 mountain crew members and conducted first aid certification courses, culminating in the certification of 1,387 mountain crew members in first aid.[26]

While KPAP's account of its achievements is positive, a survey of porters and porter unions brought a more nuanced assessment. Contrary to the purported claims of unmitigated success, porter unions hold that KPAP has been doing nothing in the area of training, as they recall no day when their members had been asked to attend the training. One surveyed leader of a porters' union told Melubo that "when you visit the KPAP office, you are welcomed by signs around the door which claim that training on customer care, the environment, and *afya* [health] is going on, but actually they are offering nothing about training. I think KPAP does this to blind the government to the fact that it is doing a great job, but in reality, it doesn't. KPAP is good at overstating its achievements, as it always paints itself as good." Pressed further, the union leader described KPAP as "[using] photos of past events to show that they are training, so when they call people for a meeting on evaluation, they use photos of such occasions as evidence of training."

The role played by the tour and guide unions such as Tanzania Association of Tour Operators (TATO), Kilimanjaro Association of Tour Operators (KIATO), Kilimanjaro Guides Associations (KGA), Tanzania Tour Guide Associations (TTGA), and Northern Tanzania Safari Guides Society (NTSGS) is also significant in improving the welfare of porters on Mt. Kilimanjaro. TATO members are the principal employers of mountain crews. TATO works closely through dialogues with porters' unions with a view to improving job skills and customer service delivery. The business consortium relies on complaints from porters' unions to enforce the rule, including paying the rates suggested by the government. In addition, TATO has provided seminars, training courses, and workshops for tour guides, porters, and cooks to advance the working condition of porters and improve service delivery on the mountain.

Porters and Park Authorities

Another key player on the mountain is the Kilimanjaro National Park Authority (KINAPA). KINAPA, which operates under the Tanzania National Parks Authority (TANAPA), manages all activities related to conservation, tourism, and extension services on Mt. Kilimanjaro. To support effective administrative development, the park headquarters at Marangu gate includes a booking office, sales shops, and equipment rental stores. TANAPA establishes policies and regulations aimed at minimizing and addressing the negative impacts of trekking tourism and related activities. It enforces laws to govern the conduct of mountain crew members and trekking companies. Although TANAPA is not the sole entity responsible for creating regulations to improve working conditions, it serves as the gatekeeper and principal regulator of who and what can enter and exit KINAPA, as well as the activities permitted within the park area. For instance, after a mutual agreement was signed by mountain stakeholders on December 12, 2015, TANAPA was directed to deny access to guides and operators accused of mistreating supportive porters and cooks. Despite the Tourism Act of 2008, which mandated that the Division of Tourism issue licenses to all professional guides, TANAPA has been issuing licenses to mountain guides. The Division of Tourism is financially under-resourced and understaffed, limiting its ability to enforce the law across all protected areas. By issuing licenses to guides, TANAPA plays a crucial role in improving the working conditions for porters. It can deny access to irresponsible guides who, for example, pressure porters to carry more than the recommended weight.

However, while porters express skepticism about the successes claimed by KPAP, they also highlight significant failures by TANAPA. For instance, porters have accused TANAPA of doing little to prevent malpractice regarding the recommended maximum weight limits. Many porters believe that guides collude with certain TANAPA gatekeepers to allow them to carry more than the 20 kg limit. Wilson Marandu, a surveyed porter, said that the "weighing of luggage is sometimes done by the company before reaching the gate and by KINAPA rangers during the ascent. However, due to inaccurate scales and collusion among KINAPA rangers—who sometimes accept payments to allow heavier loads—it's not surprising to find porters overloaded with 35 to 40 kg [77 to 88 pounds]."

To achieve the desired positive outcomes for quality tourism, KINAPA conducts annual meetings with mountain porters, guides, and cooks during the low season, typically in May and November. At these meetings, KINAPA shares its registered achievements regarding tourism trends, mountain routes, and conservation efforts on Mt. Kilimanjaro, while also receiving critical feedback from mountain crews about their work environments. Although KINAPA believes it has made notable progress in improving the working conditions for porters, it acknowledges that some issues are beyond its control. Sometimes KINAPA, in collaboration with training institutions such as the College of African Wildlife Management, Mweka, organizes training courses and workshops for tour guides, porters, and cooks to enhance customer service and motivate mountain crews to promote tourism. The training covers topics such as mountain ecology, customer care and tour guiding, plant and animal identification, and first aid. To qualify as a mountain guide, candidates must climb Uhuru Peak and pass a written examination. The names of porters who successfully pass the examination are forwarded to KINAPA for licensing. However, many porters feel that the tuition fee of 800,000 TZS (over $300) charged by Mweka College is prohibitively expensive.

Surveyed porters expressed additional grievances against both TANAPA and KINAPA. They accused TANAPA of discrimination when considering the rescuing of sick individuals on the mountain. When KINAPA rescue drivers learn that a patient needing rescue is not a tourist but rather a porter or cook, they tend to delay their response, while tourists receive urgent attention. Porters felt that KINAPA rescue drivers viewed them as insignificant, likening them to donkeys of no commercial value.

Additionally, surveyed porters claimed that KINAPA rangers punished them publicly, allegedly for being dirty and for leaving trash behind in camps and huts. Such punishments could take the form of verbal harassment or forcing them to do push-ups or carry heavy luggage. As was mentioned, porters are often the primary suspects when theft occurs against tourists on Mt. Kilimanjaro. Occasionally,

KINAPA rangers collude with guides to unjustly target porters with one kind of blame or another without sufficient evidence. Crimes against tourists include pickpocketing and stealing valuable items like cameras and money during the night. Surveyed porters also accused KINAPA rangers of working with guides to secretly sell them water at exorbitant prices. When faced with water scarcity on the mountain, guides send porters downstream to collect water for trekkers to use for drinking, cleaning, and cooking. Yet, in other situations, the same porters are made to purchase water for their own use. For example, a water shortage at Barranco Point (13,044 ft/3,976 m) along the Machame route may force porters to purchase water from KINAPA rangers instead of fetching it from the distant Karanga camp.

Environmental Considerations

While sometimes there may be friction between KINAPA and mountain crews, it is essential for both parties, particularly the porters, to unite in addressing a significant challenge on the mountain: environmental conservation. The collaboration of mountain crews is vital to guaranteeing a sustainable future for the region. Over the years, in addition to guiding thousands of climbers to the summit, porters and guides have actively contributed to conservation efforts. They help extinguish fires, remove litter from the mountain, and plant trees. Furthermore, they report incidents of poaching and assist injured animals in need of rescue.

Mt. Kilimanjaro is relatively species-poor compared to Tanzania's other protected areas, such as Ngorongoro and the Serengeti. However, its stunning landscape and diverse climate zones support various mammal and bird species as well as a rich array of flora, which presents an attractive potential for nature-based tourism development. Excerpts from guest books indicate that climbers appreciate the striking and unusual flora and fauna they encounter on their ascent and descent. The forest belt through the heath moorland is home to 2,500 viable populations of trees, shrubs, epiphytes, lianas, and pteridophytes, with 900 species found within the forest belt alone. Sensitive flora on Mt. Kilimanjaro includes *Protea kilimandscharica*, found in the heath zone; red-hot poker (torch lily); giant lobelia (*Lobelia deckenii*), which thrives between 12,000 and 15,000 ft/3650 m and 4570 m; and groundsel (*Dendrosenecio kilimanjari*), which inhabits the middle altitudes on the Shira Plateau and around Barranco Camp. At about 13,000 ft/4,000 m above sea level, the subalpine cloud forest, primarily composed of the giant heather

(*Erica trimera*), represents the highest forest in Africa. The mountain also boasts a rich animal life, with 140 mammal species, including seven primates, twenty-five carnivores, twenty-five antelopes, and twenty-four bat species. The most common mammals are the Kilimanjaro tree hyrax, grey duiker, eland, bushbuck, red duiker, and buffalo. On the mountain, one occasionally spots elephant herds and the endangered Abbott's duiker.

There are several threats to mountain flora and fauna, including invasive species. The increased number of visitors to the mountain is being blamed for the spread of invasive plant species. The presence of *Poa annua*, a cosmopolitan weed of European origin that restricts climbing routes, serves as strong evidence that tourism facilitates its spread. TANAPA spent 567,600,000 TZS ($225,000) on invasive species management at all Tanzanian parks in the 2018/19 fiscal year and approximately 2 billion TZS (nearly $800,000) over the last eleven years, highlighting the magnitude of the problem across the country.[27] Other human activities include illegal logging in lower and middle montane forests for thatching materials, timber, poles, animal fodder, and firewood, as well as poaching for both subsistence and commercial purposes. Consequently, tree species such as *Entandrophragma excelsum*, the tallest trees in Africa, and the critically endangered *Garcinia tanzaniensis*, along with Camphor (*Ocotea usambarensis*), have been significantly destroyed. Urbanization and the expansion of human settlements, highways, and agricultural activities to the park boundary—combined with the unrestricted utilization of biodiversity from livestock grazing—have led to the blockage and shrinkage of wildlife corridors between KINAPA and Amboseli National Park in Kenya, KINAPA and Lake Natron, KINAPA and Tsavo West in Kenya, as well as KINAPA and Mkomazi National Park. These factors pose major threats to animal movement and population stability, increasingly isolating Kilimanjaro from surrounding ecosystems and intensifying human-wildlife interactions. The park's isolation has significant consequences, including hindering species movement, which can lead to inbreeding depression and a decline in genetic variability.

In participating in conservation efforts, porters and guides combine more global environmental movements with their local understandings and values. Just over half of the oral history interview participants gave some indication (indirectly or directly) about how they thought and felt about Kilimanjaro. Around twenty talked about how the mountain brought them employment, with seven of those mentioning the revenue or business that it brought to the broader community. This income is what gave Emmaline N. Swai hope to live. Similarly, Kapanya Kitaba said, "The white mountain that shines gives us hope and is our comfort and joy."[28] While Kitaba talked about the employment the mountain brought, he broadened his appreciation of the mountain. He included the water that gave life to plants, which in turn fed the cattle. People also benefitted from the water. When asked what Kilimanjaro was to him, Joshua Clement Ruhimbi said, "It is my life, it is everything, everything that I have comes from Kilimanjaro."[29] Goodluck Swai said he felt "fresh" on the mountain. It gave him heart to go there, in part because of the livelihood he obtained.[30]

Goodluck Swai and Ruhimbi were among those who appreciated the beauty and inspiration that Kilimanjaro offers. Ruhimbi shared how being on the mountain alleviated his stress. He mentioned a specific spot where, if one remains quiet, it was possible to hear the wind. He advised visitors to pause and take in the view at that location. He went on to say that the mountain was where you could see the whole world as you cross the different climate zones. He often gazed at the clouds, which he likened to "an ocean on the ground," expressing a sense of awe that was difficult to articulate. The moon could shine as brightly as the sun. The phenomenon led him to conclude that individuals of all faiths could find it a spiritual place. He described it as a paradise where one can forget their past and enjoy a cup of tea, though he acknowledged that the cold was quite intense.[31]

Fifteen other interview participants shared their views of the mountain, discussing its beauty and fascinating nature. Aratas Syril Massawe described himself as passionate about the environment. He expressed his love for the forest where he grew up and his happiness regarding the conservation efforts aimed at restoring it.[32] Several participants referred to the mountain as a place to appreciate God's creations or witness the wonders of God. Allen Godfrey noted that, upon reaching Uhuru Peak, "one can see the almighty God's creations, and as He said, His thoughts are higher."[33] Dennis Mallya echoed this sentiment, describing the mountain as a wonder of God. Emeline N. Swai appreciated the flowers and rocks on the mountain, stating that if one sees all those things, one might say, "God, you have really worked here on earth."[34]

These kinds of views led some porters and guides to share similar ideas about the importance of environmental conservation on Kilimanjaro and concern over particular issues also raised by the international community. One of the more prominent of the environmental issues on the mountain is the melting of Kibo's glaciers. Kilimanjaro is located only 3° south of the equator. According to records, the ice on Kibo peak has been thinning since the end of the Little Ice Age around 1850.

Between 1962 and 2000, Kilimanjaro lost approximately 55 percent of its glaciers. In 2011, only 1.76 km^2 of ice-covered mountaintop remained from the 11.40 km of ice-covered mountaintop in 1912. There is evidence that temperatures have been rising. While reduced cold temperatures may result in a warmer climate favorable to climbing conditions, attracting many visitors and even a greater abundance of birds, the long-term effects will be negative.[35]

Historian Matthew V. Bender wrote about how the world has often used the diminishing glaciers of Kilimanjaro as a sign of dangerous global climate change. While this particular alarm has been raised in the early twenty-first century, Bender shows that mountaineers and scientists have long charted the melting of Kilimanjaro's glaciers, predicting their disappearance in a few short years multiple times. There has been debate about the exact cause of this glacier melt—rising temperatures versus the drying out of East Africa—and its impact on water availability in the lowlands. However, the glaciers, relics of colder and wetter climates but a rare occurrence in equatorial regions, are clearly disappearing. Kilimanjaro has also seen a significant change in the mountain's forests and water supplies.[36]

A clear trend in oral history interviews from participants who worked in different generations was the environmental changes they have witnessed on the mountain. Of the forty-seven who commented about environmental changes, thirty-six talked about the reduction in the snow or glaciers on the mountain in one way or the other, an observation that was made even by those who started working in the early 2000s. Ten remembered the snow reaching the lower camps like Mandara in years past. Twelve remarked that they had noticed how the glaciers were melting. Zakaria Fataeli Mtui said the "barafu" used to start at 14,760 ft/4,500 m.[37] Joshua Mwakalinga remembered that when he first started working in the mid-1990s, he could reach out and touch the glaciers as they walked on the rim to Uhuru Peak.[38] His son, Hudson Mwakalinga, who started working on the mountain around 2010, remembered one year when it was very hot in September and the water running off a melting glacier formed a waterfall. It made him "really sad" to see and hear the water coming off the glaciers in such great amounts.[39] Joshua Clement Ruhimbi talked about a huge glacier in the crater that used to be "big and tall like a tree," but now has seen pieces vanish.[40] Kapanya Kitaba noted how the Rebmann and Shark Tooth glaciers were reducing drastically.[41] Mountain crew members fear that large tourist numbers will be short-lived because the presence of snow on Kibo is a significant attraction, and its absence will make Kilimanjaro less appealing.

Other negative environmental developments on Kilimanjaro include changes in land cover types, such as a 15 percent reduction in montane forest, a 38 percent increase in heathlands (170 km^2), and a 9.5 km^2 increase in alpine desert.[42] These changes in land cover and altitudinal zonation of vegetation communities have had an impact on tourism because of less wildlife to admire, dry rivers, dry riverbeds, water scarcity, and an increase in the frequency of forest fires. Oral history interview participants also noticed the reduction in forests and change in water on the mountain. Joshua Clement Ruhimbi noted that nowadays, the Machame route could be dusty, whereas before it almost always rained on that route. A few of the interview participants linked the number of trees on the mountain or in its foothills to the climate change they witnessed. Some observed that the reduction of the forest led to the reduction of rain and snow, while others asserted that reforestation efforts had or would help restore the environment. Somewhat in conjunction with these observations, six mentioned that switching to using gas instead of firewood helped, presumably because it stopped the cutting or burning of trees. Still, five mentioned the negative effects of fires that continued to occur on Kilimanjaro.

Wildfires occur in and around the mountain almost in every dry season. All the wildfires on Mt. Kilimanjaro are human caused, either accidentally by the carelessness of some people or the deliberate action of others. Poachers, cattle rustlers, honey collectors, and campers are the suspects for the cause of wildfires on the mountain. The frequency and intensity of fires started by campers on Kilimanjaro's slopes have grown in recent years. During the last ten years, fire that was lit to prepare food took no vacation and caused more devastation on the drier upper montane and subalpine zones of the mountain. In particular, all the fires that destroyed up to 34 km^2 of forest and important moorland on Kilimanjaro between October 2020 and October 2022 resulted from human activities on top of the mountain.[43] The burning has had an impact on biodiversity distribution; reduced fog trapping and thus water yielding, soil protection, and timber provision; increased patchiness of the previously closed *Podocarpus*, *Juniperus*, *Hagenia*, and *Erica* forest; and opened land for downward migration of alpine flora. The threat of meeting fire on the mountain has also deterred tourists and smoke has polluted the air.[44]

In the event of a fire break, porters have been the front liners in containing the burning, as they are known for their hardiness and experience at high altitudes. For example, in October 2020, hundreds of volunteers, including porters from local communities, raced to stop a blaze using shovels and machetes. That particular fire ended up destroying the Kifinuka Hill, two homes, two bathroom facilities, and two solar panels. The tourism private sector and TANAPA provided food, water, and equipment to the firefighting crew in the battle against the raging fire, sometimes leasing helicopters and fire extinguishers.[45]

The considerable increase in the number of tourists and supporting staff visiting Kilimanjaro has led to the development and use of access tracks, campsites, and refuges, which has resulted in vegetation clearing and soil erosion, as well as changes to landscapes and water flows, water and air pollution, the introduction of invasive species, and waste. Litter is one of the most serious environmental issues confronting Mt. Kilimanjaro. Much of the litter from supplies and equipment—such as tin cans, glass and plastic bottles, food packaging, oxygen bottles, batteries, plastic bags, drums, discarded ropes and tents, pharmaceuticals, personal care items, and cleaning supplies like detergents—generated on the mountain is often discarded and cannot be recycled, thus scarifying the picturesque mountain landscapes. Litter such as food scraps left in camps and huts can attract opportunistic wildlife such as birds, disease vectors (rats, mice, and other pests), and disrupt the feeding pattern of some animals such as primates.[46] Comments in recent visitors' books about the trash range from "littering is not desirable, please work on it," to "litter should be monitored," "waste management should find an alternative means for litter," and "put a sign saying 'no litter.'" Researchers Mengiseny E. Kaseva and Josia L. Moirana estimate that solid waste on Kilimanjaro "increased from about 87 tonnes in 2003 to about 125 tonnes in 2006," adding that this "increase of about 30% is attributed mainly to the increase in the number of visitors/tourists." The identified solid waste included plastic bottles, candy wrappers, cigarette butts, juice boxes, straws, shoe sole particles, and rubber pieces.[47] The exhaustion and difficulty of operating at higher altitudes and logistical challenges like remoteness are probably part of the reason why mountain users dump waste on Kilimanjaro. There is also a lack of adequate infrastructure to collect and dispose of the waste generated by visitors from the hilly terrain down to landfills located in Moshi. As a result of these challenges, there is an increase in dumping, including illegal dumping, and the open burning of plastic waste on the mountain.

Human waste (excreta and urine) is by far the most cited waste problem and is caused by a lack of toilets along the trails and rocky terrain, which makes digging pit latrines difficult. According to tourism management researcher Michal Apollo, between 1990 and 2007, hikers left behind more than 107.5 tons of feces and 6 million liters of urine on Kilimanjaro.[48] The significant amount of waste adversely affects the environment when absorbed by nature. The available pit latrines, of which there were 114 in 2004, are shallow and fill up quickly. Due to atmospheric conditions and soil characteristics, human waste can remain unrecompensed for up to a year. Concerns have been raised regarding the environmental sustainability and effectiveness of these toilets. In 2007, the park introduced long drop–type toilets, replacing the pit latrines in all campsites, picnic areas, and rest areas. These dug toilets, which feature a wooden shelter built above, are often viewed as unpleasant and unsanitary. Regardless of their use, dislodging septic tanks continues to pose a challenge, highlighting the need for appropriate technology. KINAPA is working to enhance existing toilet facilities, focusing on privacy as well as the size and design of the huts, kitchen, and dining areas at various locations, including Horombo, Umbwe, Machame, Lemosho Gate, Londorosi, Marangu, Jiwe la Ukoyo, and Kikelelwa.

Eighteen participants in the oral history interviews addressed the issue of trash on the mountain, highlighting that many workers in the area recognize the importance of maintaining a litter-free environment. Some participants recalled how dirty the mountain had been in the past, while others noted the introduction of new trash-in, trash-out regulations and shared their personal involvement in cleanup efforts. Porters play a vital role in removing much of the unwanted litter, particularly the plastic waste generated during climbing. Estimates based on experiences in the Annapurna Conservation Area in Nepal show that "an average trekking group of 15 people generates about 15 kilos of non-biodegradable and non-burnable garbage in 10 days trek, producing tons of garbage in mountain regions annually."[49] In the absence of similar data processed from the local experience, it can be presumed that the reality is not entirely different on Kilimanjaro. The types of waste that porters must transport down from the mountain include food scraps left in huts, plastic bottles, steel cans, tissue paper, textiles, metal, glass, and human feces.

To address litter, park management has been implementing "bring back-your-waste policies," commonly known as Trash In, Trash Out (TITO), since 2001. TITO mandates that mountain users, especially support staff, carry all trash with them when they descend. KINAPA management is tasked with providing solid waste collection bags that are water- and odor-proof. However, there has been limited success in supplying these bags and sacks for waste disposal, leading porters to rely on sacks provided by their companies as well as plastic bags or mat baskets on occasion. The TITO initiative has reportedly yielded positive results in reducing trash accumulation along trails, at hiker rest stops, and around campsites and huts.[50] Other measures taken to control litter include providing incinerators for burning waste and implementing a penalty system to ensure compliance with environmental standards. To help maintain the fragile ecosystem, some environmentally conscious operators offer bonuses to porters for collecting leftover trash, educate climbers on proper behavior to respect the mountain, dedicate one day each month to a Keep Kili Clean campaign aimed at removing litter from Kilimanjaro, and promote the use of refillable water bottles. Luckily, due to the efforts of the porters who carry waste off the mountain, 2003–2006 statistics indicated that over 94 percent of waste disposal was efficiently removed from Kilimanjaro.[51]

Mountain Crews and the Future of the Industry

The actions or inactions of tourists can significantly shape the nature of tourism in a given destination. Tourists have the power to influence, drive, and create responsible practices. Furthermore, many contemporary travelers seek holidays that minimize negative environmental impacts and provide opportunities for underprivileged communities. By choosing which tour company to engage with, tourists can encourage these companies to positively interact with local communities and their surroundings. Generally, tourism activities are tailored to meet tourist demand, including aspects such as climbing routes, timings, necessary equipment, and pricing. The activities available are contingent on their ongoing popularity among tourists. By deciding against traveling with companies that have poor records or unclear policies regarding the treatment of porters, tourists can ensure that their journeys contribute more positively than negatively. The recommendations included after this chapter are designed to facilitate this process by outlining concrete ways to engage ethically with Kilimanjaro mountain climbing.

A significant number of visitors have expressed favorable perceptions of the operators on Mt. Kilimanjaro. On the other hand, most visitors appear to be aware of the porters serving on Mt. Kilimanjaro as being underpaid, overburdened, underfed, and provided with poor sleeping conditions without proper clothing. Visitors are happy to assist by offering generous tips at the end, by teaming up with socially responsible operators, and by several other ethical practices outlined in the recommendations provided at the end of this book. When guided by appropriate knowledge, visitors' positive dispositions and deliberate action can counter the urge of unscrupulous companies to benefit from porters' poor working conditions and limited welfare assurances.[52]

Despite ongoing shortcomings, some improvements in porters' welfare may stem from Tanzania's tourism regulations, which require that mountain businesses be citizen operated; however, the reality is different. As previously noted, budget companies—often small scale and locally owned—offer low-cost climbs to attract customers but are frequently accused of mistreating porters, who are visible to tourists. This mistreatment may arise from a lack of financial skills, marketing expertise, effective short- and long-term planning, and international connections that ensure a consistent client base each year, compounded by the seasonal nature of tourism. Consequently, budget operators do not employ porters, cooks, and guides on a permanent basis; instead, they maintain a list of names and contacts to hire when work is available.

In addition to actions taken by tourists, other stakeholders—including porter unions, KINAPA, KPAP, and training institutions within the Kilimanjaro tourism sector—can take further steps to improve conditions for porters. At the beginning of 2026, four porters' organizations merged to form a new Tanzanian Association of Porters (TAP) to unify these efforts among unions (TPO, MKPS, the Mount Meru Porters Association [MMPA] and Ngurdoto Crater Porters Association [NCPA]). A new configuration of unions could provide porters with more power. This may involve addressing mistreatment, being more vigilant about permitted luggage weights, conducting unannounced gear checks, implementing policy recommendations, investigating allegations of corruption, and ensuring the ethical treatment of mountain crews. To be effective, various unions that coordinate Kilimanjaro mountain crews may need to grant their members more voice on matters that affect them and the running of the unions. Government agencies such as the Tanzania Tourism Diplomatic Police may need to continue dealing with cases involving tourism and porters, scaling up both the number of complaints processed and the speed with which they are resolved. Training institutions can find ways of empowering porters by providing training on various subjects at an affordable fee, including life skills, business and entrepreneurial skills, interpretation, ecology, customer care, regulations, and conservation.

It truly requires the involvement of all parties to enhance the working conditions of mountain crews and reduce the negative environmental impact of the Kilimanjaro mountain-climbing industry. Many people have come to Kilimanjaro and its foothills over the past century and a half. The Chagga moved there to take advantage of the life-giving environment; traders and travelers came to the region for relief and refreshment; European explorers, missionaries, and mountaineers followed with their fascination with the highest peak in hot tropical Africa capped with snow. Then, the mountain-climbing industry developed out of the colonial period into post–World War II global tourism.[53] After independence, Tanzania owned the industry just as Kilimanjaro became the mountain of the nation. Beyond Tanzania, many called Kilimanjaro the roof of Africa, and the world claimed it as a natural heritage site for all humanity. At the beginning of the twenty-first century, the mountain continued to capture the world's attention with continuously expanding numbers of people coming to climb, earn, achieve, and endure. Those that seek to partake of what Kilimanjaro offers and wish to sustain its future must not forget those who have made this all possible with their invaluable work on the mountain.

Further Reading

ALTHOUGH THERE HAS BEEN SOME ATTENTION TO YOHANE KINYALA LAUWO AS ONE of the first local guides on Kilimanjaro, most histories of climbing Kilimanjaro in academic journals and climbing and tourism literature start with the first Europeans to write about and ascend the mountain. They often begin with Johannes Rebmann, the first European credited with citing Kilimanjaro in 1848, and climax with the first successful ascent of the highest peak by Hans Meyer in 1889.

Burns, Cameron M. *Kilimanjaro & East Africa: A Climbing and Trekking Guide*, 2nd ed. Seattle: Mountaineers Books, 2006.

Lenoble-Bart, Annie, and François Constantin. "Mount Kilimanjaro: From History to Symbol," in *Mount Kilimanjaro: Mountain, Memory, Modernity*, edited by François Bart, François Devenne, and Milline J. Mbonile. Translated by Taffy Martin. Dar es Salaam: Mkuki na Nyota Publishers, 2006, 5–20.

Musa, Ghazali, James Higham, and Anna Thompson-Carr, eds. *Mountaineering Tourism*. London: Routledge, 2015.

Salkeld, Audrey. *Kilimanjaro: To the Roof of Africa*. Washington, D.C.: National Geographic, 2002.

Much of the other literature on Kilimanjaro and mountain-climbing support crews largely focuses either on animals, biological conservation, and environmental history. As Brent Lovelock wrote, in the literature about mountain-guiding operations in general, "there has been more detailed coverage of the conditions for pack animals" than the conditions for porters (275). Kokel Melubo has similarly observed that more research has been done on conservation biology and climatology on Mt. Kilimanjaro than porters. Melubo, Lovelock, and David Peaty are the few who have addressed Kilimanjaro porters in the modern climbing industry.

Lovelock, Brent. "Climbing Kili: Ethical Mountain Guides on the Roof of Africa." In *Mountaineering Tourism*, edited by Musa, G., J. E. S. Higham, Anna Thompson-Carr. London: Routledge, 2015, 272–84.

Melubo, Kokel. "Case study 9. The working conditions of 'Wagumu' (high altitude porters) on Mt Kilimanjaro." In *Mountaineering Tourism*, edited by G. Musa, J. E. S. Higham, and A. Thompson-Carr. London: Routledge, 2017, 285–92.

Peaty, David. "Kilimanjaro Tourism and What It Means for Local Porters and for the Local Environment," *Journal of Ritsumeikan Social Sciences and Humanities* 4 (2012), 1–11.

A few historians have examined pre-colonial porterage in different parts of the African continent, including the use of enslaved people to traverse long distances.

Lovejoy, Paul E., and Catherine Coquery-Vidrovitch. *The Workers of African Trade*. Beverly Hills: Sage Publications, 1985.

Rockel, Stephen J. "'A Nation of Porters': The Nyamwezi and the Labour Market in Nineteenth-Century Tanzania," *Journal of African History* 41 (2000), 173–95.

Rockel, Stephen J. *Carriers of Culture: Labor on the Road in Nineteenth-Century East Africa*, Portsmouth: Heinemann, 2006.

For a more recent summary of porter work across the continent, see: Bellucci, Stefano. "Transport." In *General Labour History of Africa: Workers, Employers and Governments 20th–21st Centuries*, edited by Stefano Bellucci and Andreas Eckert. Oxford: James Currey, 2019, 195–219.

The literature on Sherpas who work as climbers and porters in the Himalaya mountains has developed with both personal and scholarly works that explore the Sherpas' history and perspective, especially after the highly publicized deaths on Mt. Everest in 1996. Edmond Hillary and Tenzing Norgay both published their autobiographies or accounts after their 1953 ascent of the summit (with Norgay's account told to different authors and published in different books). Thus, Norgay's words, perspective, and history as a Sherpa entered the written record along with Hillary's. Jon Krakauer's account of his personal experience on Everest with the deaths of fellow climbers caught in a dangerous storm sparked more interest in Sherpa work and Sherpas. In 1999 and 2001, both scholarly and more personal works focused on Sherpa history from a Sherpa perspective were published. Sherry B. Ortner's *Life and Death on Mt. Everest: Sherpas and Himalayan Mountaineering* was an anthropological work taking off from Ortner's work on Sherpa culture to focus on the story of mountaineering from the Sherpa point of view, including the way they have shaped, not just supported, the ventures and the role it plays in their lives more broadly. Relatives of Tenzing Norgay published their own works in 2001. Jamling Tenzing Norgay, son of Tenzing Norgay, published a memoir of his experiences with his father and his own climbing career. The grandson of Tenzing Norgay, Tashi Tenzing, and his then-wife published a book moving the work of Norgay and other Sherpa to the forefront, with a focus on the personal stories of prominent Sherpa climbers and an aim to recognize the work of Sherpas involved in many other aspects of high-altitude mountaineering. Another memoir of the Sherpa Ang Tharkay added to the growing literature a decade and a half later. Babu Adhikari and Pradeep Bashyal sought to fill out the history of Sherpas as well with their 2022 publication that brought the history up to the present day. Much of this work celebrated Sherpa achievements, explained Sherpa culture, and focused on how intertwined the Sherpa were with Himalayan mountaineering.

Adhikari, Ankit Babu, and Pradeep Bashyal. *Sherpa: Stories of Life and Death from the Forgotten Guardians of Everest*. Sydney: Hachette, 2022.

Hillary, Sir Edmund. *High Adventure*. New York: Oxford University Press, 2003.

Krakauer, Jon. *Into Thin Air: A Personal Account of the Mount Everest Disaster*. New York: Random House (Villard Books), 1997.

Norgay, Jamling Tenzing, with Broughton Coburn. *Touching My Father's Soul: A Sherpa's Journey to the Top of Everest*. San Francisco: Harper San Francisco, 2001.

Ortner, Sherry B. *Life and Death on Mt. Everest: Sherpas and Himalayan Mountaineering*. Princeton: Princeton University Press, 2001.

Tenzing, Judy, and Tashi Tenzing. *Tenzing and the Sherpas of Everest*. New Delhi: Harper Collins Publishers, 2001.

Tharkay, Ang. *Sherpa: The Memoir of Ang Tharkay*. Seattle: Mountaineers Books, 2016.

Ullman, James Ramsey, and Tenzing Norgay. *Man of Everest: The Autobiography of Tenzing Norgay*. London: Reprint Society, 1956.

Mountaineering history was often recorded in the account of explorers, naturalists, or mountaineers themselves who were pioneers in exploring certain mountain ranges with the highest peaks. Scholars who have studied this history have often focused on those mountaineers and their writings. More recently, historians have highlighted the gendered, racial, and national or imperial aspects of mountaineering. Much of the literature has focused on the European Alps, the Americas, and the Himalayas, although there is some literature on mountaineering and mountain clubs in different parts of South Africa. Outside of the literature on Sherpas, few have considered the role of porters and guides.

Bayers, Peter L. *Imperial Ascent: Masculinity, Mountaineering, and Empire*. Boulder: University Press of Colorado, 2003.

Carruthers, Jane. "The Royal National Park, KwaZulu Natal: Mountaineering, Tourism and Nature Conservation in South Africa's First National Park c. 1896 to c. 1947," *Environment and History* 19, no. 4 (November 2013): 459–86.

Debarbieux, Bernard, and Gilles Rudaz. *The Mountain: A Political History from the Enlightenment to the Present*. Chicago: University of Chicago Press, 2015.

Gilchrist, Paul. "Gender and British Climbing Histories: Introduction," *Sport in History* 33, no. 3 (2013): 223–35.

Hansen, Peter H. "Partners: Guides and Sherpas in the Alps and Himalayas, 1850s–1950s." In *Voyages and Visions: Towards a Cultural History of Travel*, eds. Jas Elsner and Joan-Pau Rubies. London: Reaktion, 1999, 210–31.

Hansen, Peter H. *The Summits of Modern Man: Mountaineering After the Enlightenment*. Cambridge: Harvard University Press, 2013.

Isserman, Maurice, and Stewart Weaver. *Fallen Giants: A History of Himalayan Mountaineering from the Age of Empire to the Age of Extremes*. New Haven: Yale University Press, 2008.

Kahn, Farieda. "A Century of Mountaineering: Race, Class and the Politics of Climbing Table Mountain," *Acta Academica* 50, no. 2 (2018): 74.

———. "Apartheid Mountaineering: Race, Politics, and the History of the University of Cape Town Mountain and Ski Club, 1933–1969," *The International Journal of the History of Sport* 36, no. 1 (2019): 48–66.

———. "From Carriers to Climbers: The Cape Province Mountain Club, 1930s to 1960s—an untold story." In *Exploring Decolonising Themes in SA Sport History: Issues and Challenges*, edited by Francois Johannes Cleophas. Stellenbosch: African Sun Media, 2018, 67–80.

———. "The Impact of Racial Inequality on the Pursuit of Mountain-Based Leisure Pursuits among Black Recreation-Seekers in Cape Town, South Africa, 1910–1969," *Recreation and*

Society in Africa, Asia and Latin America 6 (2018): 32.

Keller, Tait. *Apostles of the Alps: Mountaineering and Nation Building in Germany and Austria.* Chapel Hill: University of North Carolina Press, 2016.

Pearse, R. O. *Barrier of Spears: Drama of the Drakensberg.* Johannesburg: Southern Book Publishers, 1989.

Schaumann, Caroline. *Peak Pursuits: The Emergence of Mountaineering in the Nineteenth Century.* New Haven: Yale University Press, 2020.

For works on tourism in Africa, both from a historical perspective and from an overview of current issues, the following sources provide a starting point with helpful summaries and citations for further reading.

Admasie, Samuel Andreas. "Sport, Tourism and Entertainment." In *General Labour History of Africa: Workers, Employers and Governments 20th–21st Centuries*, edited by Stefano Bellucci and Andreas Eckert. Woodbridge: James Currey, 2019, 405–21.

Chen, Joseph S., and Nina K. Prebensen, eds. *Nature Tourism.* London; New York: Routledge, 2017.

Christie, Iain Thornto, Eneida Herrera Fernandes, Hannah R. Messerli, and Louise D. Twining-Ward. *Tourism in Africa: Harnessing Tourism for Growth and Improved Livelihood.* Washington, D.C.: The World Bank, 2014.

Cleveland, Todd. *A History of Tourism in Africa: Exoticization, Exploitation, and Enrichment.* Athens: Ohio University Press, 2021.

Pirie, Gordon. "Tourism Histories in Africa." In *The Oxford Handbook of Tourism History*, edited by Eric G. E. Zuelow and Kevin J. James. Oxford: Oxford University Press, 2025, 447–68.

Finally, historians have written illuminating histories on colonial conservation, the origins of national parks, and their relation to African social history, particularly in relation to Tanzania's history.

Adams, William Mark, and Martin Mulligan, eds. *Decolonizing Nature: Strategies for Conservation in a Post-colonial Era.* London: Earthscane, 2003.

Beinart, William. *The Rise of Conservation in South Africa: Settlers, Livestock, and the Environment, 1770–1950.* Oxford: Oxford University Press, 2008.

Beinart, William, and Peter Coates. *Environment and History: The Taming of Nature in the USA and South Africa.* London; New York: Routledge, 1995.

Bender-Shetler, Jan. *Imagining Serengeti: A History of Landscape Memory in Tanzania from*

Earliest Times to the Present. Athens: Ohio University Press, 2007.

Brockington, Dan, Hassan Sachedina, and Katherine Scholfield. "Preserving the New Tanzania: Conservation and Land Use Change," *The International Journal of African Historical Studies* 41, no. 3 (2008): 557–79.

Carruthers, Jane. "Conservation and Wildlife Management in South African National Parks, 1930s–1960s," *Journal of the History of Biology* 41, no. 2 (2008): 203–36.

———. *The Kruger National Park: A Social and Political History*. Pietermaritzburg: University of Natal Press, 1995.

Cock, Jacklyn, and David Fig, "From Colonial to Community-Based Conservation: Environmental Justice and the National Parks of South Africa," *Society in Transition* 31, no. 1 (2000): 22–35.

Conte, Christopher A. *Highland Sanctuary: Environmental History in Tanzania's Usambara Mountains*. Athens: Ohio University Press, 2004.

Dlamini, Jacob. *Safari Nation: A Social History of the Kruger National Park*. Athens: Ohio University Press, 2020.

Gissibl, Bernhard. *The Nature of German Colonialism: Conservation and the Politics of Wildlife in Colonial East Africa*. New York: Berghahn Books, 2016.

Lekan, Thomas N. *Our Gigantic Zoo: A German Quest to Save the Serengeti*. Oxford: Oxford University Press, 2020.

MacKenzie, John M. *The Empire of Nature: Hunting, Conservation, and British Imperialism*. Manchester: Manchester University Press, 1997.

Munro, Paul. "Colonial Wildlife Conservation and National Parks in Sub-Saharan Africa." *Oxford Research Encyclopedia of African History*. November 29, 2021. https://oxfordre.com/africanhistory/view/10.1093/acrefore/9780190277734.001.0001/acrefore-9780190277734-e-195.

Neumann, Roderick P. "Africa's 'Last Wilderness': Reordering Space for Political and Economic Control in Colonial Tanzania," *Africa* 71, no. 4 (November 2001): 641–65.

Prendergast, David K., and William M. Adams. "Colonial Wildlife Conservation and the Origins of the Society for the Preservation of the Wild Fauna of the Empire (1903–1914)," *Oryx* 37, no. 2 (April 2003): 251–60.

Schauer, Jeff. *Wildlife between Empire and Nation in Twentieth-Century Africa*. London: Palgrave MacMillan, 2018.

Recommendations for Engaging in Ethical Tourism on Kilimanjaro

MANY VISITORS TO KILIMANJARO ARE CONCERNED ABOUT HAVING THE BEST EXPErience on the mountain that is also cost-effective and ethical. The history outlined in this book also compels us to do our best to ensure the industry takes care of those on which it relies the most and has the most impact. Visitors can have a significant influence in two key areas: choosing a tour company and interacting with the mountain crews.

Choosing a locally owned and operated company with ethical practices can be daunting. Some visitors have reported being scammed by companies offering prices far below the market average of $1,850–$1,900. The majority of these accusations involve local operators, as guests often feel uncertain about how to hold them accountable. Yet locally-owned operators can more directly support local Tanzanians. Such unfortunate client experiences could be avoided with greater diligence in gathering the right information and planning a realistic budget. Based on various sources, particularly the accounts of those we interviewed, we propose a list of simple rules for selecting a reliable and trustworthy operator:

1. Do not get hooked by the incredibly low prices.
2. Do not send deposits by Western Union or other similar means. A legitimate

tour operator is required by law to have a business bank account with one of the reputable country banks. In Tanzania, these banks are commonly CRDB, Equity, NMB (National Microfinance Bank), DTB (Diamond Trust Bank), Exim and KCB. Preferably, the account should be in the company name, not in the name of a private individual.

3. Read the reviews on TripAdvisor or other similarly trusted platforms. TripAdvisor is generally known to be the most reliable platform for collecting reviews about adventure trips. However, do not rely on it entirely. Some reviews are misleading. Some tips to evaluate the authenticity of the review include:
   i. Verify the company account registration date. The older the company, the more likely it is a legitimate business.
   ii. Pay attention to the dates of the first reviews. If they were all gathered in a year (or worse, a month), the company is most likely a sham unless it is clearly declared to be a new company.
   iii. It might be helpful if the tour operator has non-English reviews. The majority of the fake ones are farmed in English only.
   iv. See if the company has reviews from “trusted” travelers; i.e., those who have left over one hundred reviews of different places in different countries. These reviews are always genuine because forging them is both technically impossible and prohibitively expensive.
4. Google search the company name to see what other travelers say on platforms like Google Reviews, Bookmundi, and TourRadar.
5. Ask the company for a license from the Ministry of Natural Resources and Tourism. Each tour operator in Tanzania is required by law to have a license. Ask for a soft copy so that in the event of a problem, the directors and managers of these companies can be easily tracked down.
6. Ask for a Tax Identification Number (TIN) and VAT Certificate. In Tanzania, all legitimate businesses are registered with the Tanzania Revenue Authority and must have a registration certificate. It is always a good idea to request one and cross-check it against a license. There is always the possibility that a license can be forged, but forging both documents is a risk that few are willing to take.
7. Be wary of friends’ recommendations. A friend’s recommendation is a good place to start your research, but make sure to do additional checks on the travel company you are dealing with, especially if your friend’s trip was several years ago. Much could have changed in the intervening years.

8. Pay Attention to internet identity:
   i. Most genuine and well established tour operators would not have an email address registered on gmail.com, yahoo.com, or other similar public domains. The vast majority would be willing to pay around $100 per year for a corporate email with the same ending as the company's website. An email with the address "XXX@gmail.com" or something similar is suspicious and should be approached more cautiously.
   ii. A majority of credible operators have websites with engaging content that is updated on a regular basis. The market becomes more competitive every year, and good tour operators invest in a high-quality website.
   iii. Most credible travel companies tend to have a Facebook or Instagram account, and most have both. Some are using these platforms to market their adventures; others simply publish photos and videos from their trips. In either case, these profiles are a great tool to see if the company has regular operations.
9. Professional communication is rare among fraudsters. Their emails are frequently inconclusive, contain numerous grammar errors, and push for the deposit to be paid as soon as possible. As you pay attention to details of the communication, take note of the following points:
   i. A legitimate business's sales manager will never refer to you as "my brother" or "my friend." Safari operators' sales staff are professionals who address clients as "Mr.," "Ms.," "Dear ____," or other appropriate terms.
   ii. The emails should be well structured, conclusive, and provide concise answers to your questions. A detailed itinerary and hotel names (rather than just "good four-star hotels") are required.
   iii. A good company will always have a corporate identity with a recognizable logo, and all-important communication (invoices, itineraries) should be done on the company letterhead.
   iv. Small details such as different signatures, use of different emails for communication, or other elements that would show a lack of professionalism are also good clues for recognizing a fraudulent business.

Tipping is another significant aspect of the Kilimanjaro experience that visitors must prepare for. If conducted well, this can be a good opportunity to support mountain crews. Given the history of tipping and the efforts to attract clients with lower costs, it is evident that for most mountain crews, tipping serves as a crucial supplement to their wages. Taking part in a tipping ceremony at the end of the adventure also allows tourists to celebrate with and express gratitude to all the crew members. To ensure the tipping experience is satisfying to visitors and all the crew, we suggest doing the following:

1. Remember that tipping is optional. It is a way to express gratitude for the quality of services provided and thus depends on the visitors' generosity and experience.
2. Do some research and prepare appropriate amounts of cash ahead of time (with monetary notes in the condition and denominations that you may need). Some operators, guidebooks, and tourist resources suggest appropriate amounts for tipping, ranging from $10 to $25 per day for porters and guides respectively.
3. Request a list of all the crew members and their positions to help you distribute appropriate tip amounts and record the transaction. Crew members generally receive different amounts according to their position (e.g., porters vs. summit porters, cooks vs. servers, guides).
4. Ask to announce the tip amounts for each position in front of the entire crew and to distribute the tips to each crew member, one by one. This can help ensure that each crew member receives their intended amount (this is also the time to have monetary notes in denominations needed to avoid having to change money). The tipping ceremony is generally held on the last day before descending or upon arrival at the bottom. If a visitor needs to descend earlier than the rest of the group, they can tip the guide and crew members who escorted them down apart from the rest of the crew who remained on the mountain.

Notes

CHAPTER 1. MOUNTAIN CREWS, THE WORLD, AND MT. KILIMANJARO

1. Alex Lemunge, interview with EM and FB, September 18, 2021, Arusha. He continued, "and . . . you become their boss, it doesn't matter how rich and powerful they are but . . . you are the BOSS!"
2. Batchi Vitalis Donat, interview with LH, May 22, 2018, Himo.
3. Simon Mtuy, interview with LH, June 6, 2022, Moshi.
4. Iain Thornto Christie, Eneida Herrera Fernandes, Hannah R. Messerli, Louise D. Twining-Ward, *Tourism in Africa: Harnessing Tourism for Growth and Improved Livelihood* (Washington, D.C.: The World Bank, 2014).
5. Samantha Jones, "A Political Ecology of Wildlife Conservation in Africa," *Review of African Political Economy* 33, no. 109 (September 2006): 483–95; Paul Andre DeGeorges and Kevin Reilly, "The Realities of Community Based Natural Resource Management and biodiversity conservation in Sub-Saharan Africa," *Sustainability* 1, no. 3 (2009): 734–88.
6. This work focuses more on Eastern and Southern Africa because that is where nature tourism and national parks came first. See, for example: Jacob Dlamini, *Safari Nation: A Social History of the Kruger National Park* (Athens: Ohio University Press, 2020); Jane Carruthers, "The Royal National Park, KwaZulu Natal: Mountaineering, Tourism and Nature Conservation in South Africa's First National Park c. 1896 to c. 1947," *Environment*

and History 19, no. 4 (November 2013), 459–86; Christopher A. Conte, *Highland Sanctuary: Environmental History in Tanzania's Usambara Mountains* (Athens: Ohio University Press, 2004); William Beinart and Peter Coates, *Environment and History: The Taming of Nature in the USA and South Africa* (London; New York: Routledge, 1995).

7. Scholars have highlighted how European enthusiasts, explorers, and scientists relied upon African experts. See Nancy Jacobs, *Birders of Africa: History of a Network* (New Haven: Yale University Press, 2016); Dane Kennedy, *The Last Blank Spaces: Exploring Africa and Australia* (Cambridge: Harvard University Press, 2013); Helen Tilley, *Africa as a Living Laboratory: Empire, Development, and the Problem of Scientific Knowledge, 1870–1950* (Chicago: University of Chicago Press, 2011).
8. Gordon Pirie, "Tourism Histories in Africa," in *The Oxford Handbook of Tourism History*, eds. Eric G. E. Zuelow and Kevin J. James (Oxford: Oxford University Press, 2025), 460; Todd Cleveland, *A History of Tourism in Africa: Exoticization, Exploitation, and Enrichment* (Athens: Ohio University Press, 2021).
9. Erick Kivelege, *Climbing Kilimanjaro with Africa's Top Guide* (Enumclaw; Moshi: Kilimanjaro Kutembea Publishing, 2021).
10. Brent Lovelock, "Climbing Kili: Ethical Mountain Guides on the Roof of Africa," in *Mountaineering Tourism*, ed. G. Musa, J. E. S. Higham, and Anna Thompson-Carr (London: Routledge, 2015), 272–84.
11. Dlamini, *Safari Nation*, 3, 12; Cleveland, *A History of Tourism in Africa*, 6.
12. Dlamini, *Safari Nation*, 29.
13. Pirie, "Tourism Histories in Africa"; Cleveland, *A History of Tourism in Africa*; Beinart and Coates, *Environment and History*; Paul Munro, "Colonial Wildlife Conservation and National Parks in Sub-Saharan Africa." *Oxford Research Encyclopedia of African History*, November 29, 2021; Roderick P. Neumann, "Africa's 'Last Wilderness': Reordering Space for Political and Economic Control in Colonial Tanzania," *Africa* 71, no. 4 (November 2001): 641–65; Jacklyn Cock and David Fig, "From Colonial to Community-Based Conservation: Environmental Justice and the National Parks of South Africa," *Society in Transition* 31, no. 1 (2000): 22–35.
14. Bernard Debarbieux and Gilles Rudaz, *The Mountain: A Political History from the Enlightenment to the Present* (Chicago: University of Chicago Press, 2015); Peter H. Hansen, *The Summits of Modern Man: Mountaineering After the Enlightenment* (Cambridge: Harvard University Press, 2013); Caroline Schaumann, *Peak Pursuits: The Emergence of Mountaineering in the Nineteenth Century* (New Haven: Yale University Press, 2020).
15. Peter L. Bayers, *Imperial Ascent: Masculinity, Mountaineering, and Empire* (Boulder:

University Press of Colorado, 2003); Paul Gilchrist, "Gender and British Climbing Histories: Introduction," *Sport in History* 33, no. 3 (2103): 223–35; Maurice Isserman and Stewart Weaver, *Fallen Giants: A History of Himalayan Mountaineering from the Age of Empire to the Age of Extremes* (New Haven: Yale University Press, 2008); Tait Keller, *Apostles of the Alps: Mountaineering and Nation Building in Germany and Austria* (Chapel Hill: University of North Carolina Press, 2016). For works on South Africa, see R. O. Pearse, *Barrier of Spears: Drama of the Drakensberg* (Johannesburg: Southern Book Publishers, 1989); Carruthers, "The Royal National Park, KwaZulu Natal," 459–86; Farieda Kahn, "From Carriers to Climbers: The Cape Province Mountain Club, 1930s to 1960s—an untold story," in *Exploring Decolonising Themes in SA Sport History: Issues and Challenges*, ed. Francois Johannes Cleophas (Stellenbosch: African Sun Media, 2018), 67–80; Farieda Khan, "Apartheid Mountaineering: Race, Politics, and the History of the University of Cape Town Mountain and Ski Club, 1933–1969," *The International Journal of the History of Sport* 36, no. 1 (2019): 48–66.

16. Audrey Salkeld, *Kilimanjaro: To the Roof of Africa* (Washington, D.C.: National Geographic, 2002); Cameron M. Burns, *Kilimanjaro & East Africa: A Climbing and Trekking Guide*, 2nd ed. (Seattle: Mountaineers Books, 2006); Francois Bart, Francois Devenne, and Milline Jethro Mbonile, eds., *Mount Kilimanjaro: Mountain, Memory, Modernity*, (Dar es Salaam: Mkuki na Nyota Publishers, 2006); Ghazali Musa, James Higham, and Anna Thompson-Carr, eds., *Mountaineering Tourism* (London: Routledge, 2015). See also Kennedy, *The Last Blank Spaces*.

17. James Ramsey Ullman and Tenzing Norgay, *Man of Everest: The Autobiography of Tenzing Norgay* (London: Reprint Society, 1956).

18. Jamling Tenzing Norgay with Broughton Coburn, *Touching My Father's Soul: A Sherpa's Journey to the Top of Everest* (San Francisco: Harper San Francisco, 2001); Judy and Tashi Tenzing, *Tenzing and the Sherpas of Everest* (New Delhi: Harper Collins Publishers, 2001); Ang Tharkay, *Sherpa: The Memoir of Ang Tharkay* (Seattle: Mountaineers Books, 2016). See also Jon Krakauer, *Into Thin Air: A Personal Account of the Mount Everest Disaster* (New York: Random House (Villard Books), 1997); Sherry B. Ortner, *Life and Death on Mt. Everest: Sherpas and Himalayan Mountaineering* (Princeton: Princeton University Press, 2001); Ankit Babu Adhikari and Pradeep Bashyal, *Sherpa: Stories of Life and Death from the Forgotten Guardians of Everest* (Sydney: Hachette, 2022).

19. Louise Hoole, *Seven Wonders: The World Heritage Sites of Tanzania*, 2nd edition (Black Ink Press, 2016).

20. Ministry of Natural Resources and Tourism (MNRT), *2024 Maliasili, Statistical Bulletin* (Dodoma, Tanzania, 2024).

21. Edwin Bernbaum, "Sacred Mountains: Themes and Teachings," *Mountain Research and Development* 26, no. 4 (2006), 304–9.
22. Charles Dundas, *Kilimanjaro and Its People* (London: Frank Cass, 1924), 39.
23. Matthew V. Bender, *Water Brings No Harm: Management Knowledge and the Struggle for the Waters of Kilimanjaro* (Athens: Ohio University Press, 2019), 35.
24. Bender, *Water Brings No Harm*, 9–10.
25. Charles Dundas, *Kilimanjaro and Its People: A History of the Wachagga, Their Laws, Customs and Legends . . . By the Hon'ble Charles Dundas* (London: H. F. and G. Witherby, 1924).

CHAPTER 2. INHABITANTS OF THE MOUNTAIN

1. Bruno Gutmann, "Chagga Folk-lore: Extracts from Two Books by Bruno Gutman," trans. J. A. Hutchinson, *Tanzania Notes and Records* 64 (1965): 50.
2. Kathleen M. Stahl, *History of the Chagga People of Kilimanjaro* (London: Mouton & Co., 1964), 19; also see Susan Geiger Rogers, "The Search for Political Focus on Kilimanjaro: A History of Chagga Politics, 1916–1962" (PhD diss., University of Dar es Salaam, 1972), 36.
3. Thomas L. M. Marealle, "The Wachagga of Kilimanjaro," *Tanganyika Notes and Records* 32 (1952): 57.
4. See Hans Meyer, *Across East African Glaciers: An Account of the First Ascent of Kilimanjaro*, trans. E. H. S. Calder (London: Longmans, Green, and Co.,1891), 1–7; Harry Hamiton Johnston, *The Kilimanjaro Expedition: A Record of Scientific Exploration in Eastern Tropical Africa* (London: Kegan and Paul, 1886), 7; A. Le Roy, *Au Kilima-Ndjaro: Histoire de la fondation d'une mission catholique en Afrique orientale* (Paris: L'Œuvre d'auteil, 1928), 11; E. Stuart-Watt, *Africa's Dome of Mystery* (London: Marshall, Morgan & Scott, 1930), 13–16; Stahl, *History of the Chagga People*, 34; and P. J. Boyd Johnson, and H. McCullum, eds., *Kilimanjaro: Africa's Beacon* (Harare: African Publishing Group International, 2004), 15.
5. Conventional English usage upholds "Chagga" as both noun (singular and plural) and adjective. We shall adhere to this form as much as possible.
6. Sally Falk Moore, *Social Facts and Fabrications: "Customary" Law on Kilimanjaro, 1880–1980* (Cambridge: Cambridge University Press, 1986), 24.
7. See A. G. Pike, "Kilimanjaro and the Furrow System," *Tanzania Notes and Records*, 64 (1965): 95–96; A. Grove, "Water Use by the Chagga on Kilimanjaro" *African Affairs* 92, no. 368 (1993): 431–48; and F. K. Vavrus, "A Shadow of the Real Thing: Furrow Societies, Water User Associations, and Democratic Practices in the Kilimanjaro Region of

Tanzania," *The Journal of African American History* 88, no. 4 (2003): 393–412.

8. John Ludwig Krapf, *Travels, Researches and Missionary Labours During Eighteen Years' Residence in Eastern Africa*, 2nd ed. (London: Frank Cass, 1968 [1860]), 254–55. The rendering of "Kibo" as snow is disputable, not least because elsewhere Rebmann says the Chagga had no word for snow. See Johannes Rebmann, "Narrative of a Journey to Jagga, the Snow Country of Eastern Africa," *Church Missionary Intelligencer* 1 (1849/50): 17.
9. Johnston, *The Kilimanjaro Expedition*, 1.
10. See J. A. Hutchinson, "The Meaning of Kilimanjaro," *Tanzania Notes and Records* 64 (1965): 65–67; and Ludger Wimmelbücker, *Kilimanjaro: A Regional History* (London: Transaction Publishers, 2002), 113–14.
11. See Le Roy, *Au Kilima-Ndjaro*, 10.
12. Ubiquitously present in Chagga stories for children, this myth is also referred to in Charles Dundas, *Kilimanjaro and Its People: A History of the Wachagga, their Laws, Customs and Legends, together with Some Account of the Highest Mountain in Africa* (London: Frank Cass & Co., 1968 [1924]), 33–37; R. Reusch, "The Menelik Legend," *Tanganyika Notes and Records* 2 (1936): 77–79; Gutmann, "Chagga Folk-lore," 53; Petro I. Marealle, *Maisha ya Mchagga Hapa Duniani na Ahera* (Dar es Salaam: Mkuki na Nyota Publishers, 2002 [1947]), 116–17; and Marealle, "The Wachagga of Kilimanjaro," 57–58.
13. Krapf, *Travels, Researches and Missionary Labours*, 234–36.
14. John Ludwig Krapf, "Mount Kenia," *Proceedings of the Royal Geographical Society and Monthly Record of Geography*, 4, no. 12 (1882 [1849/50]): 747–53.
15. R. Thornton, "Notes on a Journey to Kilima-njaro, Made in Company of the Baron von der Decken," *Journal of the Royal Geographical Society of London* 35 (1865): 21.
16. Johnston, *The Kilimanjaro Expedition*, 8, 96.
17. Anon, "Recent Changes in the Map of East Africa," *Proceedings of the Royal Geographical Society and Monthly Record of Geography*, New Monthly Series 9, no. 8 (1887): 491.
18. Le Roy, *Au Kilima-Ndjaro*, 179.
19. Meyer, *Across East African Glaciers*, vii, 112.
20. C. Hollis, "Notes on the History and Customs of the People of Taveta, East Africa," *Journal of the Royal African Society* 1, no. 1 (1901): 101–3.
21. F. R. Cana, "Frontiers of German East Africa." *The Geographical Journal* 47, no. 4 (1916): 299.
22. Thornton, "Notes on a Journey to Kilima-njaro," 49.
23. Charles P. Rigby, "Mr. J. M. Hildebrandt on His Travels in East Africa." *Proceedings of the Royal Geographical Society of London* 22, no. 6 (1877/78): 449.
24. Krapf, *Travels, Researches and Missionary Labours*, 259.

25. Johannes Rebmann, "Narrative of a Journey to Madjame, in Jagga," *Church Missionary Intelligencer* 1, no. 272–76 (1849/50): 275.
26. Krapf, *Travels, Researches and Missionary Labours*, 262.
27. Le Roy, *Au Kilima-Ndjaro*, 10.
28. See Meyer, *Across East African Glaciers*, 103 and *passim*.
29. Hollis, "Notes on the History and Customs," 118.
30. See Stahl, *History of the Chagga People*, 38; and Wimmelbücker, *Kilimanjaro*, 99.
31. C. W. Hobley, "People, Places, and Prospects in British East Africa." *The Geographical Journal* 4, no. 2 (1894): 115.
32. Krapf, *Travels, Researches and Missionary Labours*, 267.
33. Krapf, *Travels, Researches and Missionary Labours*, 265. Rebmann translated "Kirima" as "Jagga" and "Wa-Kirima" as "People of Jagga," which he could have rendered "Wa-Jagga." As already suggested, by "Kirima" and "Wa-Kirima," King Maina likely meant "Mountain" and "Mountain-dwellers," respectively.
34. Johnston, *The Kilimanjaro Expedition*, 95, 109, and *passim*.
35. H. A. Fosbrooke and H. Sassoon, "Archaeological Remains on Kilimanjaro," *Tanzania Notes and Records* 64 (1965): 62.
36. See Dundas, *Kilimanjaro and Its People*, 41, 51; Stuart-Watt, *Africa's Dome of Mystery*, 21–22; J. E. G. Sutton, "The Archaeology and Early Peoples of the Highlands of Kenya and Northern Tanzania," *Azania* 1 (1966): 45; and K. Odner, "A Preliminary Report on an Archaeological Survey on the Slopes of Kilimanjaro," *Azania* 6 (1971): 133.
37. P. J. Wood, "The Forest Glades of West Kilimanjaro," *Tanzania Notes and Records* 64 (1965): 108.
38. Odner, "A Preliminary Report on an Archaeological Survey," 148.
39. T. L. Marealle and R. S. Kishimba, trans. and eds., *Historia ya Kanisa la Kiinjili la Kilutheri Africa Mashariki, 1902–1912: Kilimanjaro, Arusha, Meru na Pare* (Moshi: Printing Services Ltd, 1997), 11.
40. Kathleen M. Stahl, *Tanganyika: Sail in the Wilderness* (The Hague: Mouton & Co., 1961), 22.
41. Odner, "A Preliminary Report on an Archaeological Survey," 133.
42. Sally Falk Moore, "The Chagga of Kilimanjaro," in *The Chagga and Meru of Tanzania*, ed. S. F. Moore and P. Ruritt (London: International African Institute, 1977), 5. See also Rogers, "The Search for Political Focus," 27; and Isaria N. Kimambo, "The Eastern Bantu Peoples," in *Zamani: A Survey of East African History*, new ed, ed. B. A. Ogot (Nairobi: East African Publishing House, 1973), 198–9.
43. See Kathleen M. Stahl, "Outline of Chagga History," *Tanzania Notes and Records* 64 (1965): 37.

44. Stahl, *Tanganyika*, 22; Stahl, "Outline of Chagga History," 37.
45. See F. J. Berg, "The Coast from the Portuguese Invasion to the Rise of the Zanzibar Sultanate," in *Zamani: A Survey of East African History*, new ed, ed. B. A. Ogot (Nairobi: East African Publishing House, 1973), 118.
46. See J. E. G. Sutton, "The Archaeology and Early Peoples of the Highlands of Kenya and Northern Tanzania," *Azania* 1 (1966): 50.
47. Dundas, *Kilimanjaro and Its People*, 41; see also Charles Dundas, *Asili na Habari za Wachagga* (London: The Sheldon Press, 1932), 31.
48. Dundas, *Kilimanjaro and Its People*, 43–44; Dundas, *Asili na Habari za Wachagga*, 7–8. See also S. J. Ntiro, *Desturi za Wachagga* (Dar es Salaam: The Eagle Press, 1953), 5–6.
49. For Nyamwezi, see Stahl, "Outline of Chagga History," 37; for Persians, see Anon, "Recent Changes," 74. The mention of Persian origins of Chagga chiefs could be an exaggeration for purposes of attracting traders from the coast, which Chagga chiefs always struggled to control.
50. Stahl, *History of the Chagga People*, 306–7.
51. Marealle, *Maisha ya Mchagga*, 80–81.
52. Ali A. Jahadhmy, *Anthology of Swahili Poetry* (London: Heinemann Educational Books, 1975), vii.
53. See Dundas, *Kilimanjaro and Its People*, 47; Dundas, *Asili na Habari za Wachagga*, 8, 33; and Stahl, *History of the Chagga People*, 227–28.
54. See Dundas, *Asili na Habari za Wachagga*, 40–41; Stahl, *History of the Chagga*, 309, 338–39; and E. E. Malya, *Wamarangu: Historia na Maendeleo* (Moshi: Northern Packages, 2002), 24.
55. Dundas, *Asili na Habari za Wachagga*, 13.
56. Odner, "A Preliminary Report on an Archaeological Survey," 132.
57. Sally Falk Moore, "The Secret of the Men: A Fiction of Chagga Initiation and its Relation to the Logic of Chagga Symbolism," *Africa* 46, no. 4 (1976): 367.
58. Marealle, *Maisha ya Mchagga*, 72.
59. Marealle, "The Wachagga of Kilimanjaro," 61–62.
60. Krapf, *Travels, Researches and Missionary Labours*, 244; see also Rogers, "The Search for Political Focus," 33–34. Rebmann's "Dafeta" and "Ugono" obviously refers to today's Wataveta and Wagweno, respectively.
61. Johnston, *The Kilimanjaro Expedition*, 404.
62. See Hans Meyer, *Across East Africa Glaciers: An Account of the First Ascent of Kilimanjaro,* trans. E. H. S. Calder (London, 1891), 113; Stahl, *History of the Chagga*, 25, 345.
63. See Krapf, *Travels, Researches and Missionary Labours,* 244–5; Moore, "The Chagga of

Kilimanjaro," 5; and Sally Falk Moore, *Social Facts and Fabrications: "Customary" Law on Kilimanjaro, 1880–1980* (Cambridge: Cambridge University Press, 1986), 25–27.

64. See E. A. Fitch and J. A. Wray, "The First Year of the Chagga Mission," *Church Missionary Intelligencer*, New Series 2 (1886): 556; and Le Roy, *Au Kilima-Ndjaro*, 279.
65. Meyer, *Across East Africa Glaciers*, 117. Also see J. R. Harding, "Nineteenth-Century Trade Beads in Tanganyika," *Man* 62 (1962): 105. Michael von Clemm, "Trade-Bead Economics in Nineteenth-Century Chaggaland," *Man* 63 (1963), 13–14.
66. K. W. Deutsch, "The Growth of Nations: Some Recurrent Patterns of Political and Social Integration," *World Politics* 5, no. 2 (1956): 169.
67. See W. H. Whiteley, "Chagga Languages," *Tanzania Notes and Records* 64 (1965): 68; and Dundas, *Asili na Habari za Wachagga*, 27.
68. See Johnston, *The Kilimanjaro Expedition*, 425; H. H. Johnston, "The People of Eastern Equatorial Africa," *The Journal of the Anthropological Institute of Great Britain and Ireland* 15 (1886): 13; G. P. Murdock, *Africa: Its Peoples and Their Culture History* (London: McGraw-Hill Book Company, Inc., 1959), 344; and Sutton, "The Archaeology and Early Peoples," 47–48.
69. See R. J. Swynnerton and A. L. B. Bennett, *All About "KNCU" Coffee* (London: Hazell, Watson & Viney, 1948), 10; and Moore, *Social Facts and Fabrications*, 65, 131–3, 215.
70. See Krapf, *Travels, Researches and Missionary Labours*, 238, 252–3; See Hollis, "Notes on the History and Customs," 118.
71. Dundas, *Kilimanjaro and Its People*, 144–5; Marealle, *Maisha ya Mchagga*, 107.
72. Cf. Judith A. Carney and Richard Nicholas Rosomoff, *In the Shadow of Slavery: Africa's Botanical Legacy in the Atlantic World* (Oakland: University of California Press, 2010), 34–37.
73. Dundas, *Kilimanjaro and Its People*, 262.
74. See Dundas, *Kilimanjaro and Its People*, 75; Marealle, *Maisha ya Mchagga*, 5, 53–54.
75. Krapf, *Travels, Researches and Missionary Labours*, 238.
76. Stahl, *History of the Chagga*, 27, 52, 60, 325. Also see F. B. Steiner, "Chagga Truth: A Note on Gutmann's Account of the Chagga Concept of Truth in Das Recht der Dschagga," *Africa* 24, no. 4 (1954): 367.
77. T. H. Swai, "Limpasalo Mchagga ni Kihamba, Sale na Nyinda," *Komkya* (August 15, 1955), 3a.
78. See Fitch and Wray, "The First Year of the Chagga Mission," 557; Meyer, *Across East African Glaciers*, 106, 114.
79. See Dundas, *Kilimanjaro and Its People*, 257.
80. Moore, *Social Facts and Fabrications*, 64.

81. Le Roy, *Au Kilima-Ndjaro*, 276.
82. Rogers, "The Search for Political Focus," 39; Moore, *Social Facts and Fabrications*, 193; Le Roy, *Au Kilima-Ndjaro*, 287; Marealle, *Maisha ya Mchagga*, 62–69; Stahl, *History of the Chagga*, 342.
83. Fitch and Wray, "The First Year of the Chagga Mission," 53; F. R. Lehman, "Some Field-Notes on the Chagga of Kilimanjaro," *Bantu Studies* 15 (1941): 390; Marealle, *Maisha ya Mchagga*, 65–66, 73–74.
84. Historian Ludger Wimmelbücker (*Kilimanjaro*, 70) suggests that, during the nineteenth century, "the farming population on Mt. Kilimanjaro" used the word "Wakirima" as a self-designation and "used the notion of Wanyika . . . for sedentary populations to the east of Kilimanjaro." This interpretation may have relied on Rebmann's single reference to the said self-designation, which as such constitutes a very weak evidence, for the root *nyika* appears foreign to Kichagga dialects. Those that others called Wanyika, the Chagga called Kyasaka.
85. See S. Feierman, *The Shambaa Kingdom: A History* (Madison: University of Wisconsin Press, 1974), 20; also see Johnston, *The Kilimanjaro Expedition*, 395.
86. R. F. Morton, 1972. "The Shungwaya Myth of Miji Kenda Origins." *The International Journal of African Historical Studies* 5, no. 3 (1972): 397, fn. 1.
87. See C. Dundas, *African Crossroads* (London: Macmillan & Co., 1955), 73.
88. See C. Peters, *New Light on Dark Africa: Being the Narrative of the German Emin Pasha Expedition*, trans. H. W. Dulken. (London: Ward, Lock and Co., 1891), 182–3; and Hobley, "People, Places, and Prospects," 115.
89. Marealle, *Maisha ya Mchagga*, 46.
90. See Rogers, "The Search for Political Focus," 49.
91. See Ntiro, *Desturi za Wachagga*, 16–17.
92. See Marealle, *Maisha ya Mchagga*, 24–25, 83; Rogers, "The Search of Political Focus," 87–91; Moore, "The Chagga of Kilimanjaro," 58.
93. See Dundas, *Kilimanjaro and Its People*, 150–5; Marealle, *Maisha ya Mchagga*, 81; Marealle, "Notes on Chagga Customs," 68.
94. Moore, *Social Facts and Fabrications*, 60.
95. See Dundas, *Asili na Habari za Wachagga*, 9; Marealle, *Maisha ya Mchagga*, 121; Marealle, "Notes on Chagga Customs," 67; Marealle, "The Wachagga of Kilimanjaro," 53; Rogers, "The Search for Political Focus," 35.
96. Dundas, *Kilimanjaro and Its People*, 49.
97. E. E. Evans-Pritchard, *The Nuer: A Description of the Modes of Livelihood and Political Institutions of a Nilotic People* (Oxford: At the Clarendon Press, 1940), 5.

98. Wimmelbücker, *Kilimanjaro*, 83; see also Stahl, *History of the Chagga*, 339.
99. B. Gutmann, "The African Standpoint," *Africa* 8, no. 1 (1935): 1.
100. See Johnston, *The Kilimanjaro Expedition*, 437–8; Moore, "The Chagga of Kilimanjaro," 30.
101. Dundas, *Kilimanjaro and Its People*, 209–10.
102. See Moore, "The Chagga of Kilimanjaro," 30; Dundas, *Kilimanjaro and Its People*, 210–11.
103. Le Roy, *Au Kilima-Ndjaro*, 179.
104. See Krapf, *Travels, Researches and Missionary Labours*, 243; Le Roy, *Au Kilima-Ndjaro*, 279; W. W. Jones, "African Dogouts," *Tanganyika Notes and Record* 11 (1941): 11–12.
105. Krapf, *Travels, Researches, and Labours*, 243.
106. See Marealle, *Maisha ya Mchagga*, 25, 39; and Marealle, "Notes on Chagga Customs," 69–70.
107. Krapf, *Travels, Researches and Missionary Labours*, 237.
108. Krapf, *Travels, Researches and Missionary Labours*, 244.
109. See Krapf, *Travels, Researches and Missionary Labours*, 243, 252.
110. Le Roy, *Au Kilima-Ndjaro*, 184–88 and *passim*.
111. Johnston, "The People of Eastern Equatorial Africa," 6.
112. Johnston, *The Kilimanjaro Expedition*, 7–8.
113. Krapf, "Mount Kenia," 749.
114. Five women chiefs stand out in Chagga history: Mashina of Mamba, early 1800s; Tarimbo, who succeeded Mashina; Msanya of Marangu, c.1850s–60s; Machaki of Moshi, c.1851–61; and Manka Lokila of Kibosho, c.1867–71.
115. See Stahl, *History of the Chagga*, 56; Stahl, "Outline of Chagga History," 38–39.
116. Wimmelbücker, *Kilimanjaro*, 277.
117. Rebmann, "Narrative of a Journey to Madjame, in Jagga." *Church Missionary Intelligencer* 1, no. 272–76 (1849/50): 22; Rogers, "The Search for Political Focus," 67–68.
118. Krapf, *Travels, Researches and Missionary Labours*, 238, 241.
119. Johnston, *The Kilimanjaro Expedition*, 110. Called Mchau in childhood, then Makindara, which evolved into Mandara, this Chagga chief was also known by his initiation name Rindi.
120. Krapf, *Travels, Researches and Missionary Labours*, 238, 253.
121. Stahl, *History of the Chagga*, 169.
122. Le Roy, *Au Kilima-Ndjaro*, 188, 190.
123. See Marealle and Kishimba, *Historia ya Kanisa la Kiinjili la Kilutheri*, 19; Wimmelbücker, *Kilimanjaro*, 291–2.
124. See Dundas, *Asili na Habari za Wachagga*, 23, 28–29.
125. Le Roy, *Au Kilima-Ndjaro*, 279; see also Johnston, *The Kilimanjaro Expedition*, 96, 101; and

Dundas, *Asili na Habari za Wachagga*, 54.

126. See Marealle, "Notes on Chagga Customs," 68; Stahl, *History of the Chagga*, 103, 107, 110, 114; Rogers, "The Search for Political Focus," 69–70.
127. Krapf, *Travels, Researches and Missionary Labours*, 238; Rebmann, "Narrative of a Journey to Jagga," 18.
128. Meyer, *Across the African Glaciers*, 111; Le Roy, *Au Kilima-Ndjaro*, 277.
129. Krapf, *Travels, Researches and Missionary Labours*, 259.
130. Johnston, *The Kilimanjaro Expedition*, 97–98.
131. Le Roy, *Au Kilima-Ndjaro*, 232.
132. Stahl, *History of the Chagga*, 106, 113; Malya, *Wamarangu*, 74.
133. Chief's councillors at Taveta were also called *wachili*. See Hollis, "Notes on the History and Customs," 106.
134. Moore, *Social Facts and Fabrications*, 148–9.
135. Dundas, *Kilimanjaro and Its People*, 32, 50; Meyer, *Across East African Glaciers*, 114. Meyer's estimates of five hundred to eight hundred residents per chiefdom and a total of forty-six thousand for the whole Chagga population seem too small to reliably explain the amount of activity described around the mountain at that time.
136. Dundas, *Kilimanjaro and Its People*, 40.
137. Johnston, *The Kilimanjaro Expedition*, 443; Johnston, "The People of Eastern Equatorial Africa," 14.
138. Stahl, *History of Kilimanjaro*, 364.
139. Dundas, *Asili na Habari za Wachagga*, 149.
140. Dundas, *Kilimanjaro and Its People*, 50; Stahl, *History of the Chagga*, 285; Rogers, "The Search for Political Focus," 95.
141. Dundas, *Asili na Habari za Wachagga*, 88–89.
142. Krapf, *Travels, Researches and Missionary Labours*, 249. On dating Rengua's reign, see Stahl, *History of the Chagga*, 94.
143. See I. N. Kimambo, "Environmental Control and Hunger in the Mountain Plains of Northeastern Tanzania," in *Custodians of the Land: Ecology and Culture in the History of Tanzania*, ed. G. Maddox, J. Giblin, and I. N. Kimambo (London: James Currey, 1996), 88–89. Also see Moore, "The Chagga of Kilimanjaro," 7–11; and Wimmelbücker, *Kilimanjaro*, 95. Rombo survives today as an administrative district and a parliamentary constituency.
144. Dundas, *Kilimanjaro and Its People*, 67–76; Dundas, *Asili na Habari za Wachagga*, 67–72; Stahl, *History of the Chagga*, 346–50; Moore, "The Chagga of Kilimanjaro," 7–11; Malya, *Wamarangu*, 27–28.

145. Moore, "The Chagga of Kilimanjaro," 11; Kimambo, "Environmental Control and Hunger," 89; Al-Amin bin Ali Mazrui, *The History of the Mazrui Dynasty of Mombasa*, trans. J. McL. Ritchie (Oxford: Oxford University Press, 1999), 5.
146. See Johnston, *The Kilimanjaro Expedition*, 441; Johnston, "The People of Eastern Equatorial Africa," 13; Le Roy, *Au Kilima-Ndjaro*, 276, 279.
147. See Le Roy, *Au Kilima-Ndjaro*, 278–9.
148. Stahl, *History of the Chagga*, 72.
149. See Dundas, *Asili na Habari za Wachagga*, 143–4.
150. Johnston, *The Kilimanjaro Expedition*, 95–96.
151. Krapf, *Travels, Researches and Missionary Labours*, 240, 242, 248–9, 259–61.
152. See Johnston, *The Kilimanjaro Expedition*, 94, 98–102; Meyer, *Across East African Glaciers*, 101; Stahl, "Outline of Chagga History," 43.
153. See Marealle and Kishimba, *Historia ya Kanisa la Kiinjili la Kilutheri*, 22; Dundas, *Asili na Habari za Wachagga*, 137.
154. Mandara, "Invitation from the King of Chagga," *Church Missionary Intelligencer*, New Series 3 (1878): 448–9; Dundas, *Kilimanjaro and Its People*, 97.
155. See Fitch and Wray, "The First Year of the Chagga Mission," 555–6; Meyer, *Across East African Glaciers*, 89; 96–98, 102; Le Roy, *Au Kilima-Ndjaro*, 202–4.
156. Le Roy, *Au Kilima-Ndjaro*, 279.
157. Dundas, *Asili na Habari za Wachagga*, 138–39; Meyer, *Across East African Glaciers*, 112.

CHAPTER 3. FACTS AND FICTION ABOUT EARLY KILIMANJARO GUIDES

Parts of this chapter originally appeared in sections of Leslie Anne Hadfield, "Historical Change in Porter Work on Kilimanjaro," in *Protected Areas in Northern Tanzania: Local Communities, Land Use Change, and Management Challenges*, ed. Jeffrey O. Durrant, Emanuel H. Martin, Kokel Melubo, Ryan R. Jensen, Leslie A. Hadfield, Perry J. Hardin, Laurie Weisler (Cham, Switzerland: Springer, 2020). https://doi.org/10.1007/978-3-030-43302-4_3.

1. Paul E. Lovejoy and Catherine Coquery-Vidrovitch, *The Workers of African Trade* (Beverly Hills: Sage Publications, 1985); Stephen J. Rockel, *Carriers of Culture: Labor on the Road in Nineteenth-Century East Africa*, Social History of Africa (Portsmouth: Heinemann, 2006); Stephen J. Rockel, "'A Nation of Porters': The Nyamwezi and the Labour Market in Nineteenth-Century Tanzania," *Journal of African History* 41, no. 2 (2000): 173–95.
2. Robert B. Munson, "The Landscape of German Colonialism: Mt. Kilimanjaro and Mt. Meru, CA. 1890–1916" (PhD diss., Boston University, 2005). Some Chagga sold enslaved

people to these caravans who may have used enslaved people as porters before selling them when they reached the coast.

3. Rockel, "A Nation of Porters," 173–95.
4. Rockel, "A Nation of Porters,"184.
5. Annie Lenoble-Bart and François Constantin, "Mount Kilimanjaro: From History to Symbol," in *Mount Kilimanjaro: Mountain, Memory, Modernity*, ed. François Bart, François Devenne, and Milline J. Mbonile, trans. Taffy Martin (Dar es Salaam: Mkuki na Nyota Publishers, 2006), 6.
6. Harry Hamilton Johnston, *The Kilimanjaro Expedition: A Record of Scientific Exploration in Eastern Equatorial Africa* (London: K. Paul, Trench, and Co., 1886), 48.
7. Hans Meyer, *Across East African Glaciers: An Account of the First Ascent of Kilimanjaro*, trans. E.H.S. Calder (London: George Philip & Son, 1891), 37, 41.
8. Johnston, *The Kilimanjaro Expedition*, 247. His promise of two men coming from the Calcutta Botanical Gardens fell through, leaving him to improvise with two Zanzibari men who "were so exacting and difficult to deal with" that he let them go when they arrived at Moshi. He complained of having to do all the work himself afterwards, since his regular porters did not do it according to his liking.
9. Johnston, *The Kilimanjaro Expedition*, 46.
10. Johnston, *The Kilimanjaro Expedition*, 57.
11. Rockel, "Nation of Porters," 182.
12. Boris Michel, "Making Mount Kilimanjaro German: Nation Building and Heroic Masculinity in the Colonial Geographies of Hans Meyer," *Transactions of the Institute of British Geographers*, 44, no. 3 (2018), 7, https://doi-org.erl.lib.byu.edu/10.1111/tran.12283.
13. Meyer, *Across East African Glaciers*, 30–31.
14. Meyer, *Across East African Glaciers*, 48.
15. Ter Ellingson, *The Myth of the Noble Savage* (Oakland: University of California Press, 2001).
16. Robert B. Munson, *The Nature of Christianity in Northern Tanzania: Environmental and Social Change 1890–1916* (Lanham: Lexington Books, 2013); Munson, "The Landscape of German Colonialism."
17. Cameron M. Burns, *Kilimanjaro & East Africa: A Climbing and Trekking Guide*, 2nd ed. (Seattle: The Mountaineers Books, 2006); Deogratias Mushi, "Do We Know These Facts About Mount Kilimanjaro?" *Tanzania Daily News*, November 13, 2011, allafrica.com.
18. Wilhelm Methner, "The Ascent of Mount Kilimanjaro: An Outline of its History by Wilhelm Methner of Stolberg (Harz), former District Officer in Moshi," n.d., Box 30, KMCA.
19. "First Woman Climber of Kilimanjaro," East Africa, February 23, 1928, *The Daily Mail*,

Gillman's Scrapbook, Box 1, KMCA.

20. Audrey Salkeld, *Kilimanjaro: To the Roof of Africa* (Washington, D.C.: National Geographic, 2002), 137–42.
21. R. A. Dummer, Letter to the Editor, "Kilimanjaro," n.d.; "The First British Ascent: Mr. West Reaches Summit in 1914," n.d. unidentified newspaper; typed note "Cape Times of 21/4/1922," Gillman's Scrapbook, Box 1, KMCA.
22. Methner, "The Ascent of Mount Kilimanjaro."
23. "The First Woman to Climb Kilimanjaro," *The Ice-Cap: The Journal of the Kilimanjaro Mountain Club*, no. 9, April 2000, Box 13, KMCA, 11.
24. "The First Woman to Climb Kilimanjaro," 14–15.
25. Clement Gillman, Letter to the Editor, *Dar-es-Salaam Times*, November 3, 1921, Gillman's Scrapbook, Box 1, KMCA.
26. "Extract from my Diary," no. 55, *Dar-es-Salaam Times*, November 5, 1921, Gillman's Scrapbook, Box 1, KMCA, 140–42.
27. "Kibo Conquered Again: The Climb on Kilimanjaro," *Dar es-Salam Times*, November 26, 1921, Gillman's Scrapbook, Box 1, KMCA.
28. See interviews with Atanus Isack, Christo Amani Fataeli Mbando, David Sifueli Mtui, Elias Andrea Minja, Heavenlight Israel Mtui, Felix Anasa Olotu, Gibson Minja, Morgan Eliakimu Minja, Samwel Toma Mosha, Stanley Mosha, and Zakaria Fataeli Mtui.
29. The following oral history participants were related directly to early guides and shared information closer to the written record: Heavenlight Israel Mtui (descendant of Jonathan Mtui), Gibson Minja (related to Lawuo and Mosha, but did not necessarily say these things), Morgan Eliakimu Minja, Samwel Toma Mosha (son of Toma Mosha), Zakaria Fataeli Mtui.
30. Basic information about the Kibo Hotel, presumably obtained from the hotel, accessed on the following websites in August 2025 list 1886 as the date it was built: travelweekly.com, atrsafari.com. This date was not confirmed by evidence. Hans Meyer did not write about the Kibo Hotel when describing his expeditions.
31. Peter von Lany, "A brief early history of von Lany family at Marangu," personal document shared with authors, July 31, 2025; "Marangu Hotel—Our Story," Marangu Hotel, http://www.maranguhotel.com/our-story. See also Frant Paul, *V Rovníkové Africe* (Prague: Orbis, 1931) and Jiří Baum, *Africkou divočinou: Autem z Prahy k Mysu Dobré Naděje* (Prague: published by the author, 1933).
32. Apparently, Reusch overheard two British officers who had not made it to the top of Kilimanjaro "disparage the soft and meek missionaries," so he decided to attempt to summit and succeeded in his first try in 1926. He was the seventh person to write his

name in the book Hans Meyer left and brought the book down with him and took a photo with a Christian flag at the top. He climbed three more times in 1926 and by the end of 1935, had reached Kibo and Mawenzi twenty-five times. "Kilimanjaro became Reusch's passion." See Daniel H. Johnson, *Loyalty: A Biography of Richard Gustavovich Reusch* (St. Cloud: SunRay Printing, 2008), 149.

33. The club initially was called the East African Mountain Club. It included Mt. Kenya and the Rwenzori mountains and liaised with sections of the club established in those places at various times.
34. "The Mountain Club of East Africa," *Ice Cap*, no. 1, 1932, Box 26, KMCA, 75.
35. "Kilimanjaro," Box 2, KMCA, 1, 7.
36. Minutes of the General Meeting of the East African Mountain Club, Mawenzi Hotel, Moshi, February 20, 1930, Box 2, KMCA.
37. Methner, "The Ascent of Mount Kilimanjaro."
38. Bernard Leeman, "Kinyala Johannes Lauwo (1871–1996): The World's Oldest Person and the First Known Successful Climber of Mount Kilimanjaro," Academia.edu, 2016. See also "Yohani Kinyala Lauwo," Mount-Kilimanjaro-Wiki, n.d., http://kilimanjaro.bplaced.net/wiki/index.php?title=Yohani_Kinyala_Lauwo; "Yohani Kinyala Lauwo," Forum, nTZ—Information about northern Tanzania, https://ntz.info.
39. Ubatizo wa Watu Wazima, 1908–1933, Mamba Kotela, year 1918, group 81, 161; Wanafunzi wa Ubatizo, 1907–1927, Mamba Kotela, 1917, group 83, 164, Evangelical Lutheran Church in Tanzanian-Northern Diocese Archive (ELCT-ND).
40. List of Guides and Porters 1938, Box 4, KMCA.
41. Gillman's Point 1953–1954 Summit Book, February 25, 1953, Box 27, KMCA.
42. "Meyer and Purtscheller Were Not Alone," January 1, 1990. *Tanzanian Affairs*, www.tzaffairs.org.
43. Meyer, *Across East African Glaciers*; Hans Meyer, "Ascent to the Summit of Kilima-Njaro," *Proceedings of the Royal Geographical Society and Monthly Record of Geography* 12, no. 6 (June 1890): 331–45.
44. Boris Michel, "Making Mount Kilimanjaro German: Nation Building and Heroic Masculinity in the Colonial Geographies of Hans Meyer," *Transactions of the Institute of British Geographers*, 2018, 1–16, https://doi-org.erl.lib.byu.edu/10.1111/tran.12283.
45. Interview participants who were related included: David Sifueli Mtui, Elias Andrea Minja, Heavenlight Israeli Mtui, Gibson Emmanuel Minja, Stanley Mosha, Zakaria Fataeli Mtui, Samson Lauwo.
46. Atanus Isak Lekule, interview with ES, August 19, 2022, Samwel Toma Mosh Mosha, interview with ES and RA, August 16, 2021, Marangu; Atanus Isak Lekule, interview with

ES, August 19, 2022, Marangu; Gibson Minja, interview with ES and LH, August 7, 2021, Marangu.

47. Elias Andrea Minja, interview with ES, August 17, 2022, Marangu.
48. Frant Paul wrote that three Chagga men who had climbed Kibo before were available to guide his group going with some of the Lany family in 1930. They employed one named "Johannu" who mobilized porters. This could have possibly been Lauwo. See Paul, *V Rovníkové Africe*, 277.
49. Samson was known by Atanus Isack as Lauwo's grandson who worked on the mountain along with many from the same clan. He established the company Kilimanjaro Bound.
50. The following said Lauwo trained their fathers or the men who trained them: Atanus Isack, Christo Amani Fataeli Mbando, and David Sifueli Mtui (who said his father married into Lauwo's family).
51. Heavenlight Israeli Mtui, interview with ES and RA, August 24, 2021, Marangu Mshiri; Fredy Solomon Mtui, interview with ES and RA, August 25, 2021, Marangu; Felix Anasa Olotu, interview with ES, June 20, 2022, Himo; Gibson Emmanuel Minja, interview with ES and LH, August 7, 2021, Marangu; interview with ES and RA, August 16, 2021, Marangu.
52. Samwel Toma Mosha said that Lauwo had a misunderstanding with Kibo Hotel. Lauwo wanted a bigger salary, so they told him to retire (Samwel Toma Mosha, interview with ES, August 18, 2022, Marangu).
53. Peter's Hut Book 1937–1943, February 10–13, 1943, Box 27, KMCA.
54. Peter's Hut Book 1943–1945, October 29–34, 1943, Box 27, KMCA.
55. Paul, *V Rovníkové Africe*, 277–93.
56. Mangi Mwitori to Bwana Yohannes Lauwo, Kiongozi Mkuu wakusaidia Wapanda Mlima Kilimanjaro, u.f.s., January 20, 1959, Box 6, KMCA.
57. One Marangu elderly guide, Morgan Eliakimu Minja, remembered Mlombare as the very first guide from Masia. Morgan Eliakimu Minja, interview with ES, August 16, 2022, Marangu.
58. He also may be listed in the mountain books in 1960 (see "Thomas Ndewigs, guide, Marangu; Hermann Mtui, acc. guide, Marangu," Gillman's Point 1959–1960 Summit Book, March 4, 1960, Box 27, KMCA).
59. Samwel Toma Mosha, interview with ES, August 18, 2022, Marangu.
60. Book for Guide Thomas Mosha, no. 3, July 14, 1947, Box 27, KMCA.
61. Book for Guide Thomas Mosha, no. 3, February 1, 1948, Box 27, KMCA.
62. Book for Guide Thomas Mosha, no. 3, July 22–August 2, 1955, Box 27, KMCA.

63. Book for Guide Thomas Mosha, no. 3, September 23–38, 1951, Box 27, KMCA.
64. Elias Andrea Minja, interview with ES, August 17, 2022, Marangu.
65. Peter's Hut Book 1937–1943, February 28—March 1, 1942, Box 27, KMCA.
66. Peter's Hut Book 1943–1945, August 25, 1944, Box 27, KMCA.
67. Peter's Hut Book 1943–1945, September 1, 1944, Box 27, KMCA.
68. Peter's Hut Book 1943–1945, November 24, 1945, Box 27, KMCA.
69. Minutes of the Committee Meeting, April 29, 1951, Box 3, KMCA.
70. Richard Reusch, "Mount Kilimanjaro and its Ascent," *Tanganyika Notes and Records* no. 64, March 1965, Kilimanjaro, 132.
71. R. J. W. Roome, "The Wondrous Beauty of The Crown of Africa," *The East African Standard*, September 1, 1928, Gillman's Scrapbook, Box 1, KMCA.
72. Hon. Secretary and Treasurer to Mangi Petro Iteshi Mareale, February 24, 1947, Box 6, KMCA.
73. In the written record, guides listed as Daudi Jonathan and Faeteli Jonathan are very likely the same people, listing their father's name as a surname, rather than the clan name, Mtui. Another guide prominent in the written record in the 1950s and 1960s, Effata—twice listed as Effata Jonathan—could also be a son of Jonathan Mtui. A 1958 list of "enlisted" mountain guides includes Johane Rauya, Thoma Ndewicho, Daudi Jonathan, Effata Jonathan, and Syara Kisaka, as well as assistant guides Fataeli and Safari Kaya Kisaka. Bruehl noted: "All of them have been up the Mountain during the last two weeks and I had to wait to find out about their fathers name" (Letter from A. Bruehl to Hon. Secr. Treas. of the Mountain Club, Mr. J. Hughes, January 24, 1958, Box 6, KMCA; Gillman's Point 1959–1960 Summit Book, March 3, 1960, Box 27, KMCA.)
74. See also Letter from Mrs. Bruehl, Kibo Hotel to Hon. Treasurer/Secretary of Kilimanjaro Mountain Club, Mr. N. Emmanuel, July 10, 1959, Box 6, KMCA (wherein Bruehl mentions Lauwo's retirement and Safari and Syara Kisaka as brothers who were both working as guides).
75. Kimatare guided Peter von Lany, grandson of Martin Bohdan von Lany, in 1972, according to Peter von Lany's personal correspondence with Hadfield in July 2025.
76. Samwel Toma Mosha, interview with ES, August 18, 2022, Marangu.
77. Gibson Emmanuel Minja, interview with ES and LH, August 7, 2021.
78. Atanus Isack, interview with ES and RA, August 23, 2021.
79. Heavenlight Israeli Mtui, interview with ES and RA, August 24, 2021, Marangu Mshiri.
80. Christo Amani Fataeli Mbando, interview with ES and RA, August 23, 2021, Marangu.
81. Zakaria Fataeli Mtui, interview with ES and RA, August 23, 2021, Marangu.

CHAPTER 4. THE KILIMANJARO CLIMBING TOURISM INDUSTRY

1. Anna Thompson-Carr, "Guided Mountaineering," in *Mountaineering Tourism*, ed. Ghazali Musa, James E. S. Higham, and Anna Thompson-Carr (London: Routledge, 2017), 85–100.
2. Paul Beedie, "A History of Mountaineering Tourism," in *Mountaineering Tourism*, ed. Ghazali Musa, James E. S. Higham, and Anna Thompson-Carr (London: Routledge, 2017), 48.
3. Jane Carruthers, "The Royal National Park, KwaZulu Natal: Mountaineering, Tourism and Nature Conservation in South Africa's First National Park c. 1896 to c. 1947," *Environment and History* 19, no. 4 (November 2013), 459–86; Farieda Kahn, "From Carriers to Climbers: The Cape Province Mountain Club, 1930s to 1960s—an untold story," in *Exploring Decolonising Themes in SA Sport History: Issues and Challenges*, ed. Francois Johannes Cleophas (Stellenbosch: African Sun Media, 2018), 67–80; Farieda Khan, "Apartheid Mountaineering: Race, Politics, and the History of the University of Cape Town Mountain and Ski Club, 1933–1969," *The International Journal of the History of Sport* 36, no. 1 (2019): 48–66.
4. Von Franz Grassler, "Hohe Ziele alpenferner Sektionen: die Dreitausender der Ostalpen und der Kilimandscharo," *Alpenvereinsjahrbuch*, 188 (1994): 235; Address by the President [Dr:] R. Reusch at the Annual General Meeting August 1953, Box 30, KMCA.
5. The Mountain Club of East Africa (Kilimanjaro Section) Information on the climbing of Kilimanjaro (Kibo and Mawenzi), n.d. Box 3, KMCA.
6. Erica's three older brothers—Martin, Ludwig, and Milan—and younger sister Ruth all spent significant time at Marangu before making their life elsewhere (although Martin junior passed away in 1930). Ruth was the youngest woman to climb Kilimanjaro in the early 1940s at the age of sixteen.
7. From Honorary Secretary and Treasurer of the Mountain Club of East Africa to Mangi Petro Itoshi, Marangu, c/o the District Officer, Moshi, July 28, 1938, Box 6, 1933–1959, KMCA; From Honorary Secretary [of Mountain Club] to Herrn. Th. Kloss, Kibo Hotel, Marangu, August 11, 1938, Box 6, 1933–1959, KMCA.
8. From Honorary Secretary and Treasurer to Mangi Petro Itosi, by Kind Favour of the District Officer Moshi, September 5, 1938, Box 6, 1933–1959, KMCA; From Mountain View, Marangu, to Honorary Secretary and Treasurer of the E. A. Mountain Club Moshi, September 11, 1938, Box 6, 1933–1959, KMCA.
9. From Honorary Secretary [of Mountain Club] to Herrn. Th. Kloss, Kibo Hotel, Marangu, August 11, 1938, Box 6, 1933–1959, KMCA.
10. From Mangi Marangu P. I. M to Honorary Secretary, E. A. Mountain Club, Moshi, March

13, 1939, Box 6, 1933–1959, KMCA. In this letter, the *mangi* pleads for the bill to be settled and writes, "I remember having written to you and request you to cease to correspond with me only on the matters that concern the climbings and porters supply for the mountain business as I feel that I have no time sufficient to meet this bit of service. I again beg to state that from now on I shall not be able to give further assistance to the club. You may in next time write to Mr Kloss or Mr Lany who will send for the porters and conduct the caravans. Excuse me for the trouble. Yours Obedient Servant."

11. Mountain Club of East Africa to Mrs. Lany, July 17, 1946, Box 6, 1933–1959, KMCA.
12. The Mountain Club of East Africa (Kilimanjaro Section) Information on the Climbing of Kilimanjaro (Kibo and Mawenzi), n.d., Box 3, KMCA; From the District Officer, Moshi, Northern Province to the Honorary Secretary, the Mountain Club of East Africa, Kilimanjaro Section, July 18, 1938, Box 6, 1933–1959, KMCA.
13. Ag Honorable Secretary to Mr. E. Luternauer, Kibo Hotel, Mrs. E. Lany Marangu Guest House, October 3, 1942, Box 6, 1933–1959, KMCA; Ag Honorable Secretary to Mrs. E. Lany, October 3, 1942, Box 6, 1933–1959, KMCA.
14. Peter's Hut Book 1943–1945, February 16, 1944, Box 27, KMCA.
15. There were other times when the guides could not accompany visitors and they did not make it all the way (such as the time Toma/Mlombare fell ill and the cook, likely Fuateli, could only take the visitor to the crater rim (Peter's Hut Book 1943–1945, February 11, 1944 and February 14, 1944, Box 27, KMCA).
16. The Mountain Club of East Africa (Kilimanjaro Section) Information on the Climbing of Kilimanjaro (Kibo and Mawenzi), n.d., Box 3, KMCA.
17. Peter's Hut Book 1943–1945, May 30, 1945–June 3, 1945, Box 27, KMCA.
18. Book for Guide Thomas Mosha, no. 2, March 1–6, 1936, Box 27, KMCA.
19. Book for Guide Thomas Mosha, no. 2, January 19, 1944, Box 27, KMCA.
20. Book for Guide Thomas Mosha, no. 2, February 9, [1940], Box 27, KMCA.
21. Book for Guide Thomas Mosha, no. 3, July 2, 1952, Box 27, KMCA.
22. Book for Guide Thomas Mosha, no. 3, March 25, 1949, Box 27, KMCA.
23. Mawenzi Hut Book 1952–1956, January 1, 1953, Box 27, KMCA.
24. The entry for January 5–January 8, [1956] reads: "along with guide Johanna + Fateli attempted the peak by a gully rout described by Johanne." Mawenzi Hut Book 1952–1956, Box 27, KMCA.
25. Book for Guide Thomas Mosha, no. 2, February 9, [1940], Box 27, KMCA.
26. Book for Guide Thomas Mosha, no. 2, January 5–19, 1941, Box 27, KMCA.
27. Peter's Hut Book 1943–1945, January 17, 1944, Box 27, KMCA.
28. Peter's Hut Book 1937–1943, January 6–9, 1942, Box 27, KMCA.

29. Book for Guide Thomas Mosha, no. 3, February 19, 1950, Box 27, KMCA.
30. Peter's Hut Book 1943–1945, August 24, 1944, Box 27, KMCA.
31. Peter's Hut Book 1937–1943, August 2, 1941, Box 27, KMCA.
32. Book for Guide Thomas Mosha, no. 3, October 15, 1952, Box 27, KMCA. It reads: "Thomas literally pulled me up the last part of the climb. Without his assistance I should never have reached the top. I am most grateful. Joan Hicks."
33. Peter's Hut Book 1943–1945, September 29–October 3, 1943, Box 27, KMCA.
34. Peter's Hut Book 1943–1945, September 16–20, 1943, Box 27, KMCA.
35. Kaiser Wilhelm Spitze Book 1941–1957, January 4, 1946, Box 27, KMCA.
36. Reusch claimed that he trained three guides in "Address by the President [Dr:] R. Reusch at the Annual General Meeting August 1953," Box 30, KMCA. Peter von Lany reported that Kimatare told him in 1972 that his father, Ludwig, taught him how to be a guide (conversation with Hadfield, July 21, 2025 and August 4, 2025). Ludwig von Lany's modeling of how to guide could be reflected in the description of Ludwig helping arrange supplies and lead the group of Jiří Baum and Frank V. Foit in 1931. See Jiří Baum, *Africkou divočinou: Autem z Prahy k Mysu Dobré Naděje* (Prague: nákladem vlastním, 1933), 145–50.
37. See also Zakaria Fataeli Mtui, interview with ES and RA, August 23, 2021, Marangu; Heavenlight Israeli Mtui, interview with ES and RA, August 24, 2021, Marangu Mshiri.
38. Gibson Emmanuel Minja, interview with ES and RA, August 16, 2021; Julius Naftali Tawa, interview with ES and RA, August 25, 2021, Marangu.
39. Interview participants who talked about death on the mountain included: David Sifueli Mtui, Elias Andrea Minja, Fredy Solomon Mtui, Kamili Iiatonga Mtui, Zakaria Fataeli Mtui.
40. Those who talked about rescue procedures included: Christoamani Fataeli Mbando, Heavenlight Israeli Mtui, Jarid Filipo Minja, George Kimaro, Stanley Meshack Mosha. Those who talked about stretchers or cars include: Anasen Ndenimfoo, George Kimaro, Gibson, Emmanuel Minja, Stanley Meshack Mosha.
41. Book for Guide Thomas Mosha, no. 2, January 29–February 2, 1945, Box 27, KMCA.
42. Book for Guide Thomas Mosha, no. 2, March 17, 1945, Box 27, KMCA.
43. Peter's Hut book 1937–1943, February 17–22, 1943, Box 27, KMCA.
44. "Another Commendable Act," Letter From Mangi Mkuu Marealle II to District Commissioner Bryce, June 27, 1955, Box 6, 1933–1959, KMCA.
45. Minutes of the Annual General Meeting of the Mountain Club of East Africa (Kilimanjaro Section) Held in the Hellenic Club, Moshi, on April 10, 1959, Box 3, KMCA.
46. Book for Guide Thomas Mosha, no. 2, January 30, 1939, February 17, 1941, Box 27, KMCA.

47. Peter's Hut Book 1937–1943, March 16–20, 1943, Box 27, KMCA.
48. Peter's Hut Book 1937–1943, March 16–20, 1943, Box 27, KMCA.
49. Peter's Hut Book 1937–1943, March 24, 1942, Box 27, KMCA.
50. Peter's Hut Book 1937–1943, March 9, 1943, Box 27, KMCA.
51. Peter's Hut Book 1943–1945, September 29–October 3, 1943, Box 27, KMCA.
52. Peter's Hut Book 1943–1945, January 17, 1944, Box 27, KMCA.
53. Letter from Hughes to Peake Regarding climbing arrangements and discussions, December 30, 1957, Box 4, KMCA. This is likely the deed for which Lauwo was honored and given a watch.
54. From Hon. Secretary and Treasurer to Mangi Petro Iteshi Mareale, February 24, 1947, Box 6, 1933–1959, KMCA; Letter from Ungerer to Mangi Marealle, February 24, 1947, Box 4, KMCA.
55. Letter from Bruehl to Ellwell-Sutton, November 29, 1949, Box 4, KMCA, Letter from Bruehl to Youngdale, September 12, 1950, Box 4, KMCA; Letter from Bruehl to Hughes, May 4, 1954, Box 4, KMCA; Letter from Bruehl to Bryce, August 5, 1955, Box 4, KMCA.
56. Peter's Hut Book 1937–1943, September 25, 1941, Box 27, KMCA.
57. Peter's Hut Book 1937–1943, June 7–9/10, 1943, Box 27, KMCA.
58. Peter's Hut Book 1943–1945, August 9, 1944, Box 27, KMCA.
59. Book for Guide Thomas Mosha, no. 2, February 12–18, 1939, Box 27, KMCA.
60. Book for Guide Thomas Mosha, no. 2, February 24, 1945, Box 27, KMCA. This man also complained that they did not follow his order or produce tea on the way—he seemed to be demanding, expecting them to meet every wish and for him to direct their actions rather than the guide.
61. Peter von Lany, Zoom conversation with Hadfield, July 21, 2025.
62. The Mountain Club of East Africa (Kilimanjaro Section) Information on the Climbing of Kilimanjaro (Kibo and Mawenzi), n.d., Box 3, KMCA.
63. Letter from Bruehl to Hughes, July 10, 1957, Box 4, KMCA. They wrote to a Mr/Mrs. McQueen, "Regarding porters the average climber is a [tourist] and requires a plush safari. If you are willing to carry most of your equipment you can manage with a guide. We are not keen on porters going without a guide."
64. Allen Godfrey, interview with EM and FB, September 3, 2021, Machame; Frank Leonard Nnko, interview with EM and FB, September 16, 2021, Arusha; Joshua Clement Ruhimbi, interview with EM and FB, September 15, 2021, Arusha.
65. Book for Guide Thomas Mosha, no. 2, February 10, 1937, Box 27, KMCA.
66. "Hero of 20,000 Ft. Climb," 1935, Box 30, KMCA.
67. Letter from Ginner to Worsley, January 11, 1938, Box 8, KMCA.

68. Matthew V. Bender, “Being ‘Chagga’: Natural Resources, Political Activism, and Identity on Kilimanjaro,” *Journal of African History* 54, no. 2 (2013): 199–220; N. Thomas Håkansson, Mats Widgren, and Lowe Börjeson, “Introduction: Historical and Regional Perspectives on Landscape Transformations in Northeastern Tanzania, 1850–2000,” *International Journal of African Historical Studies* 41, no. 3 (2008): 369–82.
69. Heavenlight Israeli Mtui, interview with ES and RA, August 24, 2021, Marangu Mshiri; Samwel Toma Mosha, interview with ES and RA, August 16, 2021, Marangu.
70. Interview participants who commented about this kind of weighing include: Christoamani Fataeli Mbando, Elias Andrea Minja, Fredy Solomon Mtui, George Kimaro, Heavenlight Israeli Mtui, Jarid Filipo Minja, Morgan Eliakimu Minja, Samwel Toma Mosha, Stanley Mosha.
71. Letter from Mrs. A. Bruehl, Kibo Hotel Kilimanjaro to P. Campbell, Esq., President, Mountain Club of Kenya, Nairobi, September 29, 1957, Box 6, 1933–1959, KMCA.
72. Paul, *V Rovníkové Africe*, 287.
73. Book for Guide Thomas Mosha, no. 2, February 12–18, 1939, Box 27, KMCA.
74. Peter’s Hut Book 1937–1943, March 24, 1942, Box 27, KMCA.
75. Kibo Hut Book 1939–1943, July 9, 1942, Box 27, KMCA.
76. Peter’s Hut Book 1943–1945, August 27, 1945, Box 27, KMCA.
77. Book for Guide Thomas Mosha, no. 3, July 14, 1947, Box 27, KMCA.
78. Book for Guide Thomas Mosha, no. 3, December 17, 1947, January 21, 1948, December 12, 1948, Box 27, KMCA. An entry on August 27, 1948, reads, “Can something be done about providing adequate clothing for the use of porters? Some of ours were in rags and felt the cold very much.”
79. Book for Guide Thomas Mosha, no. 3, September 23–28, 1951, Box 27, KMCA.
80. Letter from Ag Honorable Secretary to Mrs. E. Lany, October 3, 1942, Box 6, 1933–1959, KMCA.
81. Letter from A. Bruehl, Kibo Hotel, Hon. Secretary and Treasurer, Mr. Ellwell-Sutton, March 24, 1950, Box 6, 1933–1959, KMCA.
82. Peter’s Hut Book 1959–1961, February 19, 1960, Box 27, KMCA.
83. John W. Stauffacher, “Kilimanjaro,” n.d., Box 2, KMCA, 5.
84. Peter’s Hut Book 1937–1943, January 29, 1941, Box 27, KMCA; Book for Guide Thomas Mosha, no. 3, December 28, 1955-January 1, 1956, Box 27, KMCA.
85. Stanley Mosha interview with ES and RA, August 16, 2021, Marangu; Zakaria Fataeli Mtui, interview with ES and RA, August 23, 2021.
86. Letter from Lany to Youngdale, June 26, 1950, Box 4, KMCA. “If the mattresses have not been made yet I suggest that they would be made of light kapok stuffing, as the porters

always complain about the bed loads being too heavy." A later letter indicates they worked on getting the kapok (see Letter from A. Lany to Youngdale, September 19, 1950, Box 4, KMCA.

87. Peter's Hut Book 1937–1943, January 5–13, 1941, Box 27, KMCA.
88. Peter's Hut Book 1937–1943, March 9, 1943, Box 27, KMCA.
89. Peter's Hut Book 1943–1945, January 6, 1944, Box 27, KMCA.
90. Emmanuel Mongi, interview with ES and RA, August 19, 2021, Marangu Mshiri.
91. Single sheets Johannnes' Hut 1937–1949, September 3, 1937, Box 27, KMCA.
92. Peter's Hut Book 1943–1945, May 30–June 3, 1945, Box 27, KMCA.
93. David Sifueli Mtui, interview with ES and RA, August 24, 2021, Marangu Mshiri.
94. Gillman's Point Book 1947–1950, September 8, 1942, Box 27, KMCA.
95. Book for Guide Thomas Mosha, no. 2, October 6, 1937, Box 27, KMCA.
96. Stanley Mosha interview with ES and RA, August 16, 2021, Marangu.
97. Peter's Hut Book 1937–1943, July 29, 1941, Box 27, KMCA.
98. Jiri Hanzelka and Miroslav Zikmund, *Afrika—Snū a Skutečnosti* (Prague: Orbis, 1953).
99. Peter's Hut Book 1937–1943, June 12–15, 1942, Box 27, KMCA.
100. Peter's Hut Book 1937–1943, August 25, 1941, Box 27, KMCA.
101. Peter's Hut Book 1937–1943, February 15, 1942, Box 27, KMCA.
102. Book for Guide Thomas Mosha, no. 2, August 29, 1936, and September 2, 1936, Box 27, KMCA; Letter from A. E. Weirich to T. Kloss, Kibo Hotel, Marangu, October 15, 1932, Box 2, KMCA.
103. Book for Guide Thomas Mosha, no. 3, December 17, 1947, Box 27, KMCA; Book for Guide Thomas Mosha, no. 3, January 18, 1951, Box 27, KMCA.
104. Peter's Hut Book 1943–1945, July 9, 1945, Box 27, KMCA.
105. Peter's Hut Book 1937–1943, November 7, 1941, Box 27, KMCA.
106. Peter's Hut Book 1943–1945, September 1, 1944, Box 27, KMCA.
107. Peter's Hut Book 1943–1945, October 26–30, 1943, Box 27, KMCA.
108. Book for Guide Thomas Mosha, no. 3, July 2, 1952, Box 27, KMCA.
109. Letter from Honorary Secretary and Treasurer to Mangi Petro Itosi, By Kind Favour of the District Officer Moshi, September 5, 1938, Box 6, 1933–1959, KMCA.
110. Letter from Honorary Secretary, Mountain Club of East Africa, to Sir/Madam Re: Blankets for Mountain Safaris, July 13, 1943, Box 6, 1933–1959, KMCA.
111. Unsigned letter to Hon. Secretary, Mountain Club of East Africa, Old Moshi, October 8, 1943, Box 6, 1933–1959, KMCA.
112. Kibo Hotel Climbing list, from Mrs. G. Ungerer? to Mr. Ginner, secretary of the Mountain-Club Old-Moshi, August 28, 1945, Box 6, KMCA; Letter from Ginner to Lany,

July 17, 1945, Box 4, KMCA.

113. Letter from Mrs. Anne Bruehl to Mr. [Ungerer], April 21, 1947, Box 6, 1933–1959, KMCA; Letter from A. Bruehl, Kibo Hotel, Hon. Secretary and Treasurer to Mr. Ellwell-Sutton, November 29, 1949, Box 6, KMCA.
114. Letter from Mrs. Anne Bruehl to Mr. [Ungerer], April 21, 1947, Box 6, 1933–1959, KMCA; Letter from A. Bruehl, Kibo Hotel, Hon. Secretary and Treasurer to Mr. Ellwell-Sutton, November 29, 1949, Box 6, KMCA.
115. Note to Dr. Reusch, July 30, 1951, Box 6, KMCA; Letter from Geologist to the District Commissioner, Moshi, October 3, 1951, Box 6, KMCA; Letter from Youngdale to Reusch, July 30, 1951, Box 6, 1933–1959, KMCA.
116. Letter from District Commissioner and Vice President of the Mountain Club, John . . ., to Mrs. E. K. Lany, November 15, 1951, Box 6, KMCA.
117. Letter from Kibo Hotel Mrs. A. Bruehl to R. Clifford, Esq., Hon. Treasurer/Secretary of the Mountain Club Moshi, July 9, 1952, Box 6, KMCA; Letter from R. H. R. Clifford to Mrs. A. Bruehl, the Kibo Hotel Kilimanjaro, July 23, 1952, Box 6, KMCA.
118. Letter from Hughes to Bruehl, February 14, 1953, Box 4, KMCA.
119. Letter from Mrs. A. Bruehl, Kibo Hotel Kilimanjaro, to Mr. Bryce, August 5, 1955, Box 6, KMCA. Bruehl wrote: "I can't go into my papers yet as my office is not yet in order again, the fundis [carpenters] all being absent for maize harvesting etc." And, "My younger guides are all prepared to do the necessary repairs now, as their fields are in order and the work at my place nearly comes to an end."
120. Letter from Anne Bruehl, Kibo Hotel Kilimanjaro to the President, the Mountain Club of E. A. Tanganyika Section, the District Commissioner, Moshi, February 10, 1954, Box 6, KMCA. See also Book for Guide Thomas Mosha, no. 3, July 30, 1951–August 3, 1951, and August 12, 1935, Box 27, KMCA.
121. Letter from Mountain Club of East Africa to Mr. Weinrich, March 28, 1954, Box 6, KMCA.
122. Letter from Anne Bruehl, Kibo Hotel Kilimanjaro to the Hon. Secretary, the Mountain Club of E. A. Kilimanjaro Section, May 4, 1954, Box 6, KMCA.
123. A guide or porter who acted as cook was given an extra fifty cents per day. The Mountain Club of East Africa (Kilimanjaro Section) Information on the Climbing of Kilimanjaro (Kibo and Mawenzi), n.d., Box 3, KMCA; Letter from Bruehl to Hughes, January 16, 1957; Letter from Hughes to Bruehl, January 17, 1957, Box 4, KMCA. The guide Syara demanded more pay for some maintenance work on the toilets at the huts to the annoyance of Hughes, who wrote to Bruehl, "It is nice to see that Syara has developed a big head and I think we shall have to find one way of reducing it for him. If guides are not prepared to help the Club then I shall have no hesitation in taking away their

license to climb with parties using the Club Huts."

124. Letter from the Labour Officer [Ben Wilmot], Moshi to the Secretary, E. A. Mountain Club Kilimanjaro Section, September 23, 1953, Box 6, KMCA.
125. For more on this concept, see Emmanuel Chukwudi Eze, ed., *Race and the Enlightenment: A Reader* (Cambridge: Blackwell, 1997); Ter Ellingson, *The Myth of the Noble Savage* (University of California Press, 2001).
126. Alex Sutton, "Primitive Accumulation in the East Africa Groundnut Scheme," *Diplomacy & Statecraft* 35, no. 2 (2024): 338–62; Nicholas Westcott, *Imperialism and Development: The East African Groundnut Scheme and Its Legacy* (Woodbridge: James Currey, 2020).
127. Book for Guide Thomas Mosha, no. 3, August 26, 1949, Box 27, KMCA.
128. Letter from A. Bruehl, Kibo Hotel, Hon. Secretary and Treasurer to Mr. Ellwell-Sutton, November 29, 1949, Box 6, KMCA.
129. The Mountain Club of East Africa (Kilimanjaro Section) Information on the Climbing of Kilimanjaro (Kibo and Mawenzi), n.d., Box 3, KMCA.
130. Letter from David L. Sampson to Mr. Millard, November 8, 1951, Box 6, KMCA.
131. Letter from Hughes to . . ., October 8, 1953, Box 4, KMCA.
132. Letter from Hughes to Bruehl, December 21, 1954, Box 4, KMCA. Some correspondence between Mangi Mwitori of Vunjo and club secretary Ungerer shows distrust and annoyance at requests for wages. Penciled in as a response to the mangi's request to hire two soldiers to take care of Bismark Hut are the remarks that the need to guard against wild animals was "nonsense" and thus the wages and overall proposition was "inacceptable." Letter from Mangi Mwitori of Vunjo to Ungerer, March 11, 1947, Box 4, KMCA.
133. John W. Stauffacher, "Kilimanjaro," n.d., Box 2, KMCA, 5.
134. Peter's Hut Book 1937–1943, July 11, 1940, Box 27, KMCA.
135. Book for Guide Thomas Mosha, no. 2, January 5–19, 1941, Box 27, KMCA.
136. Book for Guide Thomas Mosha, no. 3, July 20–26, [1949], Box 27, KMCA.
137. Book for Guide Thomas Mosha, no. 3, August 26, 1949, Box 27, KMCA.
138. Paul, *V Rovníkové Africe*, 277–93.
139. Jiří Baum, *Africkou Divočinou*, 146, 148–50.
140. Hanzelka and Zikmund, *Afrika*, 118.
141. D. L. Busk, "Kilimanjaro," *Alpine Journal*, vol. 60 (1955), 100.
142. Book for Guide Thomas Mosha, no. 2, October 12–16, 1945, Box 27, KMCA.
143. Sometimes the guides and porters were listed with the pack animals. See Wilhelm Methner, "The Ascent of Mount Kilimanjaro: An Outline of its History by Wilhelm Methner of Stolberg (Harz), former District Officer in Moshi," n.d., Box 30, KMCA and

"Hero of 20,000 Ft. Climb," 1935, n.p., Box 30, KMCA.

144. John W. Stauffacher, "Kilimanjaro," n.d., Box 2, KMCA.
145. Book for Guide Thomas Mosha, no. 2, February 4, 1939, Box 27, KMCA.
146. "Planting the Jewel on the Snowy Crown of Africa: The Bible on the Empire's Summit," *Ice Cap*, no. 1, 1932, Box 26, KMCA, 27–28.
147. Peter's Hut Book 1943–1945, June 10, 1943, Box 27, KMCA. (Presumably, this entry was in 1944 because it is in the 1944 year entries.)
148. The Mountain Club of East Africa Annual General Meeting, February 26, 1938, Box 3, KMCA.
149. Address by the President [Dr.] R. Reusch at the Annual General Meeting August 1953, Box 30, KMCA.
150. Lecture by the President Dr. R. Reusch, August 1953, at Moshi, Box 30, KMCA.
151. Letter from Honorary Secretary and Treasurer to P. Wyn Harris, Esq., Nairobi, August 29, 1938, Box 6, 1933–1959, KMCA.; The Mountain Club of East Africa Annual General Meeting, February 26, 1938, Box 3, KMCA.
152. Letter to Marangu Hotel, Kibo Hotel, December 1, 1951, Box 4, KMCA. "Personally, I would say that if there should happen to be no other parties of Europeans on those dates, or if you think such Europeans would not mind, it will be OK with the Club. This, however, remains for your decisions. If it is impossible I think we must plainly inform Mr. Lake thus," the club representative wrote.
153. Letter to Mr. R. A. Lake, December 1, 1951, Box 4, KMCA.

CHAPTER 5. WAGUMU IN POST-INDEPENDENCE TANZANIA

Parts of this chapter originally appeared in sections of Leslie Anne Hadfield, "Historical Change in Porter Work on Kilimanjaro," in *Protected Areas in Northern Tanzania: Local Communities, Land Use Change, and Management Challenges*, ed. Jeffrey O. Durrant, Emanuel H. Martin, Kokel Melubo, Ryan R. Jensen, Leslie A. Hadfield, Perry J. Hardin, Laurie Weisler (Cham, Switzerland: Springer, 2020). https://doi.org/10.1007/978-3-030-43302-4_3.

1. The Mountain Club of East Africa Annual General Meeting, June 17, 1939, Box 3, KMCA.
2. Letter 126 from Youngdale to Bruehl, May 26, 1951, Box 4, KMCA.
3. Minutes of the Annual General Meeting of the Mountain Club of East Africa (Kilimanjaro Section), March 21, 1958, Box 3, KMCA.
4. F. R. Brooke, "Alpine Notes—Kilimanjaro," *The Alpine Journal*, 68, nos. 306–7 (1963): 301; Cameron M. Burns, *Kilimanjaro & East Africa: A Climbing and Trekking Guide*, 2nd ed. (Seattle: The Mountaineers Books, 2006), 20.

5. Gillman's Point 1959–1960 Summit Book, December 14, 1959, Box 27, KMCA.
6. Letter from Mangi Mwitori to Hughes, April 19, 1956, Box 6, KMCA.
7. This rule seems to go back to 1938. See Letter from Ginner to Feuerheerd, February 8, 1938, Box 8, KMCA.
8. Letter from Hughes to Bruehl, November 30, 1957, Box 4, KMCA; Letter from Hughes to Lany, December 30, 1957, Box 6, KMCA; Letter from Hughes to Peake, December 30, 1957, Box 4, KMCA.
9. Letter from Hughes to Peake, December 30, 1957, Box 6, KMCA. This is likely the help for which Lauwo was honored for and given a watch.
10. Julius K. Nyerere, *Freedom and Unity: A Selection of Writings and Speeches, 1952–65* (Dar es Salaam: Oxford University Press, 1967), 72.
11. Letter from Marealle, Mangi Mkuu to Vicars-Harris, February 15, 1958, Box 6, KMCA (listed as 1958–02–18 in digital archive).
12. Letter from Vicars-Harris to Mangi Mkuu, February 20, 1958, Box 6, KMCA.
13. "Minutes of the Annual General Meeting of the Mountain Club of East Africa (Kilimanjaro Section) Held in the Hellenic Club, Moshi, on 10th April, 1959," Box 3, KMCA. See also "Kilimanjaro Mountain Club. Minutes of the Committee Meeting Held at 5 p.m. at the Hellenic Club, Moshi, on 15th May 1958," Box 3, KMCA. "The proposal of the Chagga Trust was discussed in length. It was decided to reply to Mr. Bennett's letter saying that the committee of the Mountain Club agree and support the idea of a Mount Kilimanjaro National Park."
14. Audrey Salkeld, *Kilimanjaro: To the Roof of Africa* (Washington, D.C.: National Geographic, 2002).
15. Kilimanjaro Mountain Club. Annual General Meeting Held on 20thFeb, 1963, Box 3, KMCA.
16. Kilimanjaro Mountain Club. The minutes of the Annual General Meeting Held on Wednesday, 8th February 1967, Box 14, KMCA.
17. See *The Ice-Cap: The Journal of the Kilimanjaro Mountain Club*, no. 2, 4, Box 26, KMCA.
18. *The Ice-Cap: The Journal of the Kilimanjaro Mountain Club*, no. 5, December 1971, Box 26, KMCA, 1.
19. Annie Lenoble-Bart and François Constantin, "Mount Kilimanjaro: From History to Symbol," in *Mount Kilimanjaro: Mountain, Memory, Modernity*, ed. François Bart, François Devenne, and Milline J. Mbonile, trans. Taffy Martin (Dar es Salaam: Mkuki na Nyota Publishers, 2006), 19.
20. Peter von Lany, "A brief early history of von Lany family at Marangu," personal document shared with authors, July 31, 2025; "Marangu Hotel—Our Story," Marangu Hotel, http://www.maranguhotel.com/our-story. The next generation of Brice-Bennetts

included Desmond, Fionnuala, and Seamus and his wife Jackie. The Marangu Hotel has also worked to build up the surrounding community. Peter von Lany felt his family's legacy was not just manifested in the tourism industry, but in agriculture as well. As evidence of this, he cited the Kwa Lany pre-school and community of Roman Catholic Sisters next door to Marangu Hotel (www.kathluzern.ch). The Marangu Hotel has also supported local charities such as the Kilimanjaro Initiative (https://kiworld.org) and provides free space for meetings for groups such as the Rotary Club of Marangu.

21. Shisauya W. Nkya, interview with EM and FB, September 3, 2021, Machame; Joel W. Nkya, EM and FB, August 31, 2021, Machame; Anasen Ndenimfoo, interview with EM and FB, September 1, 2021, Machame; James Nkya, interview with EM and FB, September 2, 2021, Machame; Coletha Abel Shirima, interview with ES and RA, September 12, 2021, Rombo.
22. Atanus Isack, interview with ES and RA, August 23, 2021, Marangu; interview with ES, August 19, 2022, Marangu.
23. Fredy Solomon Mtui, interview with ES and RA, August 25, 2021, Marangu; Shisauya W. Nkya, interview with EM and FB, September 3, 2021, Machame; Stanley Mosha, interview with ES and RA, August 16, 2021, Marangu; Samson Lauwo, interview with LH, May 18 and 19, 2023, Moshi.
24. Anasen Ndenimfoo, interview with EM and FB, September 1, 2021, Machame.
25. Fredy Solomon Mtui, interview with ES and RA, August 25, 2021, Marangu; Steven Matero, interview with LH, May 30, 2019, Himo. For the last information, see especially Emmanuel Makule, interview with ES and RA, August 18, 2021, Marangu.
26. David Munguatosha, interview with, ES and RA, August 19, 2021, Marangu. Julius Naftali Tawa also talked about using wet wood as long as they could start the fire with dry wood (in interview with ES and RA, August 25, 2021, Marangu).
27. David Munguatosha, interview with ES and RA, August 19, 2021, Marangu.
28. Zakaria Fataeli Mtui, interview with ES and RA, August 23, 2021, Marangu.
29. Shisauya W. Nkya, interview with EM and FB, September 3, 2021, Machame; George Eliapenda Kimaro, interview with LH and ES, August 7, 2021, Marangu.
30. Samson Lauwo, interview with LH, May 18 and 19, 2023, Moshi.
31. Ezron Samuel Nkya, interview with EM and FB, September 3, 2021, Machame.
32. Remsi William Nkya, interview with EM and FB, September 2, 2021, Machame.
33. Emmanuel Makule, interview with ES and RA, August 18, 2021, Marangu.
34. Steven Matero, interview with LH, May 30, 2019, Himo; Ezron Samwel Nkya, interview with EM and FB, September 3, 2021, Machame.
35. Iain Thornto Christie, Eneida Herrera Fernandes, Hannah R. Messerli, Louise D. Twining-Ward, *Tourism in Africa: Harnessing Tourism for Growth and Improved*

Livelihoods (Washington, D.C.: The World Bank, 2013), 230; Kokel Melubo, "Case study 9. The working conditions of 'Wagumu' (high altitude porters) on Mt Kilimanjaro," in *Mountaineering Tourism*, eds. G. Musa, J. E. S. Higham, and A. Thompson-Carr, eds. (London: Routledge, 2017), 285.

36. Alex Lemunge, interview with EM and FB, September 18, 2021, Arusha; Mathew Laurent and Joshua Enock Mwakalinga, interview with LH, May 21, 2018, Moshi; Batchi Vitalis Donat, interview with LH, May 22, 2018, Himo; Hassan Sakweli Buga, EM and FB, September 24, 2021, Moshi; Aratas Syril Massawe, interview with EM and FB, August 31, 2021, Moshi.
37. Alex Lemunge, interview with EM and FB, September 18, 2021, Arusha; Batchi Vitalis Donat, interview with LH, May 22, 2018, Himo.
38. Joshua Mwakalinga, interview with LH, May 21, 2018, Mt. Kilimanjaro.
39. Kapanya Kitaba, interview with EM and FB, September 13, 2021; Arusha Batchi Vitalis Donat, interview with LH, May 22, 2018, Himo.
40. Samwel Toma Mosha, interview with ES and RA, August 16, 2021, Marangu.
41. Heavenlight Israeli Mtui, interview with ES and RA, August 24, 2021, Marangu Mshiri.
42. Frank Leonard Nnko, interview with EM and FB, September 16, 2021, Arusha; Laurine Shuwa, interview with ES and RA, September 12, 2021, Moshi; Steven Matero, interview with LH, May 30, 2019, Himo; Nuru Samson, interview with EM and FB, September 23, 2021, Moshi; David Munguatosha, interview with, ES and RA, August 19, 2021, Marangu; Fredy Solomon Mtui, interview with ES and RA, August 25, 2021, Marangu; David Sifueli Mtui, interview with ES and RA, August 24, 2021, Marangu Mshiri.
43. Emeline N. Swai, interview with EM and FB, September 5, 2021, Machame.
44. Eunice A. Kimario, interview with ES and RA, September 13, 2021, Tarakea-Rombo.
45. Mary Pallanjo, interview with ES and RA, August 7, 2021, Tarakea.
46. Coletha Abel Shirima, interview with ES and RA, September 12, 2021, Rombo.
47. Lightness Filex, interview with ES and RA, September 12, 2021, Moshi.
48. Jacqline Shuma, interview with ES and RA, September 9, 2021, Rombo; Lightness Filex, interview with ES and RA, September 12, 2021, Moshi; Mary Pallanjo, interview with ES and RA, August 7, 2021, Tarakea.
49. Mary Pallanjo, interview with ES and RA, August 7, 2021, Tarakea.
50. Eunice A. Kimario, interview with ES and RA, September 13, 2021, Tarakea-Rombo.
51. Joice Baktalemo, interview with ES and RA, September 14, 2021, Mbuyuni; Jacqline Shuma, interview with ES and RA, September 9, 2021, Rombo;
52. See interviews cited above as well as Lightness Dominick Philipo Shuma, interview with EM and FB, September 5, 2021, Machame.
53. See the organization's website where they provide more information on the

local Tanzanian groups and other groups around the world: https://www.mountainwomenoftheworld.org/.

54. Christo Amani Fataeli Mbando, interview with ES and RA, August 23, 2021, Marangu; Lamerck Samwel Minja, interview with ES and RA, August 18, 2021, Marangu; Alex Lemunge, interview with EM and FB, September 18, 2021, Arusha; Alberto Jonas Haramba, interview with EM and FB, September 9, 2021, Arusha.
55. "Kilimanjaro National Park," UNESCO World Heritage Convention List, UNESCO website. https://whc.unesco.org/en/list/403/.
56. Lenoble-Bart and Constantin, "Mount Kilimanjaro"; Alan A. Lew and Guosheng Han, "A World Geography of Mountain Trekking," in *Mountaineering Tourism*, G. Musa, J. E. S. Higham, and A. Thompson-Carr, eds. (London: Routledge, 2017), 25; Brent Lovelock, "Climbing Kili: Ethical Mountain Guides on the Roof of Africa," in *Mountaineering Tourism*, ed. G. Musa, J. E. S. Higham, and Anna Thompson-Carr (London: Routledge, 2015), 272–84; David Peaty, "Kilimanjaro Tourism and What It Means for Local Porters and for the Local Environment," *Journal of Ritsumeikan Social Sciences and Humanities* 4 (2012): 1–11.
57. Melubo, "Case study 9"; Peaty, "Kilimanjaro Tourism and What It Means."
58. Lovelock, "Climbing Kili."
59. "Mount Kilimanjaro Porters Society—About Us," www.kilimanjaro-porters.org.
60. Joshua Clement Ruhimbi, interview with EM and FB, September 15, 2021, Arusha.
61. Simon Mtuy, interview with LH, June 6, 2022, Moshi.
62. Peaty, "Kilimanjaro Tourism and What It Means," 2.
63. Melubo, "Case study 9," 286; Salkeld, *Kilimanjaro: To the Roof of Africa*, 48.
64. Iain Thornto Christie, Eneida Herrera Fernandes, Hannah R. Messerli, Louise D. Twining-Ward, *Tourism in Africa: Harnessing Tourism for Growth and Improved Livelihood* (Washington, D.C.: The World Bank, 2014), 230; Peaty, "Kilimanjaro Tourism and What It Means," 3.
65. Melubo, "Case study 9," 289.
66. Peaty, "Kilimanjaro Tourism and What It Means."
67. Melubo, "Case study 9," 289.

CHAPTER 6. THE PRESENT AND FUTURE OF THE KILIMANJARO CLIMBING INDUSTRY

1. Cf. UNDP, *Human Development Report 2022/2023* (New York, NY: United Nations Development Program, 2024), 274–7.

2. Thomas Fisher, "Chagga Elites and the Politics of Ethnicity in Kilimanjaro, Tanzania" (PhD diss., University of Edinburgh, 2012), iii and *passim*.
3. See The United Republic of Tanzania, *The 2022 Population and Housing Census; Tanzania Basic Demographic and Social Economic Profile*, vol 4A (Ministry of Finance, Tanzania National Bureau of Statistics and President's Office, Finance and Planning, Office of the Chief Government Statistician, Zanzibar, 2024), 55–56.
4. Chairperson of Tanzania Porters Organization (TPO), Loshiye Mollel, personal communication with Kokel Melubo, November 19, 2019.
5. Yurii Bogorodskiy, "Mount Kilimanjaro deaths. How many people die on the highest mountain in Africa?" *Altezza Travel*, June 18, 2024 (revised April 1, 2025), https://altezzatravel.com/articles/deaths-on-kilimanjaro.
6. Kilimanjaro National Park General Management Plan 2016 (TANAPA, 2016).
7. Yurii Bogorodskiy, "Legendary Kilimanjaro Records," *Altezza Travel*, September 3, 2024 (revised October 30, 2024), https://altezzatravel.com/articles/kilimanjaro-records.
8. "Tusker's Origin Story," Tusker Trail website, www.tusker.com.
9. Kilimanjaro Visitors' Books, 2013–2020, KINAPA, Marangu Gate.
10. Aratas Syril Massawe, interview with EM and FB, August 31, 2021, Moshi.
11. Estomi Nkya, interview with EM and FB, September 1, 2021, Machame.
12. Sifuel G. Moshi, interview with EM and FB, September 16, 2021, Arusha.
13. Allen Godfrey, interview with EM and FB, September 3, 2021, Machame.
14. Aseri Aiwinjia Mosha, interview with LH, August 8, 2021, Marangu.
15. Simon Mtuy, interview with LH, June 6, 2022, Moshi.
16. Enock Mwakalinga and Hudson Mwakalinga, interview with LH, May 9, 2018, Mt. Kilimanjaro.
17. Enock Mwakalinga and Hudson Mwakalinga, interview with LH, May 9, 2018, Mt. Kilimanjaro.
18. Aratas Syril Massawe, interview with EM and FB, August 31, 2021, Moshi.
19. Sifuel G. Moshi, interview with EM and FB, September 16, 2021, Arusha.
20. Joshua Clement Ruhimbi, interview with EM and FB, September 15, 2021, Arusha.
21. See reviews of various companies, including the websites of Ultimate Kilimanjaro (www.ultimatekilimanjaro.com), Climbing Kilimanjaro (https://www.climbing-kilimanjaro.com/), Trip Advisor, and the Kilimanjaro Porters Assistance Project (https://kiliporters.org/).
22. Victoria Frances Kernot Cunningham, Mahjabeen Haji Kanz, and Jacques Morisset, "Tanzania Economic Update: The Elephant in the Room—Unlocking the Potential of the Tourism Industry for Tanzanians," *Tanzania Economic Update*, no. 6 (Washington,

D.C.: World Bank Group, 2015), 26. http://documents.worldbank.org/curated/en/716911468305677763.

23. See lists of operators on the International Mountain Explorers Connection (IMEC) website under "Partnership for Responsible Travel" (also accessible through the Kilimanjaro Responsible Trekking Organization website of KPAP). In "How Much Does it Cost to Climb Kilimanjaro?" on the Ultimate Kilimanjaro company website (a large operator company headquartered in the United States), under the section titled, "Budget Kilimanjaro Operators," the company writes, "Avoid the cheap, low budget operators; they are downright dangerous." In the following section, "Why You Should Care about Porter Abuse," the article reads, "Only climb with KPAP member companies, like Ultimate Kilimanjaro . . . KPAP partner companies, like Ultimate Kilimanjaro, are leading the industry to improve working conditions for all porters on Mount Kilimanjaro."
24. This is not just a Kilimanjaro problem as Basnyat and Litch show in Buddha Basnyat and James A. Litch, "Medical problems of porters and trekkers in the Nepal Himalaya," *Wilderness & Environmental Medicine*, 8, no. 2 (1997): 78–81.
25. "Mount Kilimanjaro deaths. How many people die on the highest mountain in Africa?" Altezza Travel website, https://altezzatravel.com/articles/deaths-on-kilimanjaro.
26. Annual Report, International Mountain Explorers Connection, mountainexplorers.org.
27. United Republic of Tanzania, Vice President's Office, *National Invasive Species Strategy and Action Plan (NISSAP) (2019–2029)* (Dodoma: Permanent Secretary, Vice President's Office, 2019), 20.
28. Kapanya Kitaba, interview with EM and FB, September 13, 2021, Arusha.
29. Joshua Clement Ruhimbi, interview with EM and FB, September 15, 2021, Arusha.
30. Goodluck Swai, interview with EM and FB, September 5, 2021, Machame.
31. Joshua Clement Ruhimbi, interview with EM and FB, September 15, 2021, Arusha.
32. Aratas Syril Massawe, interview with EM and FB, August 31, 2021, Moshi.
33. Allen Godfrey, interview with EM and FB, September 3, 2021, Machame.
34. Emeline N. Swai, interview with EM and FB, September 5, 2021, Machame.
35. Hamadi I. Dulle, Stefan W. Ferger, Norbert J. Cordeiro, et. al, "Changes in abundances of forest understorey birds on Africa's highest mountain suggest subtle effects of climate change," *Diversity and Distributions*, 22 (206): 288–99. High temperatures at high elevations have favored bird abundances and distribution in the 20 years between 1991 and 2001.
36. Bender, *Water Brings No Harm*, chap 8.
37. Zakaria Fataeli Mtui, interview with ES and RA, August 23, 2021, Marangu.

38. Joshua Enock Mwakalinga, interview with LH, May 8, 2018, Mt. Kilimanjaro.
39. Enock Mwakalinga and Hudson Mwakalinga, interview with LH, May 9, 2018, Mt. Kilimanjaro.
40. Joshua Clement Ruhimbi, interview with EM and FB, September 15, 2021, Arusha. What Ruhimbi refers to here could be the Furtwangler glacier that is known to have reduced by more than half.
41. Kapanya Kitaba, interview with EM and FB, September 13, 2021, Arusha.
42. Halima Kilungu, Rik Leemans, Pantaleo K. T. Munishi, Sarah Nicholls, and Bas Amelung, "Forty Years of Climate and Land-Cover Change and its Effects on Tourism Resources in Kilimanjaro National Park," in *Sustainable Tourism Policy and Planning in Africa*, ed. Emmanuel Akwasi Adu-Ampong and Albert Nsom Kimbu (Routledge, 2021), 127–45.
43. Edward Qorro, "Fire Ravages 34.2 sq km of Mount Kilimanjaro Ecosystem," *Daily News*, November 28, 2022, https://dailynews.co.tz/fire-ravages-34–2-sqkm-of-mount kilimanjaro-ecosystem/.
44. Aside from the environmental consequences, smoke from fires emits ultrafine particles that can travel up to 1,000 km/620 mi and affect people's respiratory health, causing coughing or difficulty breathing. Fires scare climbers, leading them to either cut their trek short or cancel a visit that was just getting started. The October 2022 wildfire in the Karanga area forced the closure of millennium base camp and the Mweka route, forcing travelers to take the lengthier Marangu route instead. The denser smokes obscure the mountain sky, making it difficult to see and less appealing for tourism.
45. TANAPA spent a significant amount of resources. Aside from military forces from TANAPA, Ngorongoro Conservation Area, and Tanzania Forest Service, a total of 885 armed forces from Tanzanian People Defense forces (TPDF) were deployed in the fire suppression operation. TPDF provided two heavily armed helicopters for surveillance purposes.
46. Rosalaura Romeo, Laura Russo, Fabio Parisi, Marcello Notarianni, Sara Manuelli and Sandra Carvao, UNWTO, *Mountain Tourism—Towards a More Sustainable Path* (Rome: FAO, 2021).
47. Mengiseny E. Kaseva and Josia L. Moirana, "Problems of Solid Waste Management on Mount Kilimanjaro: A Challenge to Tourism" *Waste Management & Research* 28, no. 8 (2010): 698.
48. Michal Apollo, "Mountaineer's Waste: Past, Present and Future," *Annals of Valahia University: Geographical Series* 16, no. 2 (2016): 24.
49. National Trust for Nature Conservation, "Annapurna Conservation Area Project (ACAP)," https://ntnc.org.np/project/annapurna-conservation-area-project-acap.

50. Cf. Kaseva and Moirana, “Problems of Solid Waste Management on Mount Kilimanjaro,” 698–701.
51. Kaseva and Moirana, “Problems of Solid Waste Management on Mount Kilimanjaro,” 695–704.
52. Lovelock, “Climbing Kili.”
53. Cf. Todd Cleveland, *A History of Tourism in Africa: Exoticization, Exploitation, and Enrichment* (Athens: Ohio University Press, 2021).

Bibliography

Archival Collections

Kilimanjaro Mountain Club Archive (hereafter KMCA)

Evangelical Lutheran Church in Tanzanian-Northern Diocese Archive (ELCT-ND)

Interviews

Oral History Interviews by Edward Simango (ES), Ester Mramba (EM), Faisal Omary Bakari (FB), Leslie Hadfield (LH), Rehema Assenga (RA)

Baktalemo, Joice, ES and RA, September 14, 2021, Mbuyuni

Buga, Hassan Sakweli, EM and FB, September 24, 2021, Moshi

Daud, Simon Haji, EM and FB, August 31, 2021, Moshi

Donat, Batchi Vitalis, LH, May 22, 2018, Himo

Filex, Lightness, ES and RA, September 12, 2021, Moshi

Godfrey, Allen, EM and FB, September 3, 2021, Machame

Haramba, Alberto Jonas, EM and FB, September 9, 2021, Arusha

Isack, Atanus, ES and RA, August 23, 2021, Marangu; ES, August 19, 2022, Marangu

Juma, Rashid, EM and FB, September 24, 2021, Moshi

Kimario, Eunice A., ES and RA, September 13, 2021, Tarakea-Rombo

Kimaro, George Eliapenda, LH and ES, August 7, 2021, Marangu

Kitaba, Kapanya, EM and FB, September 13, 2021, Arusha

Laurent, Mathew and Joshua Enock Mwakalinga, LH, May 21, 2018, Moshi

Lauwo, Samson, LH, May 18 and 19, 2023, Moshi

Lemunge, Alex, EM and FB, September 18, 2021, Arusha

Makule, Emmanuel, ES and RA, August 18, 2021, Marangu

Mallya, Denis, EM and FB, September 21, 2021, Arusha

Massawe, Aratas Syril, EM and FB, August 31, 2021, Moshi

Matero, Steven, LH, May 30, 2019, Himo

Mbando, Christo Amani Fataeli, ES and RA, August 23, 2021, Marangu

Mbando, Joseph E., ES and RA, August 16, 2021, Marangu

Minja, Eliandra or Elias Andrea, ES and RA, August 18, 2021, Marangu; ES, August 17, 2022, Marangu

Minja, Gibson Emmanuel, ES and LH, August 7, 2021, Marangu; ES and RA, August 16, 2021, Marangu

Minja, James Emmanuel, ES and RA, August 26, 2021, Marangu

Minja, Jarid Filipo, ES and RA, August 26, 2021, Marangu

Minja, Lamerck Samwel, ES and RA, August 18, 2021, Marangu

Minja, Morgan Eliakimu, ES, August 16, 2022, Marangu

Mollel, Long'ida M., EM and FB, September 9, 2021, Arusha

Mongi, Emmanuel, ES and RA, August 19, 2021, Marangu Mshiri

Mosha, Aseri Aiwinjia, LH, August 8, 2021, Marangu

Mosha, Samwel Toma, ES and RA, August 16, 2021, Marangu; ES, August 18, 2022, Marangu

Mosha, Stanley, ES and RA, August 16, 2021, Marangu; ES, August 18, 2022, Marangu

Moshi, Hansira Crispine, ES and RA, September 12, 2021, Rombo

Moshi, Sifuel G., EM and FB, September 16, 2021, Arusha

Mtui, David Sifueli, ES and RA, August 24, 2021, Marangu Mshiri

Mtui, Fredy Solomon, ES and RA, August 25, 2021, Marangu

Mtui, Hea/Evenlight Israel, ES and RA, August 24, 2021, Marangu Mshiri

Mtui, Kamili Liatonga, ES and RA, August 23, 2021, Marangu Mshiri

Mtui, Zakaria Fataeli, ES and RA, August 23, 2021, Marangu

Mtuy, Simon, LH, June 6, 2022, Moshi

Munguatosha, David, ES and RA, August 19, 2021, Marangu

Mwakalinga, Enock and Hudson Mwakalinga, LH, May 9, 2018, Mt. Kilimanjaro

Mwakalinga, Joshua Enock, LH, May 8, 2018, Mt. Kilimanjaro

Ndenimfoo, Anasen, EM and FB, September 1, 2021, Machame

Ngatunga, Frank Joseph, EM and FB, August 31, 2021, Moshi

Nkya, Estomii, EM and FB, September 1, 2021, Machame

Nkya, Ezron Samwel, EM and FB, September 3, 2021, Machame

Nkya, James, EM and FB, September 2, 2021, Machame

Nkya, Joel W., EM and FB, August 31, 2021, Machame

Nkya, Remsi William, EM and FB, September 2, 2021, Machame

Nkya, Shisauya W., EM and FB, September 3, 2021, Machame

Nnko, Frank Leonard, EM and FB, September 16, 2021, Arusha

Olotu, Felix Anasa, ES, June 20, 2022, Himo

Pallanjo, Mary, ES and RA, August 7, 2021, Tarakea

Ruhimbi, Joshua Clement, EM and FB, September 15, 2021, Arusha

Samson, Nuru, EM and FB, September 23, 2021, Moshi

Shirima, Coletha Abel, ES and RA, September 12, 2021, Rombo

Shuma, Jacqline, ES and RA, September 9, 2021, Rombo

Shuma, Lightness Dominick Philipo, EM and FB, September 5, 2021, Machame

Shuwa, Laurine, ES and RA, September 12, 2021, Moshi

Swai, Emeline N., EM and FB, September 5, 2021, Machame

Swai, Goodluck, EM and FB, September 5, 2021, Machame

Tawa, Julius Naftali, ES and RA, August 25, 2021, Marangu

Published Sources

Adams, William Mark, and Martin Mulligan, eds. *Decolonizing Nature: Strategies for Conservation in a Post-colonial Era*. London: Earthscane, 2003.

Admasie, Samuel Andreas. "Sport, Tourism and Entertainment." In *General Labour History of Africa: Workers, Employers and Governments 20th–21st Centuries*, edited by Stefano Bellucci and Andreas Eckert. Woodbridge: James Currey, 2019, 405–21.

Adhikari, Ankit Babu, and Pradeep Bashyal. *Sherpa: Stories of Life and Death from the Forgotten Guardians of Everest*. Sydney: Hachette, 2022.

Apollo, Michal. "Mountaineer's Waste: Past, Present and Future," *Annals of Valahia University: Geographical Series* 16, no. 2 (2016): 13–32.

Bart, Francois, Francois Devenne, Milline Jethro Mbonile, eds. *Mount Kilimanjaro: Mountain, Memory, Modernity*. Dar es Salaam: Mkuki na Nyota Publishers, 2006.

Basnyat, Buddha, and James A. Litch. "Medical problems of porters and trekkers in the Nepal Himalaya." *Wilderness & Environmental Medicine*, 8, no. 2 (1997): 78–81.

Baum, Jiří. *Africkou divočinou: Autem z Prahy k Mysu Dobré Naděje*. Prague, published by the author, 1933.

Bayers, Peter L. *Imperial Ascent: Masculinity, Mountaineering, and Empire*. Boulder: University Press of Colorado, 2003.

Beedie, Paul. "A History of Mountaineering Tourism." In *Mountaineering Tourism*, edited by

Ghazali Musa, James E. S. Higham, and Anna Thompson-Carr. London: Routledge, 2015, 40–54.

Beinart, William, and Peter Coates. *Environment and History: The Taming of Nature in the USA and South Africa*. New York: Routledge, 1995.

Beinart, William. *The Rise of Conservation in South Africa: Settlers, Livestock, and The Environment, 1770–1950*. Oxford: Oxford University Press, 2008.

Bellucci, Stefano. "Transport." In *General Labour History of Africa: Workers, Employers and Governments 20th–21st Centuries*, edited by Stefano Bellucci and Andreas Eckert. Oxford: James Currey, 2019, 195–219.

Bender, Matthew V. "Being 'Chagga': Natural Resources, Political Activism, and Identity on Kilimanjaro." *Journal of African History* 54, no. 2 (2013): 199–220.

———. *Water Brings No Harm: Management Knowledge and the Struggle for the Waters of Kilimanjaro*. Athens: Ohio University Press, 2019.

Bender-Shetler, Jan. *Imagining Serengeti: A History of Landscape Memory in Tanzania from Earliest Times to the Present*. Athens: Ohio University Press, 2007.

Berg, F. J. "The Coast from the Portuguese Invasion to the Rise of the Zanzibar Sultanate." In *Zamani: A Survey of East African History*, new ed, edited by Bethwell A. Ogot. Nairobi: East African Publishing House, 1973, 115–34.

Bernbaum, Edwin. "Sacred Mountains: Themes and Teachings." *Mountain Research and Development* 26, no. 4 (2006), 304–9.

Brockington, Dan, Hassan Sachedina, and Katherine Scholfield. "Preserving the New Tanzania: Conservation and Land Use Change," *The International Journal of African Historical Studies* 41, no. 3 (2008): 557–79.

Brooke, F. R. "Alpine Notes—Kilimanjaro." *The Alpine Journal* 68, no. 306–7 (1963): 301–2.

Burns, Cameron M. *Kilimanjaro & East Africa: A Climbing and Trekking Guide*, 2nd ed. Seattle: Mountaineers Books, 2006.

Busk, D. L. "Kilimanjaro." *Alpine Journal* 60 (1955): 96–104.

Cana, Frank R. "Frontiers of German East Africa." *The Geographical Journal* 47, no. 4 (1916): 297–303.

Carney, Judith A., and Richard Nicholas Rosomoff. *In the Shadow of Slavery: Africa's Botanical Legacy in the Atlantic World*. Oakland: University of California Press, 2010.

Carruthers, Jane. "Conservation and Wildlife Management in South African National Parks, 1930s–1960s." *Journal of the History of Biology* 41, no. 2 (2008): 203–36.

———. *The Kruger National Park: A Social and Political History*. Pietermaritzburg: University of Natal Press, 1995.

———. "The Royal National Park, KwaZulu Natal: Mountaineering, Tourism and Nature

Conservation in South Africa's First National Park c. 1896 to c. 1947." *Environment and History* 19, no. 4 (November 2013): 459–86.

Chen, Joseph S., and Nina K. Prebensen, eds. *Nature Tourism*. New York: Routledge, 2017.

Christie, Iain, Eneida Fernandes, Hannah R. Messerli, and Louise D. Twining-Ward. *Tourism in Africa: Harnessing Tourism for Growth and Improved Livelihood*. Washington, D.C.: The World Bank. 2014.

Cleveland, Todd. *A History of Tourism in Africa: Exoticization, Exploitation, and Enrichment*. Athens: Ohio University Press, 2021.

Cock, Jacklyn, and David Fig, "From Colonial to Community-Based Conservation: Environmental Justice and the National Parks of South Africa." *Society in Transition* 31, no. 1 (2000): 22–35.

Conte, Christopher A. *Highland Sanctuary: Environmental History in Tanzania's Usambara Mountains*. Athens: Ohio University Press, 2004.

Cunningham, Victoria Frances Kernot, Mahjabeen Haji Kanz, and Jacques Morisset. "Tanzania Economic Update: The Elephant in the Room—Unlocking the Potential of the Tourism Industry for Tanzanians." *Tanzania Economic Update, no. 6*, Washington, D.C.: World Bank Group, 2015. http://documents.worldbank.org/curated/en/716911468305677763.

Debarbieux, Bernard, and Gilles Rudaz. *The Mountain: A Political History from the Enlightenment to the Present*. Chicago: University of Chicago Press, 2015.

DeGeorges, Paul Andre, and Kevin Reilly. "The Realities of Community Based Natural Resource Management and Biodiversity Conservation in Sub-Saharan Africa." *Sustainability* 1, no. 3 (2009): 734–88.

Deutsch, K. W. "The Growth of Nations: Some Recurrent Patterns of Political and Social Integration." *World Politics* 5, no. 2 (1956): 168–95.

Dlamini, Jacob. *Safari Nation: A Social History of the Kruger National Park*. Athens: Ohio University Press, 2020.

Dulle, Hamadi I., Stefan W. Ferger, Norbert J. Cordeiro, Kim M. Howell, Matthias Schleuning, Katrin Böhning-Gaese, and Christian Hof. "Changes in abundances of forest understorey birds on Africa's highest mountain suggest subtle effects of climate change." *Diversity and Distributions* 22 (206): 288–99.

Dundas, Charles. *African Crossroads*. London: Macmillan & Co., 1955.

———. *Asili na Habari za Wachagga*. London: The Sheldon Press, 1932.

———. *Kilimanjaro and Its People*. London: Frank Cass, 1924.

———. *Kilimanjaro and Its People: A History of the Wachagga, Their Laws, Customs and Legends . . . By the Hon'ble Charles Dundas*. London: H. F. and G. Witherby, 1924.

Ellingson, Ter. *The Myth of the Noble Savage*. Oakland: University of California Press, 2001.

Evans-Pritchard, E. E. *The Nuer: A Description of the Modes of Livelihood and Political Institutions of a Nilotic People*. Oxford: At the Clarendon Press, 1940.

Eze, Emmanuel Chukwudi, ed. *Race and the Enlightenment: A Reader*. Cambridge: Blackwell, 1997.

Feierman, Steven. *The Shambaa Kingdom: A History*. Madison: University of Wisconsin Press, 1974.

Fisher, Thomas. "Chagga Elites and the Politics of Ethnicity in Kilimanjaro, Tanzania." PhD diss., University of Edinburgh, 2012.

Fitch, E. A. and J. A. Wray. "The First Year of the Chagga Mission." *Church Missionary Intelligencer*, New Series 2 (1886): 555–62.

Fosbrooke, H. A. and H. Sassoon. "Archaeological Remains on Kilimanjaro." *Tanzania Notes and Records* 64 (1965): 62–3.

Gilchrist, Paul. "Gender and British Climbing Histories: Introduction." *Sport in History* 33, no. 3 (2103): 223–35.

Gissibl, Bernhard. *The Nature of German Colonialism: Conservation and the Politics of Wildlife in Colonial East Africa*. New York: Berghahn Books, 2016.

Grassler, Von Franz. "Hohe Ziele alpenferner Sektionen: die Dreitausender der Ostalpen und der Kilimandscharo." *Alpenvereinsjahrbuch* 188 (1994), 235.

Grove, Alison. "Water Use by the Chagga on Kilimanjaro." *African Affairs* 92, no. 368 (1993): 431–48.

Gutmann, Bruno. "Chagga Folk-lore: Extracts from Two Books by Bruno Gutman." Translated by J. A. Hutchinson. *Tanzania Notes and Records* 64 (1965): 50–55.

———. "The African Standpoint." *Africa* 8, no. 1 (1935): 1–19.

Hadfield, Leslie Anne. "Historical Change in Porter Work on Kilimanjaro." In *Protected Areas in Northern Tanzania: Local Communities, Land Use Change, and Management Challenges*, edited by Jeffrey O. Durrant, Emanuel Martin, Kokel Melubo, Ryan Jensen, Leslie A. Hadfield, Perry J. Hardin, and Laurie Weisler. New York: Springer Nature, 2020, 29–44.

Håkansson, N. Thomas, Mats Widgren, and Lowe Börjeson. "Introduction: Historical and Regional Perspectives on Landscape Transformations in Northeastern Tanzania, 1850–2000." *International Journal of African Historical Studies* 41, no. 3 (2008): 369–82.

Hall, Henry S. "Kilimanjaro and Other African Climbs." *American Alpine Journal* 2 (1936): 455–61.

Hansen, Peter H. "Partners: Guides and Sherpas in the Alps and Himalayas, 1850s-1950s." In *Voyages and Visions: Towards a Cultural History of Travel*, eds. Jas Elsner and Joan-Pau Rubies. London: Reaktion, 1999, 210–31.

———. *The Summits of Modern Man: Mountaineering After the Enlightenment*. Cambridge: Harvard University Press, 2013.

Hanzelka, Jiri, and Miroslav Zikmund. *Afrika—Snū a Skutečnosti*. Prague: Orbis, 1953.

Hanzelka, Jiri, and Miroslav Zikmund. *Afrika: Traum und Wirklichkeit*. Translated by Adolf Langer. Berlin: Verlag Volk und Welt, 1959.

Harding, J. R. "Nineteenth-Century Trade Beads in Tanganyika." *Man* 62 (1962): 104–6.

Hemp, Andreas. "Vegetation of Kilimanjaro: Hidden Endemics and Missing Bamboo." *African Journal of Ecology* 44 (2006): 305–28.

Hillary, Sir Edmund. *High Adventure*. New York: Oxford University Press, 2003.

Hobley, C. W. "People, Places, and Prospects in British East Africa." *The Geographical Journal* 4, no. 2 (1894): 97–123.

Hollis, C. "Notes on the History and Customs of the People of Taveta, East Africa." *Journal of the Royal African Society* 1, no. 1 (1901): 98–125.

Hoole, Louise. *Seven Wonders: The World Heritage Sites of Tanzania*, 2nd edition. Black Ink Press, 2016.

Hutchinson, J. A. "The Meaning of Kilimanjaro." *Tanzania Notes and Records* 64 (1965): 65–7.

Isserman, Maurice, and Stewart Weaver. *Fallen Giants: A History of Himalayan Mountaineering from the Age of Empire to the Age of Extremes*. New Haven: Yale University Press, 2008.

Jacobs, Nancy. *Birders of Africa: History of a Network*. New Haven: Yale University Press, 2016.

Jahadhmy, Ali A. *Anthology of Swahili Poetry*. London: Heinemann Educational Books, 1975.

Johnson, Daniel H. *Loyalty: A Biography of Richard Gustavovich Reusch*. St. Cloud: SunRay Printing, 2008.

Johnson, P. J. Boyd, and H. McCullum, eds. *Kilimanjaro: Africa's Beacon*. Harare: African Publishing Group International, 2004.

Johnston, Harry Hamilton. *The Kilimanjaro Expedition: A Record of Scientific Exploration in Eastern Tropical Africa*. London: Kegan and Paul, 1886.

———. "The People of Eastern Equatorial Africa." *The Journal of the Anthropological Institute of Great Britain and Ireland* 15 (1886): 3–15.

Jones, Samantha. "A Political Ecology of Wildlife Conservation in Africa." *Review of African Political Economy* 33, no. 109 (September 2006): 483–95.

Jones, W. W. "African Dogouts." *Tanganyika Notes and Record* 11 (1941): 11–12.

Kahn, Farieda. "A Century of Mountaineering: Race, Class and the Politics of Climbing Table Mountain." *Acta Academica* 50, no. 2 (2018): 52–74.

———. "Apartheid Mountaineering: Race, Politics, and the History of the University of Cape Town Mountain and Ski Club, 1933–1969." *The International Journal of the History of Sport* 36, no. 1 (2019): 48–66.

———. "From Carriers to Climbers: The Cape Province Mountain Club, 1930s to 1960s—an untold story." In *Exploring Decolonising Themes in SA Sport History: Issues and Challenges*, edited by Francois Johannes Cleophas. Stellenbosch: African Sun Media, 2018, 67–80.

———. "The Impact of Racial Inequality on the Pursuit of Mountain-Based Leisure Pursuits among Black Recreation-Seekers in Cape Town, South Africa, 1910–1969." *Recreation and Society in Africa, Asia and Latin America* 6 (2018): 32.

Kaseva, Mengiseny E., and Josia L. Moirana. "Problems of Solid Waste Management on Mount Kilimanjaro: A Challenge to Tourism." *Waste Management & Research* 28, no. 8 (2010): 695–704.

Keller, Tait. *Apostles of the Alps: Mountaineering and Nation Building in Germany and Austria.* Chapel Hill: University of North Carolina Press, 2016.

Kennedy, Dane. *The Last Blank Spaces: Exploring Africa and Australia.* Cambridge: Harvard University Press, 2013.

Kilungu, Halima, Rik Leemans, Pantaleo K. T. Munishi, Sarah Nicholls, and Bas Amelung. "Forty Years of Climate and Land-Cover Change and its Effects on Tourism Resources in Kilimanjaro National Park." In *Sustainable Tourism Policy and Planning in Africa*, edited by Emmanuel Akwasi Adu-Ampong and Albert Nsom Kimbu. Abingdon, UK: Routledge, 2021, 127–45.

Kimambo, Isaria N. "Environmental Control and Hunger in the Mountain Plains of Northeastern Tanzania." In *Custodians of the Land: Ecology and Culture in the History of Tanzania*, edited by G. Maddox, J. Giblin, and I. N. Kimambo. London: James Currey, 1996, 71–96.

———. "The Eastern Bantu Peoples." In *Zamani: A Survey of East African History*, new ed, edited by B. A. Ogot. Nairobi: East African Publishing House, 1973, 195–209.

Kivelege, Erick. *Climbing Kilimanjaro with Africa's Top Guide*. Enumclaw; Moshi: Kilimanjaro Kutembea Publishing, 2021.

Krakauer, Jon. *Into Thin Air: A Personal Account of the Mount Everest Disaster*. New York: Random House (Villard Books), 1997.

Krapf, John Ludwig. "Mount Kenia." *Proceedings of the Royal Geographical Society and Monthly Record of Geography* 4, no. 12 (1882 [1849/50]): 747–53.

———. *Travels, Researches and Missionary Labours During Eighteen Years' Residence in Eastern Africa*, 2nd ed. London: Frank Cass, 1968 [1860].

Le Roy, Alexandre. *Au Kilima-Ndjaro: Histoire de la fondation d'une mission catholique en Afrique orientale.* Paris: L'Œuvre d'auteil, 1928.

Leeman, Bernard. "Kinyala Johannes Lauwo (1871–1996): The world's oldest person and the first known successful climber of Mount Kilimanjaro." Academia.edu, 2016.

Lehman, F. R. "Some Field-Notes on the Chagga of Kilimanjaro." *Bantu Studies* 15 (1941): 385–96.

Lekan, Thomas N. *Our Gigantic Zoo: A German Quest to Save the Serengeti.* Oxford: Oxford University Press, 2020.

Lenoble-Bart, Annie, and François Constantin. "Mount Kilimanjaro: From History to Symbol." In *Mount Kilimanjaro: Mountain, Memory, Modernity*, edited by François Bart, François Devenne, and Milline J. Mbonile, translated by Taffy Martin. Dar es Salaam: Mkuki na Nyota Publishers, 2006, 5–20.

Lew, Alan A., and Guosheng Han. "A World Geography of Mountain Trekking." In *Mountaineering Tourism*, edited by G. Musa, J. E. S. Higham and Anna Thompson-Carr. London: Routledge, 2017, 19–39.

Lovejoy, Paul E., and Catherine Coquery-Vidrovitch. *The Workers of African Trade*. Sage Publications, Beverly Hills, 1985.

Lovelock, Brent. "Climbing Kili: Ethical Mountain Guides on the Roof of Africa." In *Mountaineering Tourism*, edited by Ghazali Musa, James E. S. Higham, and Anna Thompson-Carr. London: Routledge, 2015, 272–84.

MacKenzie, John M. *The Empire of Nature: Hunting, Conservation, and British Imperialism*. Manchester: Manchester University Press, 1997.

Malya, Exaud E. *Wamarangu: Historia na Maendeleo*. Moshi: Northern Packages, 2002.

Mandara. "Invitation from the King of Chagga." *Church Missionary Intelligencer* 3 (1878): 448–9.

Marealle, Petro I. *Maisha ya Mchagga Hapa Duniani na Ahera*. Dar es Salaam: Mkuki na Nyota Publishers, 2002 [1947].

Marealle, Thomas Lenana, and Rusk S. Kishimba, trans. and eds. *Historia ya Kanisa la Kiinjili la Kilutheri Africa Mashariki, 1902–1912: Kilimanjaro, Arusha, Meru na Pare*. Moshi: Printing Services Ltd, 1997.

Marealle, Thomas L. M. "The Wachagga of Kilimanjaro." *Tanganyika Notes and Records* 32 (1952): 47–64.

Mazrui, Al-Amin bin Ali. *The History of the Mazrui Dynasty of Mombasa*. Translated by James McL. Ritchie. Oxford: Oxford University Press, 1999.

Melubo, Kokel. "Case study 9. The working conditions of 'Wagumu' (high altitude porters) on Mt Kilimanjaro." In *Mountaineering Tourism*, edited by Ghazali Musa, James E. S. Higham, and Anna Thompson-Carr. London: Routledge, 2017, 285–92.

Meyer, Hans. "Ascent to the Summit of Kilima-Njaro." *Proceedings of the Royal Geographical Society and Monthly Record of Geography* 12, no. 6 (June 1890): 331–45.

———. *Across East African Glaciers: An Account of the First Ascent of Kilimanjaro*. Translated by E. H. S. Calder. London, 1891.

Michel, Boris. "Making Mount Kilimanjaro German: Nation Building and Heroic Masculinity in the Colonial Geographies of Hans Meyer." *Transactions of the Institute of British Geographers* 44, no. 3 (2018): 1–16. https://doi-org.erl.lib.byu.edu/10.1111/tran.12283.

Ministry of Natural Resources and Tourism (MNRT), *2024 Maliasili, Statistical Bulletin*.

Dodoma, Tanzania, 2024.

Moore, Sally Falk. *Social Facts and Fabrications: "Customary" Law on Kilimanjaro, 1880–1980*. Cambridge: Cambridge University Press, 1986.

———. "The Chagga of Kilimanjaro." In *The Chagga and Meru of Tanzania*, edited by S. F. Moore and P. Ruritt. London: International African Institute, 1977, 1–85.

———. "The Secret of the Men: A Fiction of Chagga Initiation and its Relation to the Logic of Chagga Symbolism." *Africa* 46, no. 4 (1976): 357–70.

Morton, R. F. "The Shungwaya Myth of Miji Kenda Origins." *The International Journal of African Historical Studies* 5, no. 3 (1972): 397–423.

Munro, Paul. "Colonial Wildlife Conservation and National Parks in Sub-Saharan Africa." *Oxford Research Encyclopedia of African History*. November 29, 2021. https://oxfordre.com/africanhistory/view/10.1093/acrefore/9780190277734.001.0001/acrefore-9780190277734-e-195.

Munson, Robert B. "The Landscape of German Colonialism: Mt. Kilimanjaro and Mt. Meru, CA. 1890–1916." PhD diss., Boston University, 2005.

———. *The Nature of Christianity in Northern Tanzania: Environmental and Social Change 1890–1916*. Lanham: Lexington Books, 2013.

Murdock, George Peter. *Africa: Its Peoples and Their Culture History*. London: McGraw-Hill Book Company, Inc., 1959.

Musa, Ghazali, James Higham, and Anna Thompson-Carr, eds. *Mountaineering Tourism*. London: Routledge, 2015.

Neumann, Roderick P. "Africa's 'Last Wilderness': Reordering Space for Political and Economic Control in Colonial Tanzania." *Africa* 71, no. 4 (November 2001): 641–65.

Norgay, Jamling Tenzing, with Broughton Coburn. *Touching My Father's Soul: A Sherpa's Journey to the Top of Everest*. San Francisco: Harper San Francisco, 2001.

Ntiro, Sam Joseph. *Desturi za Wachagga*. Dar es Salaam: The Eagle Press, 1953.

Nyerere, Julius K. *Freedom and Unity: A Selection of Writings and Speeches, 1952–65*. Dar es Salaam: Oxford University Press, 1967.

Odner, Knut. "A Preliminary Report on an Archaeological Survey on the Slopes of Kilimanjaro." *Azania* 6 (1971): 131–49.

Ortner, Sherry B. *Life and Death on Mt. Everest: Sherpas and Himalayan Mountaineering*. Princeton: Princeton University Press, 2001.

Paul, Frant. *V Rovníkové Africe*. Prague: Orbis, 1931.

Pearse, R. O. *Barrier of Spears: Drama of the Drakensberg*. Johannesburg: Southern Book Publishers, 1989.

Peaty, David. "Kilimanjaro Tourism and What It Means for Local Porters and for the Local

Environment." *Journal of Ritsumeikan Social Sciences and Humanities* 4 (2012): 1–11.

Peters, Carl. *New Light on Dark Africa: Being the Narrative of the German Emin Pasha Expedition.* Translated by H. W. Dulken. London: Ward, Lock and Co., 1891.

Pike, A. G. "Kilimanjaro and the Furrow System." *Tanzania Notes and Records* 64 (1965): 95–6.

Pirie, Gordon. "Tourism Histories in Africa." In *The Oxford Handbook of Tourism History*, edited by Eric G. E. Zuelow and Kevin J. James. Oxford: Oxford University Press, 2025, 447–68.

Prendergast, David K., and William M. Adams. "Colonial Wildlife Conservation and the Origins of the Society for the Preservation of the Wild Fauna of the Empire (1903–1914)." *Oryx* 37, no. 2 (April 2003): 251–60.

Rebmann, Johannes. "Narrative of a Journey to Jagga, the Snow Country of Eastern Africa." *Church Missionary Intelligencer* 1 (1849/50): 12–23.

———. "Narrative of a Journey to Madjame, In Jagga." *Church Missionary Intelligencer* 1, no. 272–76 (1849/50): 307–12.

"Recent Changes in the Map of East Africa." *Proceedings of the Royal Geographical Society and Monthly Record of Geography* 9, no. 8 (1887): 490–96.

Reusch, Richard. "Mount Kilimanjaro and its Ascent." *Tanganyika Notes and Records* no. 64 (March 1965): 132.

———. "The Menelik Legend." *Tanganyika Notes and Records* 2 (1936): 77–9.

Rigby, Charles P. "Mr. J. M. Hildebrandt on His Travels in East Africa." *Proceedings of the Royal Geographical Society of London* 22, no. 6 (1877/78): 449.

Rockel, Stephen J. "'A Nation of Porters': The Nyamwezi and the Labour Market in Nineteenth-Century Tanzania." *Journal of African History* 41 (2000): 173–95.

———. *Carriers of Culture: Labor on the Road in Nineteenth-Century East Africa*, Social History of Africa. Portsmouth: Heinemann, 2006.

Rogers, Susan Geiger. "The Search for Political Focus on Kilimanjaro: A History of Chagga Politics, 1916–1962." PhD diss., University of Dar es Salaam, 1972.

Romeo, Rosalaura, Laura Russo, Fabio Parisi, Marcello Notarianni, Sara Manuelli, and Sandra Carvao. *Mountain Tourism—Towards a More Sustainable Path.* Rome: Food and Agriculture Organization of the United Nations and United Nations World Tourism Organization , 2021.

Salkeld, Audrey. *Kilimanjaro: To the Roof of Africa.* Washington, D.C.: National Geographic, 2002.

Schauer, Jeff. *Wildlife between Empire and Nation in Twentieth-Century Africa.* London: Palgrave MacMillan, 2018.

Schaumann, Caroline. *Peak Pursuits: The Emergence of Mountaineering in the Nineteenth Century.* New Haven: Yale University Press, 2020.

Stahl, Kathleen M. *History of the Chagga People of Kilimanjaro*. London: Mouton, 1964.

———. "Outline of Chagga History." *Tanzania Notes and Records* 64 (1965): 35–49.

———. *Tanganyika: Sail in the Wilderness*. The Hague: Mouton & Co., 1961.

Steiner, Franz Baermann. "Chagga Truth: A Note on Gutmann's Account of the Chagga Concept of Truth in Das Recht der Dschagga." *Africa* 24, no. 4 (1954): 364–69.

Stuart-Watt, Eva. *Africa's Dome of Mystery*. London: Marshall, Morgan & Scott, 1930.

Sutton, Alex. "Primitive Accumulation in the East Africa Groundnut Scheme," *Diplomacy & Statecraft* 35, no. 2 (2024): 338–62.

Sutton, John E. G. "The Archaeology and Early Peoples of the Highlands of Kenya and Northern Tanzania." *Azania* 1 (1966): 37–57.

Swai, T. H. "Limpasalo Mchagga ni Kihamba, Sale na Nyinda." *Komkya* (August 15, 1955): 3a.

Swynnerton, R. J. M., A. L. B. Bennett, and H. B. Stent. *All About "KNCU" Coffee*. Moshi: Moshi Native Coffee Board, 1948.

Tenzing, Judy, and Tashi. *Tenzing and the Sherpas of Everest*. New Delhi: Harper Collins Publishers, 2001.

Tharkay, Ang. *Sherpa: The Memoir of Ang Tharkay*. Seattle: Mountaineers Books, 2016.

"The East African Mountain Club," *American Alpine Journal* 1 (1931): 423.

The United Republic of Tanzania, *The 2022 Population and Housing Census; Tanzania Basic Demographic and Social Economic Profile*, vol. 4A (Ministry of Finance, Tanzania National Bureau of Statistics and President's Office, Finance and Planning, Office of the Chief Government Statistician, Zanzibar, 2024), 55–56.

Thompson-Carr, Anna. "Guided Mountaineering." In *Mountaineering Tourism*, edited by Ghazali Musa, James E. S. Higham, and Anna Thompson-Carr. London: Routledge, 2017, 85–100.

Thornton, Richard. "Notes on a Journey to Kilima-njaro, Made in Company of the Baron von der Decken." *Journal of the Royal Geographical Society of London* 35 (1865): 15–21.

Tilley, Helen. *Africa as a Living Laboratory: Empire, Development, and the Problem of Scientific Knowledge, 1870–1950*. Chicago: University of Chicago Press, 2011.

Ullman, James Ramsey, and Tenzing Norgay. *Man of Everest: The Autobiography of Tenzing Norgay*. London: Reprint Society, 1956.

Vavrus, Frances K. "A Shadow of the Real Thing: Furrow Societies, Water User Associations, and Democratic Practices in the Kilimanjaro Region of Tanzania." *The Journal of African American History* 88, no. 4 (2003): 393–412.

von Clemm, Michael. "Trade-Bead Economics in Nineteenth-Century Chaggaland," *Man* 63 (1963), 13–14.

Wakibara, James, Kimaro Ndesari, and Nyamakumbati Mafuru. "Tourism-Related Impacts on Mount Kilimanjaro, Tanzania: Implications for Tourism Management on Mountain Ecosystems." *Journal of Tourism Challenges and Trends* 2, no. 1 (2009): 111–23.

Westcott, Nicholas. *Imperialism and Development: The East African Groundnut Scheme and Its Legacy*. Woodbridge: James Currey, 2020.

Whiteley, Wilfred Howell. "Chagga Languages," *Tanzania Notes and Records* 64 (1965): 68.

Wimmelbücker, Ludger. *Kilimanjaro: A Regional History*. London: Transaction Publishers, 2002.

Wood, P. J. "The Forest Glades of West Kilimanjaro." *Tanzania Notes and Records* 64 (1965): 108–11.

Index

V

W

Z